D0053923

PEGASUS

PEGASUS

HOW A SPY IN YOUR POCKET
THREATENS THE END OF PRIVACY,
DIGNITY, AND DEMOCRACY

LAURENT RICHARD AND
SANDRINE RIGAUD

HENRY HOLT AND COMPANY
NEW YORK

Henry Holt and Company
Publishers since 1866
120 Broadway
New York, New York 10271
www.henryholt.com

Henry Holt® and Ⓗ® are registered trademarks of
Macmillan Publishing Group, LLC.

Library of Congress Cataloging-in-Publication Data is available.

ISBN: 9781250858696

Our books may be purchased in bulk for promotional, educational, or business use. Please contact
your local bookseller or the Macmillan Corporate and Premium Sales Department at (800) 221-7945,
extension 5442, or by e-mail at MacmillanSpecialMarkets@macmillan.com.

First Edition 2023

Designed by Kelly S. Too

Printed in the United States of America

1   3   5   7   9   10   8   6   4   2

CONTENTS

INTRODUCTION

Rachel Maddow

The call appeared urgent, in that it was coming at close to midnight Tel Aviv time, August 5, 2020, from somebody in senior management at the NSO Group. Cherie Blair, former First Lady of the United Kingdom, longtime barrister, noted advocate for women entrepreneurs in Africa, South Asia, and the Middle East, a prominent voice for human rights worldwide, was obliged to pick up the phone. Mrs. Blair had recently signed on as a paid consultant to the Israeli firm NSO to help "incorporate human rights considerations into NSO activities, including interactions with customers and deployment of NSO products."

This was a delicate high-wire act, ethically speaking, because NSO's signature product, cybersurveillance software called Pegasus, was a remarkable and remarkably unregulated tool—extraordinarily lucrative to the company (NSO grossed around $250 million that year) and dangerously seductive to its clients. Successfully deployed, Pegasus essentially owns a mobile phone; it can break down defenses built into a cell phone, including encryption, and gain something close to free rein on the device, without ever tipping off the owner to its presence. That includes all text and voice communications to and from the phone, location data, photos and videos, notes, browsing history, even turning on the camera and the microphone of the device while the user has no idea it's happening. Complete remote personal surveillance, at the push of a button.

NSO insists its software and support services are licensed to sovereign states only, to be used for law enforcement and intelligence purposes. They insist that's true, because—my God—imagine if it weren't.

The cybersurveillance system the company created and continually updates and upgrades for its sixty-plus clients in more than forty different countries has made the world a much safer place, says NSO. Tens of thousands of lives have been saved, they say, because terrorists, criminals, and pedophiles (pedophiles is a big company talking point the last few years) can be spied on and stopped before they act. The numbers are impossible to verify, but the way NSO describes it, the upsides of Pegasus, used within legal and ethical boundaries, are pretty much inarguable. Who doesn't want to stop pedophiles? Or terrorists? Who could be against it?

"Mission Control, we have a problem," was the message Cherie Blair got from the call that warm summer evening in August 2020.

"It had come to the attention of NSO that their software may have been misused to monitor the mobile phone of Baroness Shackleton and her client, Her Royal Highness Princess Haya," Blair explained in a London court proceeding some months later. "The NSO Senior Manager told me that NSO were very concerned about this."

NSO's concern appeared to be twofold, according to the evidence elicited in that London court. The first was a question of profile. Pegasus had been deployed against a woman who was a member of *two* powerful Middle Eastern royal families, as well as her very well-connected British attorney, Baroness Fiona Shackleton. Shackleton was not only a renowned divorce lawyer to the rich and famous—including Paul McCartney, Madonna, Prince Andrew, and Prince Charles—she was also herself a member of the House of Lords. Even more problematic for NSO, it was an outside cybersecurity researcher who had discovered the attacks on the baroness and the princess. If he'd figured out this one piece of how Pegasus was being used, what else had he figured out? And how much of this was about to become public knowledge?

The caller from NSO asked Cherie Blair "to contact Baroness Shackleton urgently so that she could notify Princess Haya," she explained in testimony. "The NSO Senior Manager told me that they had taken steps to ensure that the phones could not be accessed again."

The details of the late-night call to Blair and the spying on the princess and her lawyer didn't really shake out into public view until more than a year later, and only then because it was part of the child custody proceedings between Princess Haya and her husband, Sheikh Mohammed bin Rashid Al Maktoum, prime minister of the United Arab Emirates and the emir of Dubai. The finding by the president of the High Court of Justice Family Division, released to the public in October 2021, held that the mobile phones of the princess, her lawyer, the baroness, and four other people in their intimate circle were attacked with cybersurveillance software, and that "the software used was NSO's Pegasus." The judge determined it was more than probable that the surveillance "was carried out by servants or agents of [the princess's husband, Sheikh Mohammed bin Rashid Al Maktoum], the Emirate of Dubai, or the UAE." The surveillance, according to the judge, "occurred with [the Sheikh's] express or implied authority."

The story of the princess, the baroness, and Pegasus might have faded into gossip columns and then into oblivion after a few weeks. A rich and powerful man used a pricey bit of software to spy on his wife and her divorce lawyer? Well, if you marry a sheikh and then cross him, you damn well might expect things to get weird. NSO also did a fairly nice job of cleanup on Aisle Spyware. The court finding pretty much accepted the word of NSO that it had terminated the UAE's ability to use its Pegasus system altogether, at a cost to the company, the judge noted, "measured in tens of millions of dollars." And maybe they did, but who can say.

A FUNNY THING happened on the way to that divorce court gossip column item, though. Because right around the time Cherie Blair got that call from Israel, a very brave source offered two journalists from Paris and two cybersecurity researchers from Berlin access to a remarkable piece of leaked data. The list included the phone numbers of not one or two or ten Emirati soon-to-be divorcees, or even twenty or fifty suspected pedophiles or drug traffickers. It was fifty *thousand* mobile phone numbers, all selected for possible Pegasus targeting by clients of that firm in Israel, NSO. Fifty thousand?

What exactly to make of that initial leaked list—that crucial first peek into the abyss—is a question that took nearly a year to answer, with a lot of risk and a lot of serious legwork to get there. The answer to the question matters. Because either this is a scandal we understand and get ahold of and come up with solutions for, or this is the future, for all of us, with no holds barred.

THIS BOOK IS the behind-the-scenes story of the Pegasus Project, the investigation into the meaning of the leaked data, as told by Laurent Richard and Sandrine Rigaud of Forbidden Stories, the two journalists who got access to the list of fifty thousand phones. With the list in hand, they gathered and coordinated an international collaboration of more than eighty investigative journalists from seventeen media organizations across four continents, eleven time zones, and about eight separate languages. "They held this thing together miraculously," says an editor from the *Guardian*, one of the partners in the Pegasus Project. "We've got, like, maybe six hundred journalists. The *Washington Post* is maybe twice the size. And to think that a small nonprofit in Paris, with just a handful of people working for it, managed to convene a global alliance of media organizations and take on not just one of the most powerful cybersurveillance companies in the world but some of the most repressive and authoritarian governments in the world, that is impressive."

In the daily back-and-forth of American news and politics—my wheelhouse—it is rare indeed to come across a news story that is both a thriller and of real catastrophic importance. Regular civilians being targeted with military-grade surveillance weapons—against their will, against their knowledge, and with no recourse—is a dystopian future we really are careening toward if we don't understand this threat and move to stop it. The Pegasus Project saga not only shows us how to stop it; it's an edge-of-your-seat procedural about the heroes who found this dragon and then set out to slay it. I have never covered a story quite like this, but Laurent and Sandrine sure have, and it is freaking compelling stuff.

The engine of the narrative you're about to read is the risky investigation itself, from the minute these guys first got access to that leaked list in the last half of 2020 to publication in July 2021. But herein also is the story of the company NSO, its Israeli government benefactors, and its client states, which takes the reader from Tel Aviv to Mexico City to Milan, Istanbul, Baku, Riyadh, Rabat, and beyond. The company's ten-year rise—from its unlikely inception, to its early fights with competitors, to its golden era of reach and profitability—reveals the full history of the development, the weaponization, and the mindless spread of a dangerous and insidious technology. "If you're selling weapons, you better make sure you're selling those to someone who is accountable for their actions," one young Israeli cybersecurity expert says. "If you're giving a police officer a gun and if that police officer starts shooting innocent people, you are not to be blamed. But if you're giving a chimpanzee a gun and the chimpanzee shoots someone, you can't blame the chimpanzee. Right? You will be to blame." Turns out this story has armed chimpanzees up the wazoo. And a lot of innocent people shot at by the proverbial police, too.

Here also is the story of the other individuals besides Laurent and Sandrine who were entrusted with full access to the leaked data, Claudio Guarnieri and Donncha Ó Cearbhaill (pronounced O'Carroll), two young, incorrigible, irrepressible cybersecurity specialists at Amnesty International's Security Lab. These men—one barely in his thirties, the other still in his twenties—shouldered incredible weight throughout the Pegasus Project. Against the most aggressive and accomplished cyber-intrusion specialists in the world, Claudio and Donncha were charged with designing and enforcing the security protocols that kept the investigation under wraps for almost a full year and kept the source that provided the list out of harm's way for good.

More than that, it was up to Claudio and Donncha to find the evidence of NSO's spyware on phones that were on the list leaked to them by that brave source. The insidious power of a Pegasus infection was that it was completely invisible to the victim—you'd have no way to know the baddies were reading your texts and emails and listening in on your calls and even your in-person meetings until they used their ability to track your exact location to send the men with guns to meet you. For the Pegasus Project to succeed in exposing the scale of the scandal, the journalists knew they would need to be able to diagnose an infection or an attempted infection on an individual phone. Claudio and Donncha figured out how to do it. Working quite literally alone, these two took on a multibillion-dollar corporation that employed 550 well-paid cyberspecialists, many with the highest levels of military cyberwarfare training. To best that Goliath, these two Davids had to fashion their own slingshot, had to invent the methods and tools of their forensics on the fly. That they succeeded is as improbable as it is important, for all our sakes.

Here also is the story of the victims of Pegasus. Among them are those who hold enough power that you might expect they'd be protected from this kind of totalist intrusion—heads of state, high-ranking royals, senior politicians, law enforcement figures. And then there's the people whom governments the world over have always liked to put in the cross-hairs: opposition figures, dissidents, human rights activists, academics. Laurent and Sandrine rack focus tight on the group most represented in the leaked data, of course: journalists.

For me, the most unforgettable characters in this story are Khadija Ismayilova, from Azerbaijan, and Omar Radi, of Morocco. Their uncommon courage proves both admirable and costly. Their stories lay bare the awful personal consequences of challenging governments in an age of unregulated cybersurveillance, and the need for more people like them.

As antidemocratic and authoritarian winds gather force all over the world, it's increasingly clear that the rule of law is only so powerful against forces hell-bent on eliminating the rule of law. If we've learned anything over the last five years, it's this: there will be no prosecutor on a white horse, no flawless court proceedings where a St. Peter in black robes opens or closes the pearly gates based on true and perfect knowledge of the sins of those in the dock. Sometimes, sure, the law is able to help. But more often, the threat evades, outmaneuvers, or just runs ahead of the law in a way that leaves us needing a different kind of protection. Again and again, it falls to journalists to lay out the facts of corruption, venality, nepotism, lawlessness, and brutality practiced by the powerful.

The dangers of doing this kind of work are real, and growing. For all the prime ministers and royal soon-to-be-ex-wives and other high-profile targets that NSO clients hit, it is no surprise that Pegasus has been turned full blast on reporters and editors in order to harass, intimidate, and silence. If this antidemocratic, authoritarian nightmare can't be safely reported upon, it won't be understood. And if it isn't understood, there's no chance that it will be stopped.

WHERE'S YOUR PHONE right now? That little device in your pocket likely operates as your personal calendar, your map and atlas, your post office, your telephone, your scratchpad, your camera—basically as your trusted confidant. Matthew Noah Smith, a professor of moral and political philosophy, wrote in 2016 that a mobile phone "is an extension of the mind. . . . There is simply no principled distinction between the processes occurring in the meaty glob in your cranium and the processes occurring in the little silicon, metal, and glass block that is your iPhone. The solid-state drive storing photos in the phone are your memories in the same way that certain groups of neurons storing images in your brain are memories. Our minds extend beyond our heads and into our phones."

Professor Smith was making the case back then for a zone of privacy that extended to our mobile phone. If the state has no right to access the thoughts in our head, why should it have the right to access the pieces of our thoughts that we keep in our mobile phone? We tell our cell phones almost anything these days, even things we aren't cognizant of telling it, and use it as the conduit to offer the most intimate glimpses of ourselves. (See sexting.) If you believe your privacy is being secured by encryption, please read this book, and consider the fifty thousand people on that horror show list, who unbeknownst to them were targeted to unwillingly share every single thing that passed through their phones with people who only had to pay for the privilege.

That list of fifty thousand was just our first keyhole view of the crime scene. If they could do it for fifty thousand, doesn't that mean they could do it for five hundred thousand? Five million? Fifty million? Where is the limit, and who is going to draw that line? Who is going to deliver us from this worldwide Orwellian nightmare? Because it turns out you don't have to be married to the emir of anything to find your every thought, every footstep, every word recorded and tracked from afar. Turns out you just need to have a phone, and a powerful enemy somewhere. Who among us is exempt from those conditions?

Where did you say your phone is right now?

PEGASUS

CHAPTER ONE

THE LIST

Laurent

Sandrine and I had been drawn to Berlin by the kind of opportunity you get maybe once in a lifetime in journalism—a shot to break a story that could have serious implications around the world. It felt kind of fitting that our taxi from the airport to the city center skirted within a few kilometers of the Stasi Museum, a complex that once housed the apparatus of the East German secret police, "The Sword and Shield of the State." This investigation, if we decided to undertake it, would have to contend with swords and shields wielded by a dozen or more very defensive state actors and by a billion-dollar private technology corporation operating under the protection of its own very powerful national government.

The taxi ride was the last leg of a trip that seemed to portend a rise of obstacles. The limitations put in place during the latest wave of Covid-19 had laid waste to familiar routines. The simple two-hour trip from Paris to Berlin had taken triple that, and included a connection through the food desert of an airport in Frankfurt, and the indignity of German soldiers shoving cotton swabs up our nasal cavities before we were allowed to exit the airport in Berlin.

By the time Sandrine and I stumbled into our sleekly modern and well-lighted little rented flat above Danziger Strasse, we were both so knackered that dark-of-the-night questions were already preying on us. Was this really the best time to dive into another difficult and all-consuming investigation? Our nine-person team at Forbidden Stories was deep into its third major project in just three years; the current investigation, the Cartel Project, was already shaping up as the most dangerous we had done to date. And we still had a lot of work to do to be ready for publication. We were developing leads on the most murderous drug gangs in Veracruz and Sinaloa and Guerrero, on the chemicals needed to produce the supercharged opioid fentanyl, which were being trafficked into the country from Asia, and on the lucrative gun trade filling the cartels' private armories (as well as the bank accounts of gun manufacturers and private gunrunners in Europe, Israel, and the United States).

We were essentially picking up reporting threads left unfinished by a handful of brave Mexican journalists who had been killed, most likely by assassins from the local drug cartels whose violent and criminal activities the reporters had been investigating. Outside of active war zones, Mexico was and remains to this day the most dangerous place in the world to be a journalist committed to telling the truth about bad guys. More than 120 journalists and media staffers had been killed in Mexico in the first two decades of the twenty-first century. Another score or so had simply disappeared without a trace.

This meant the Cartel Project tied seamlessly to the mission of Forbidden Stories: we aim to put bad actors and repugnant governments on notice that killing the messenger will not kill the message. Which means collaboration is an indispensable tool. There is strength and safety in numbers. The more journalists who are working the story, the more certain it is to see print. We had begun inviting into the Cartel Project reporters from our trusted media partners, including *Le Monde* in Paris, the *Guardian* in London, and *Die Zeit* and *Süddeutsche Zeitung* in Germany. The team would eventually grow to more than sixty reporters from twenty-five different media outlets in eighteen countries. But the beating heart of the project, already, was Jorge Carrasco, who was the director of the most intrepid investigative publication in Mexico, the weekly magazine *Proceso*. A stubborn and celebrated reporter himself, Jorge was also a colleague, and an exact contemporary of the woman who was emerging as a figure at the center of our investigation, Regina Martínez.

Carrasco was still a reporter at *Proceso* in April 2012 when the news reached him that his co-worker had been beaten and strangled to death in her home. Regina had been a journalist for nearly a quarter century by then and had spent much of the previous four years dogging the powerful and dangerous drug cartel that had essentially taken over Veracruz. Cash was flowing into the region, along with waves of violence that convulsed the state's teeming port city and spread into the surrounding area. A large portion of Martínez's final reporting was in uncovering the destabilizing relationships growing up between local politicians, local law enforcement, and local drug lords. She hadn't really gone looking for the story, but if you were a sentient being in Veracruz in those years, it was hard to miss. And once she was on it, Regina had a hard time backing off even after she knew she was on perilous ground. She had confided to her closest friends, just a few months before her death, that she might have gone too far, and she feared for her safety. She was worried enough to stop using a byline on the most incendiary of her stories, but she refused to quit reporting.

A few weeks before she was found strangled to death, Regina had published a damning report detailing the personal assets amassed by two public officials who had allied themselves with the Los Zetas cartel in Veracruz. (Three thousand copies of that issue of *Proceso* were removed from the kiosk shelves before they ever made it into the hands of local readers.) At the time of her murder, she was in the middle of investigating the story of the thousands of people who had mysteriously disappeared from Veracruz in the previous few months. "Her death marked a before and after for the profession," one of Martínez's friends and colleagues would tell us. "She was part of a major national magazine. We thought she was protected."

Jorge had already traveled to our offices in Paris to brief the Forbidden Stories team and our early partners on the state of investigative reporting in Mexico and the outlines of the Regina Martínez story. The fifty-six-year-old journalist spoke with a soft, measured cadence befitting a classics scholar, but his message to us was sharp and compelling.

"Regina's murder was a point of no return," Jorge had explained. "A very clear message that the [cartels] could continue to kill journalists and nothing happens."

The police and prosecutors in Veracruz, Jorge told us, basically punted Regina's case in 2012, pinning her murder on a low-rent criminal who quickly recanted his confession (which the suspect claimed he made only after hours of physical torture by local police). For most of the eight years since, Jorge had been determined to get to the bottom of Regina's killing. He had taken to heart the admonition of Julio Scherer García, the founding editor of *Proceso* and the godfather of investigative journalism in Mexico. "The world has hardened, and I think journalism will have to harden," Scherer said not long before he died in 2015. "If the rivers turn red and the valleys fill with corpses . . . journalism will have to tell that story with images and words. Heavy tasks await us."

Jorge Carrasco worked the story for years in spite of threats and intimidation, and even after the murder of a second *Proceso* contributor, who also demanded answers from the government about Martínez, but with little success. By January 2020, when Sandrine and I first visited the Mexico City offices of *Proceso*—offices with a security protocol you might expect at a bunkered police station, with a guard at the front gate and bars on every window—Jorge's ardor had cooled. He admitted to us that they had discussed it in the newsroom, as a staff, and decided chasing the truth about Regina Martínez's murder was too dangerous. If they kept it up, others were likely to die at the hands of the local drug lords.

Once he learned an international consortium of journalists was willing to take up the story, though, Jorge seemed reenergized. He had dispatched his chief archivist to dig up all of Regina's stories from *Proceso* in the years before her death, and he asked us to loop another of his reporters into the top-secret Signal group used by key members of the Cartel Project. But the last Sandrine had heard from Jorge on the Signal app, not long before our trip to Berlin, he had sounded a little shaky—lamenting the ongoing damage done by Covid-19 to his magazine's already slim and always wobbly profit margin. "I'm okay but worried," he wrote. "Sales of *Proceso* are really falling."

▉▉▉▉▉▉▉

I WAS KEYED up when the buzzer to our East Berlin flat rang the next morning. We hadn't yet mastered the electronic entry system to our short-term rental, so I raced down the stairs and opened the front door for our two guests. The first I saw was a pale, wraithlike, thirtysomething man with wire-rim glasses and a ski cap pulled tight atop his skull. He looked like the kind of guy who spent a lot of time indoors at a computer screen. I welcomed him with a cheery hello and stuck my hand out in greeting. Claudio Guarnieri, senior technologist at Amnesty International's Security Lab, didn't offer any pleasantries in response, didn't shake my hand, didn't even really pause long enough to make eye contact. He simply bade me to direct him and the skinny young fellow with him up the stairs and into our flat, where we could get down to business at the dining room table.

But there would be *no* business, Claudio explained, until we all powered down our phones and our laptops, put them in the next room, and closed the door on them. The cloak-and-dagger aspect of these instructions was not entirely unexpected, given the reason for this meeting, but I was surprised by Claudio's brusque tone. He was polite enough, but not long on social niceties; in fact, he didn't seem to be much concerned whether we liked him or not. This was an *alliance de circonstance*, after all, and compatibility mattered a lot less than viability.

We hastily stowed our electronic devices in the next room, but not before I took note of the sticker on Claudio's own laptop, a quote from the Mexican political dissident Subcomandante Marcos: "We are sorry for the inconvenience, but this is a revolution." Back at the table, Claudio waved away any attempt at small talk and turned immediately to the reason we were all there. We had been chosen—Forbidden Stories and Amnesty International's Security Lab—as the only two groups with access to a document we had taken to calling the List. Sandrine and I had each been given to understand that the data might help us uncover the existence of a system of truly insidious surveillance, made possible by a private for-profit corporation, that touched thousands of unsuspecting individuals on almost every continent.

We were a long way from proving that, we all knew, at our table in Berlin that morning. The data in this list was a bit of a cipher: a scroll of tens of thousands of phone numbers from all over the world, as well as some time stamps. Only a handful of those numbers had been matched to actual names or identities. What we did know was that each number represented a person whose cell phone had been selected for potential infection with the most potent cybersurveillance weapon on the market: a malware called Pegasus, which had been developed, marketed, and supplied to law enforcement and national security agencies in more than forty countries around the world by the alpha dog in the burgeoning industry—the Israeli tech company NSO.

Pegasus was coveted by national security specialists around the globe because it was regarded as state-of-the-art spyware; if a country wanted to catch the bad guys in criminal or terrorist acts, or to prevent those acts before they happened, Pegasus was a godsend. Each successful infection allowed its operator, or end user, to essentially take over a cell phone. Law enforcement or national security agencies would have access to every jot and tittle in that phone, *before* any outgoing communication was encrypted and *after* any incoming communication was decrypted. The operators of Pegasus could track that cell phone's geolocation and exfiltrate email messages, text messages, data, photographs, and videos. Pegasus also allowed its users to gain control of the device's microphones and cameras; these recording apps could be turned on remotely, at will, at the pleasure and convenience of the end user.

The dangerous hitch in the Pegasus system was that it had not been limited to spying on bad guys. By the time we sat down in Berlin with Claudio and his number two, Donncha Ó Cearbhaill, a few dozen cases of misuse had already been documented. Cybersecurity experts at the University of Toronto's Citizen Lab and at Claudio's Amnesty International's Security Lab had found cases of Pegasus being used to target human rights defenders, lawyers, and journalists. The specialists in those forensic labs had not only elucidated many of the mechanics and capabilities of Pegasus but had called out some of its most pernicious end users. WhatsApp had filed suit against NSO, claiming fourteen hundred of its users had been surreptitiously targeted by Pegasus in just one two-week period. Amnesty International had a pending suit also. The public domain was filling with information gleaned from legal filings in courts from the United States to France to Israel to Canada.

There had also been some really good journalism and a growing body of scholarship on the rise of the for-profit "Intrusion as a Service" industry in general and NSO in particular. These multiple investigations, taken together, were starting to look like a more successful edition of the Blind Men and the Elephant parable. The combination of cybersecurity experts, academics, journalists, and justice-seeking victims, working separately and in concert, had managed to sketch a pretty complete picture of the cybersurveillance elephant at work.

The outlines alone made crystal clear the threats to human rights and privacy, and yet, even the most dismaying headlines and the most granular forensic analyses had had little to no real impact. Outside of calls from Amnesty International and Citizen Lab and the United Nations special rapporteur on the promotion and protection of the right to freedom of opinion and expression, there was virtually no public outcry and very little actual attention. No governing body of consequence was putting any fetters on the industry. NSO's profits and its client base were growing faster than ever, with customers across Europe, North America, the Middle East, and Africa. "The few of us invested in these issues warned again and again how the commodification of surveillance was paving the way to systemic abuse," Claudio would later say, reflecting on a decade's worth of consistent effort and consistent frustration. "Very few listened; most were just indifferent. Every new report, every new case, felt so inconsequential that I started questioning whether insisting on them was serving anything other than our own egos."

That's what made this leak so enticing.

Claudio never grew particularly animated our first day together in Berlin, or any other day thereafter. He was always careful not to betray any outward sense of excitement. But he clearly held hope that this leaked list might finally help him get the goods on NSO and allow us to draw the sort of public attention this unfolding crisis truly deserved. Claudio and Donncha were slightly ahead of us in their understanding of the list itself, partly because of the technical skills they had developed over the last decade and partly because the Security Lab had access to digital tools that Forbidden Stories lacked. Claudio set the agenda for much of that first day at that dining room table in Berlin, sitting on a sleek wooden bench, explaining the big picture of this story as he apprehended it at that moment.

Time stamps in the data went back almost five years and extended right up to the past few weeks, Claudio explained, which meant the attacks were fresh—and possibly even ongoing. We were likely to be investigating a crime in progress. He and Donncha had already started the laborious process of identifying exactly who was attempting to spy on whom. And exactly when. And exactly where. The list of phone numbers was arranged in clusters, suggesting which of NSO's many client countries was targeting any specific individual. The governments selecting targets ranged from murderous dictatorships to would-be autocracies to the largest democracy on the planet. The most active client state by far was Mexico, with more than fifteen thousand separate numbers selected for possible targeting.

The list no doubt contained hundreds of cell phone numbers of authentic drug lords, terrorists, criminals, and national security threats—the sort of malefactors NSO spokespeople claimed Pegasus was designed to thwart. But what Claudio and Donncha had already learned about the range of targets selected for attack was eye-popping. When the two had started the process of identifying some of the phone numbers on the list, Claudio explained to us, it turned out that many belonged to academics, human rights defenders, political dissidents, government officials, diplomats, businessmen, and high-ranking military officers. Claudio and Donncha had already found hundreds of noncriminal, non-terrorist targets selected for possible Pegasus infection, and they had barely scratched the surface. The group with the largest number of targets on its collective back—well over 120 and counting—was journalists.

If the data in this list led us to the hard evidence necessary for publication, we all understood, we would not only be able to reconfirm the already-known fact that cyberintrusion and cybersurveillance were being weaponized to stifle the free press and to undermine and intimidate political dissent. We would be able to reveal that it was being weaponized at a sweep and scale that astounds—and horrifies.

As Claudio, Donncha, Sandrine, and I scrolled down through page after page after page of possibly compromised cell phone numbers, it occurred to me that we were not merely groping around to help define the outlines of a single rogue elephant. We were looking at a herd of hundreds, thousands, maybe even tens of thousands of elephants thundering unimpeded across the plains, prodded by some of the most vicious political regimes on the planet, and headed right for cherished and necessary pillars of civil society. The large-scale, unchecked, systematic abuse of cybersurveillance weapons was a clear and present danger to the most basic human rights, including privacy, political dissent, freedom of expression, and freedom of the press; it was a threat to democracy itself, at a time when the world's most stable democracies were under relentless attack from without and from within.

THE FIRST LOOK at the list was slightly disorienting. The pull was magnetic, almost like a physical sensation. I reminded myself to take a deep breath occasionally, as Claudio kept talking, noting, for instance, that it looked like Moroccan intelligence had targeted an extraordinary number of French cell phones. I had to tell myself not to let my imagination get too far ahead of me. Skepticism is crucial for any reporter—a stopgap to embarrassing mistakes, like being played by an unscrupulous source with an axe to grind, or letting excitement about a potentially big story outrun good sense and rigorous vetting. Vetting the data in this list would take months. Finding victims who were willing to allow us to analyze their phones for evidence of Pegasus targeting (and to keep quiet about it while we developed the story) would be a delicate operation. Claudio and Donncha faced a more daunting task, even with potentially compromised phones in hand to analyze. NSO had designed Pegasus as more than a Trojan horse; it was engineered to be an *invisible* Trojan horse. Top-shelf cybersurveillance exploits aim to leave behind no detectable traces, and NSO was believed to be the best in the business at covering its tracks. Gathering unassailable forensic evidence was going to be an uphill battle, and forensics was only half the battle.

Claudio, Donncha, Sandrine, and I were talking about embarking on an investigation of a private company whose entire reason for being is digital surveillance, a company that trumpeted its ability to "Find anyone, anywhere." Considering that foreign governments on five continents had been paying NSO as much as a quarter of a billion dollars a year to do just that, the company's spyware system was probably very good at it. The four of us understood what we would be stepping into by the time our first meeting came to a close, Claudio most of all. He issued Sandrine and me another brusque set of instructions before we parted: he told us we needed to go out and buy new devices—no SIM cards!—dedicated solely to communicating with one another. There would be no cell phone calls among the four of us or anybody else who came onto the project. No iMessages, no Signal messages, no WhatsApp calls. We had already, at Claudio's insistence, bought new dedicated laptops—PCs, not Macs—so that we could keep a hard wall between the Pegasus Project and all the other work we were doing. If we went ahead with this project, it occurred to me, the main driver of the operation would be paranoia.

When Claudio and Donncha left that evening, after we set a time to meet again the next day, the difficulties of tackling this investigation were already spinning in my head. The list itself was a big unknown. We had plenty of faith in the source of the leak, but that was beside the point. We were looking at months of authenticating the data on the list, double-checking every fact and story that hove up out of those tens of thousands of phone numbers. We were going to have to do this work while attempting to live within the physical and social restrictions imposed on us by the most lethal global heath pandemic in a century. I was also having a hard time imagining forming a comfortable working relationship with Claudio, who had not shown even a hint of a smile that first day. Donncha was much more open and easygoing, but the twenty-seven-year-old cyber-researcher, as we later learned, also had good reason to be wary of reporters. Add to that, this investigation would have to be done within a bubble of absolute secrecy—a bubble easily popped by a single careless mistake.

▪▪▪▪▪▪▪

CLAUDIO SUGGESTED AN interesting exercise for our second-day meeting in Berlin, a whack at low-hanging fruit. He pulled from his bag an unused USB stick, still in its packaging, and helped me to safely download a backup of the entirety of my digital contacts file from my personal cell phone. Then Claudio plugged the untainted USB stick into the secure laptop computer he was using to access the list, and ran an automated program that matched cell phone numbers from my contacts file with cell phone numbers in the data. The first to come up a match was for an official in Turkey's foreign ministry. I had his number because I had requested an interview with him while working on a story about secret arms transfers between the Turkish secret service and jihadist groups in northern Syria.

The next match to come up was the phone number of Khadija Ismayilova, who was the most famous and fearless investigative reporter in Azerbaijan. I knew her well. Khadija had been reporting on the financial corruption of Azeri president Ilham Aliyev for more than fifteen years. The forty-four-year-old Ismayilova had won multiple international press awards for her journalism. She had also earned the wrath of Aliyev and his secret police. Khadija had been harassed, blackmailed, and imprisoned by the Aliyev government; she was at that precise moment living under house arrest in Baku. She had been under almost constant physical surveillance for years.

I had actually seen some of the spooks on Khadija watch—beefy guys with bushy mustaches and ill-fitting trench coats—when I was on a reporting trip in Azerbaijan back in 2014. I was on the lookout for them because the first thing Khadija did when we met was alert me to Aliyev's iron dome of surveillance. Anybody who had been seen in her company, Khadija explained, would likely be spied on. "Don't do anything in your hotel room you wouldn't want to see published," she told me. She wasn't joking.

I had two separate numbers for Khadija, but I had always been careful to only call or text her special secret number, the one I identified as "Khadija-Safe" in my contacts file. Turns out that the number in the leaked data, the number selected for targeting by the Azeri government, was "Khadija-Safe." The possibility that Khadija was still under surveillance was no real surprise. The possibility that she was being stalked by Pegasus was.

NSO was reported to have licensed its spyware system to more than forty countries, but Azerbaijan had never been on anybody's list. If NSO had sold licenses to cybersurveillance weapons to government agencies in Azerbaijan—a country whose annual record of civil liberties violations, political repression, and outright torture put it consistently near the top ten of bad actors alongside China, North Korea, Somalia, and Syria— there was no telling how far and wide Pegasus had flown. That was a chilling thought, because in the short history of the cyberweapons-for-sale industry, surveillance was only the beginning of the problem. Where cybersurveillance was in wide use, serious casualties often followed.

I had first become aware of this industry back in the summer of 2011, when two *Wall Street Journal* reporters had stumbled into a warren of computers in Tripoli a week after rebels had deposed the murderous Libyan dictator Muammar Gadhafi. The office turned out to be the hub of a massive cybermonitoring program. "The recently abandoned room," the *Journal* reporters wrote in their initial story, "is lined with posters and English-language training manuals stamped with the name Amesys, a unit of French technology firm Bull SA, which installed the monitoring center."

Turns out the French company (with the blessing of the French government) had sold Gadhafi an internet surveillance system that allowed his agents to monitor the emails, chats, and messages of anybody in Libya. The Gadhafi regime was able to identify and track the dictator's many political opponents almost at will. "Whereas many Internet interception systems carry out basic filtering on IP addresses and extract only those communications from the global flow (Lawful Interception)," read an Amesys-produced poster hanging in the office in Tripoli, "EAGLE Interception system analyzes and stores all the communications from the monitored link (Massive Interception)."

Libyan security tactics didn't stop at surveillance. Being caught entering a chat room filled with critics of Gadhafi could have serious consequences—starting with arrest and questioning. According to the testimony of several detainees in a French court in 2013, Gadhafi's interrogators were able to quote back to them—verbatim—their emails, SMS exchanges, Facebook threads, chat-room conversations, even private phone conversations. The security agents usually demanded from their captives the identities behind the various user names they had been communicating with online or on the phone. If threats, beatings, electric shock, and other torture weren't enough to convince the detainees to reveal the names of otherwise anonymous comrades, Gadhafi's agents would ship them off to prison. Threats and beatings continued there, along with brief field trips to a courtyard to witness the executions of other prisoners.

When these revelations started to come out in France, Bull SA made the prudent business move. They simply off-loaded the technology that ran the Eagle system to another French company, Nexa Technologies—which continued to make it available on the open market. Egyptian president Abdel Fattah al-Sisi, who seized power following the chaos of the Arab Spring, became one of the French cyberweapon's most enthusiastic end users. (The surveillance system was reported to be a $12 million gift from al-Sisi's friends in the United Arab Emirates.) "The grave human rights violations committed to this day by the various branches of the [Egyptian] security services include arbitrary mass arrests, with the incarceration of at least 60,000 political prisoners since 2013; extrajudicial executions; enforced disappearances . . . and the systematic use of torture," the Paris-based International Federation for Human Rights had noted in a recent report, *Egypt: A Repression Made in France*. "This modus operandi of the security forces, aimed at eliminating all possibility of dissent, has become everyday reality for all Egyptians, and it specifically targets political opponents and civil society: members of political parties, the Muslim Brotherhood and their supporters, activists in revolutionary movements and of all stripes, human rights defenders, lawyers, journalists, writers, researchers, in addition to LGBTQ people or those perceived as such."

The Bull/Amesys/Nexa axis was hardly alone in selling spyware systems to questionable regimes—regimes that had nevertheless been designated by France as "a bulwark against Islamic fundamentalism," according to the report. "The enormous increase of arms sales beginning in 2013 and al-Sisi's arrival in power in Egypt in 2014 have proven profitable for at least eight French companies that have sold equipment—both conventional weapons and surveillance equipment—to Egypt."

By 2020, cybersurveillance weapons had become an international growth sector, with dozens of countries engaging in active cybersurveillance measures, almost all of them customers of private corporations who were happy to tailor the systems to their clients' needs and wants. So long as the price was right.

The leading spyware technology companies had, by 2020, adjusted their focus from personal computers to cell phones, with NSO Group right out front. The consequences had been predictable. Security researchers first found evidence of a cell phone infected with NSO's Pegasus in 2016—in an iPhone owned by a human rights activist in the United Arab Emirates—but that revelation proved no great boon to the victim, Ahmed Mansoor. In the aftermath of the report, Mansoor lost his job, his passport, his car, his savings, and his freedom to the UAE security forces. He was beaten by unknown assailants twice in a single week. While Claudio, Donncha, Sandrine, and I sat in a comfortable flat in Berlin matching my contacts to numbers on the list, Mansoor was serving a ten-year prison term for threatening the "unity" of the state and damaging "the status and prestige of the UAE and its symbols." He was reportedly being kept in solitary confinement and sporadically subjected to torture. "Mansoor's wife, Nadia," Reuters had reported in early 2019, "lived in social isolation in Abu Dhabi. Neighbors are avoiding her out of fear security forces are watching."

The evidence already out there made things clear: Pegasus and other cybersurveillance systems had become favorite toys of some of the most vicious leaders in the world, men who would not hesitate to destroy the lives of anybody who crossed them. We were contemplating crossing them in a very big way.

When Claudio's automated matching program finished its work on my files, we went through the same exercise with Sandrine's. She had spent much of her early career in journalism covering politics, so her contact list was different from mine, which turned out to be helpful that day. A few French political figures in her contacts were also on the list of potential Pegasus targets. Then came the match that really jolted us: among several Mexican journalists in the data was Jorge Carrasco, the crucial lead partner in our current project.

Jorge's phone had likely been targeted by somebody in Mexican law enforcement or the Mexican military. But Pegasus was like loose nukes, gettable for the right amount of money, so it was also possible he was being watched by one or more of the corrupt and dangerous Mexican officials we were secretly investigating. Whoever had done the targeting might also be able to track us, and our team, and all the other collaborators on the Cartel Project, through Jorge.

We asked Claudio if Jorge should switch out his phone, and he said that was probably a good idea, but unlikely to solve the problem. NSO's customers could infect a new iPhone just as easily.

Sandrine contacted a colleague of Jorge's in Mexico right away and asked him to get a message to him: Jorge needed to replace his phone, and he needed to get off and stay off the Cartel Project Signal loop— immediately. We could not tell Jorge exactly why this was necessary, but he had to trust us. We would be in touch as soon as we had a new and secure way to communicate.

When Sandrine and I parted from Claudio and Donncha and started preparing for the long trip back home, we were left with two big questions:

How in the world could we do this story? And how could we not?

CHAPTER TWO

"I'M COUNTING ON YOU TO FINISH IT"

Laurent

Just a few days after we arrived back in Paris, Sandrine and I gathered the members of our small staff to brief them on our trip to Berlin. My first point of emphasis was that everyone in the room needed to be bound by a solemn promise. Nobody outside of Forbidden Stories could know anything about what we were about to say. I knew the temptation from personal experience: when a big story like this presents itself, it's human nature to want to confide in a few close colleagues, or your spouse, or your closest friend—the people you know you can trust. In this instance, trust was a luxury we could not afford. We understood, as did Claudio's team at the Security Lab, that if the existence of the list was divulged, the project would be over before it started. The source was risking life and limb, and if the source felt unprotected, our access to the list would end.

"You might be out having drinks with friends and after about four beers you might be tempted to tell them about this amazing story you're working on," I told them. "Don't. You can't tell your family, the person you're living with, your best friend. Nobody. People's lives are at stake."

Then I told them what Sandrine and I had learned in Berlin. As I began to explain the nature of the leak, and the work we had in front of us, I was mindful of the fact that this investigation was likely to be both difficult and dangerous—and possibly an undue burden on a group of young reporters up to their necks in the Mexico project. We had built a very capable team in a very short time, but this new undertaking was going to test everybody in this room like never before. I also knew that while I was mulling the big picture, Sandrine was thinking through how to organize the flow of this new project in a way that gave us the greatest chance of success: Which team members were best suited to the various tasks in front of us? Who could we count on to categorize the numbers and information we gathered into data sets that revealed new and interesting patterns? Who could convince wary victims to give us total access to all the private data in their cell phones? Who could help pick up the thread of an entirely new story, in a place they had never been?

As I talked through the basic facts about the leak, and NSO, and the remarkable number of private citizens selected for targeting, I was also scanning the faces in the room—wondering what our future together would be. Not counting Sandrine and myself, our core group of reporters was only five, ranging in age from twenty-three to thirty-one. They were each multilingual, or at least bilingual. They were all smart and enthusiastic to a fault, but very different in individual style and demeanor. Their personalities and their abilities complemented one another, and the group had already proven greater than the sum of its parts.

Some, like twenty-three-year-old Paloma de Dinechin, were blessed with a natural facility to talk to people, to get sources to open up to them; others had a genius for digging information out of the deepest recesses of the internet. Audrey Travère, for instance, had just opened a new line of reporting in the Cartel Project for us by turning up a database that held records of shipments of chemicals from China and other countries into Mexico. I always think of Audrey, her brows furrowed, staring at the screen, in the compelling glow of a computer terminal.

Phineas Rueckert was an American from Brooklyn who studied Latin America in France. He was a committed internationalist with a boundless curiosity about the world, which made him a key swing man for Forbidden Stories. Sandrine was confident we could dispatch Phineas to Latin America or Eastern Europe or the Middle East or India, and he would immerse himself in the local culture and customs, develop friendships and sources, and generally be a good ambassador for our mission.

The elder statesman of the team was thirty-one-year-old Arthur Bouvart, who was already an established reporter and director of documentaries. He had worked on Forbidden Stories' first big investigative projects, before Sandrine came on as our managing editor. My personal connection to Arthur was probably deeper than my connection to anybody else in that room. We had first worked together almost ten years earlier, when he was a young trainee at the Paris-based television production company Premières Lignes. The two of us had also been together on one of the most traumatic days either of us had ever faced, and from which neither of us had entirely recovered.

If there was one person Sandrine and I thought of as the glue for this team, it was Cécile Schilis-Gallego, who signed on with Forbidden Stories in 2018, as one of my first hires. Cécile arrived with a master's degree in journalism from Columbia University and an expertise at data scraping and utilizing digital tools like fraud-detection algorithms. Still in her twenties, she had already contributed to some of the biggest international investigations of the previous five years, including the Implant Files, the Paradise Papers, and (biggest of them all) the Panama Papers.

She also came to us as a committed environmentalist, and an uncompromising one. Cécile may have had one of the smallest energy footprints in the West. She did not have a refrigerator or Wi-Fi at home. She refused to travel on airplanes or trains.

Cécile had slowly become the weather in our office, and it was usually sunny and pleasant. If there was a birthday, or an anniversary, or a big accomplishment to celebrate, Cécile brought the cake, and the candles, and the festive decorations. Her insistence on personal kindness was infectious in our small office, as was her sense of humor. "This will be painful but brief," she would say of one of her presentations, "as opposed to glorious and never-ending."

At some point during the meeting, Sandrine took over and started to tell our team about the extraordinary amount of cell phone numbers in the data—fifty thousand numbers selected for possible targeting by Pegasus. She explained the outlines of the first identifications the Security

Lab had already made: human rights lawyers, diplomats, officials at the United Nations. Mexico was by far the biggest client of NSO, but Morocco was not far behind, and neither was Saudi Arabia. We were going to want to get Jamal Khashoggi's phone number, Sandrine explained, to see if the Saudis had targeted him for cybersurveillance before they assassinated him. There were some recent public accusations that Amazon chieftain Jeff Bezos, who also owned Khashoggi's sometime employer, the *Washington Post*, was a target of the Saudis also. The reports were sketchy, and NSO always claimed that Pegasus could not be used on a cell phone with a US number (any number with a plus-1 country code), but the list gave us a way to check. So we wanted to get Bezos's personal cell phone number if possible. Sandrine explained that Claudio's team at the Security Lab, with a little help from our personal contact list, had already identified a total of 122 journalists from around the world. Among them was *Proceso*'s Jorge Carrasco, which should solve the mystery of why we asked him to get off the Cartel Project Signal group a few days earlier. Also on the list, we told the team, was the celebrated investigative reporter from Azerbaijan, Khadija Ismayilova.

I don't remember if Sandrine stopped to note it at the time—though everybody in the room would have known it already—but it was not a stretch to say that Forbidden Stories might not exist at all if not for Khadija Ismayilova. Khadija and I did not have a long history, but at least for me, the relationship was intense and meaningful. She was both a personal hero and an inspiration—the sort of journalist I most admire: the first to charge the hill, with courage that drew others to her standard. I think of Khadija as one of the two interwoven strands in the double helix of the Forbidden Stories' DNA.

I first met Khadija here in Paris when she spoke at a UNESCO conference in the spring of 2014, a week or so before I was to travel to her home country of Azerbaijan as part of French president François Hollande's press contingent. I was working on a documentary for a television investigative magazine I had co-created—*Cash Investigation*—about France's increasingly cozy relations with corrupt governments in former Soviet republics in the Caucasus. When I expressed some interest in talking to critics of the repressive family-run Azeri government while I was there,

Khadija encouraged me to come and see her in Baku. Getting people to talk on the record, for the camera, would not be easy, she said. But she gave me the number of another local journalist, a friend of hers named Leyla Mustafayeva, and said the two of them could help.

My trip to Azerbaijan started just about as I expected. Hollande was received in Baku on a crystalline May day with great pomp and circumstance by Azeri president Ilham Aliyev, who was clearly anxious to expand his country's already prodigious trade relations with France. (Aliyev was in his glory that day because Azerbaijan was about to assume the rotating presidency of the Council of Europe, a multinational institution whose stated mission is to promote democracy and to protect human rights.) The day rolled out as a series of photo ops and walks near the Caspian Sea and banqueting. There was, of course, much happy talk of potential new exploration and production contracts among Azeri government officials and the French energy company executives who were also part of Hollande's presidential junket. My cameraman, Emmanuel, and I managed to evade official security and get ourselves into a private meeting, so we were in the room to watch and record as the Azeri energy minister opined that once the newest pipelines were in place in 2019, oil and gas from Azerbaijan would begin flowing into Europe in unprecedented quantities—to the tune of about $50 billion, at a minimum. The minister didn't have to be explicit; the unspoken pitch was that Azerbaijan's longtime French partners, with their technological prowess and marketing skills in the energy field, were in line for an expanding share of those expanding profits.

Hollande then jetted off to his next destination, accompanied by a host of salivating energy company mavens. Emmanuel and I decided to peel off from President Hollande's official traveling press gaggle and, with Leyla's assistance, stick around in Baku to try to interview some of the Azeris who had been victimized by their own government. Most had agreed to meet with us because of their respect for Khadija and Leyla.

It was an intense few days, in part because the critics of the Aliyev government's escalating brutality were so compelling. ("They tied me up with my hands behind my back and put a bag on my head," one told us. "I was hit with a tool on the ribs, the back, and the chest. And they constantly demanded that I stop writing about Ilham Aliyev.") And it was an intense few days in part because Emmanuel, Leyla, and I could sense we were being watched. This sort of reporting was not something President Aliyev and his henchmen were apt to let go unchallenged, some of our interviewees explained, even in the case of a pair of journalists under French protection. In fact, Khadija called me just as we were preparing to leave Baku and said Emmanuel and I were likely to be arrested. I should make a copy of all of my hard drives, she advised, and slip them to Leyla. Then erase all the sensitive footage from the drives we were going to carry back home. Khadija told me she would personally make sure the fruits of our reporting were held safe.

So I wasn't entirely surprised to see a set of unfamiliar large men in dark suits hanging around the lobby of our hotel while I checked out. Or to see that Leyla—who already had the duplicates of our drives—had absented herself from the premises. The Azeri security team tailed our taxi all the way to the airport, and I have to admit I was a little fearful. I frantically ripped pages out of my notes and tossed them out the taxi window so they wouldn't have my notes to use against me if I was arrested. They didn't bother to stop to pick up the papers flying out the window of our moving car and pursued us all the way to the airport. When I saw a dozen or so armed secret police follow us into the terminal, I called my editor in Paris and asked him to stay on the line, just in case things went sideways. There wasn't much he could do by remote, but he did promise to alert President Hollande's office. Meanwhile the Azeri secret police grabbed us and led us into a small holding room, where they claimed we were being detained because we had neglected to pay our customs taxes—which was a lie.

Then they rifled through our baggage, set aside our camera equipment and our hard drives, and informed us we would be departing without all of it. We refused to leave our gear behind and insisted on contacting the French embassy in Baku. But the Azeri police shoved us down the jetway and onto the plane empty-handed. Our work was gone, confiscated.

What saved our bacon was Khadija, who somehow managed to ship the duplicate drives back to our office in Paris. Not only that, but

Khadija had also provided us with an interview of her own in which she had directly called out Ilham Aliyev as corrupt: "The president's family has a lot of money, which they cannot explain where that money comes from," Khadija had told me. "In Panama the daughters have eleven companies. Basically, they monopolize a huge deal of the businesses inside [Azerbaijan] and they invest money outside the country." This a dangerous thing for an Azeri journalist to broadcast all over Europe, but Khadija seemed unfazed at the certainty that she was inviting trouble.

She had already posted on her Facebook page a message titled IF I GET ARRESTED: "TO DEMOCRATIC COUNTRIES, DIPLOMATS, INTERNATIONAL ORGANIZATIONS," she wrote. "Some of you want to help, but can do it only with private diplomacy. Thank you, but No. . . . If you can, please support by standing for freedom of speech and freedom of privacy in this country as loudly as possible. Otherwise, I rather prefer you not to act at all. I don't believe in human rights advocacy behind closed doors. People of my country need to know that human rights are supported."

In the meantime, while I worked on my film, Khadija continued to report a new story of how the Aliyev family had looted a pile of assets from the largest mobile phone operator in Azerbaijan; a new story about a secret gold mining operation that was providing handsome profits to the Aliyev daughters; and a few others that were sure to enrage the Azeri president.

I was still in production on the documentary six months later, on December 5, 2014, and was actually on another trip with President Hollande and the French energy company executives, this one to Kazakhstan, another oil-soaked semi-dictatorship, when I got a text from Leyla: "Khadija was arrested."

"When?" I answered. "What happened?"

Leyla explained that the Aliyev government had earlier tried to charge Khadija with espionage, for sharing secret documents from the Ministry of Security with the United States and others. But they didn't have the evidence to back up the allegation. This time she was arrested by a city prosecutor in Baku, who charged her with the unlikely crime of inducing a co-worker to attempt suicide. This was a wacky allegation, but it was enough for a judge to order her to jail for a three-month pretrial detention. There was little I could do besides raise the issue with my own government in Paris. Khadija was still sitting in that jail in Baku in early January, while I was at work in the edit room to shape the film in which she had played such a crucial role, "My President Is on a Business Trip."

I was late getting to the office on Wednesday, January 7, 2015; it was about twenty minutes to noon when I turned the corner onto Rue Nicolas-Appert to head toward the main entrance of the building where I was working. The chef of the restaurant at that corner was outside having a smoke and he seemed very nervous. His eyes were darting, his hands shaking. "You don't want to go down there," he told me, explaining that there had been a lot of gunfire from one of the buildings down the street. I looked up at our office building, saw almost all of my colleagues from the Premières Lignes production office gathered on the rooftop, and started in that direction. The chef warned me again not to go, but the street was completely empty, and all was quiet, so I decided to see what was happening.

As I neared the entrance of the building, a young man from the maintenance department came running out onto the street. His jeans were covered in blood. "They just shot my colleague," he told me. The first thing I saw at the entrance was the body of the maintenance supervisor lying in a pool of blood. Things seemed to start moving in slow motion. I was trying to figure out how to start doing CPR, when I heard a motor scooter roar up behind me. The chief of the local fire station was driving it, and a doctor from the French emergency unit was on the back. The doctor, Patrick Pelloux, who had been called to the scene by a friend inside the building, was already shouting at me: "We have to go in and have a look up there."

He didn't have much information, he told me, but there had been a barrage of gunshots just five minutes earlier. He thought there might be more victims up on the second floor of the building. I had no time to think. I pulled out my door-pass badge and we raced in, took the stairs at a gallop, two or three steps at a time up two full flights.

Like the street below, the second-floor corridor was unpeopled— not what I was used to seeing in the middle of a workday. The door to

Premières Lignes was closed tight, and I remembered everybody from my company was on the roof. So I followed Dr. Pelloux across the hall to a different office.

When Dr. Pelloux and I gently pushed open the front door of that office, I was immediately struck by a pungent, unfamiliar odor. A haze of black smoke dissipated as we walked in. The room was eerily silent, and I could sense a hint of movement behind some of the upright partitions. There was blood everywhere. The floor was covered with limp and lifeless bodies. Dr. Pelloux had friends in this office, a number of whom lay dead in front of him. He managed, through his tears, to tell me to go downstairs and bring the firemen who were running to the building from their station down the block. I propped open the front door of the office and on the way to the staircase stopped to bang on the door of my own office. My colleague Edouard Perrin was barricaded behind it.

"Laurent, I see you," Edouard said, looking through the peephole. He opened the door slowly, and I could see he was wearing one of the bulletproof vests we had stored in our office. "You have to come and help," I told him; "there are dead people everywhere." When Edouard came out, a few of my other colleagues followed. They went to the offices across the corridor to help, while I raced back to the ground floor and found the firemen. One was making a futile attempt to save the maintenance supervisor I had seen. I yelled at them to get to the second floor right away and raced upstairs ahead of them, as fast as I could.

When I got back to the scene of the shooting and scanned the room, I noticed movement by a chair that had been knocked sideways on the floor. I made my way over and found another of my colleagues, Matthieu Goasguen, with a young man who was lying on his back. The victim was having a lot of trouble breathing, but he was breathing. He was barely conscious, in shock, and frightened. I sat down by him, took his hand, and asked his name. When he tried to talk, his voice was so thin and small that Matthieu and I could barely understand what he was saying, but we did hear, "Simon." He managed to tell us that he couldn't feel his legs. I lifted up his T-shirt and tried not to gasp at the hole in his upper torso by his clavicle, where a bullet had torn through him.

I was with him for three or four minutes, even after the arrival of the firefighters and medics who knew better how to handle the situation. Then I looked up and saw Edouard moving across the room, checking other bodies to see if anyone else was alive. I also noticed another movement on the floor across the room and went toward to it. Fabrice Nicolino was just opening his eyes when I got to him. Fabrice, I later learned, had been caught in an attack thirty years before, so when he heard the first shots, he dove for the floor. He had been hit with at least three bullets that morning, and I could see into his pants leg enough to know that one of his bones was shattered. I took his hand and told him he was going to be all right. Fabrice kept asking me to check his torso, to make sure he hadn't been shot in any major organs.

I could see a few other people from my own office were still in the room, too, moving among the other casualties, checking for any signs of life. One of them was twenty-five-year-old Arthur Bouvart, who looked determined to help, but was clearly shaken. I mean, even the medics were stunned by this scene. This was a lot of death and blood and gore in a very cramped little area; it was clear none of these hardened EMTs had ever seen anything like it. I narrowed my focus again to this one survivor in front of me. A doctor from the fire department had written a "2" on Fabrice's head. I figured it was his way of organizing the lifesaving operation; Fabrice was apparently the second survivor the doctor had found. Suddenly I heard a voice cut through the air. "To all the living," was the command from the police officer who had arrived at the scene and taken charge, "get out!"

This place was clearly about to turn into a crime scene, but when I got up to leave, one of the medics asked me to hold the bag to an IV line they had hooked into Fabrice. It seemed like I was there forever, until somebody in charge of the medical team finally asked Edouard and me to help carry Fabrice out to a waiting ambulance. I put his glasses in my pocket and, because there was no stretcher available, gently put my hands under his shattered leg and supported it as best I could as we helped carry him out onto a gurney in the street, where a host of news photographers were snapping pictures. I would have been out of that room of death for good, except that as we were putting Fabrice into the ambulance, he realized he didn't have his wallet. He begged me to go back up and get it. I went running back up, forgetting I still had his eyeglasses.

I'm not even sure why the officials on the scene let me cross back through the police tape, but they must have seen the blood splattered across my clothing and assumed I was part of the rescue team. They let me back up and into the crime scene.

Searching for that wallet might have been the hardest thing I did that day. All the survivors were out by then, including several who had taken cover behind the partitions when the shooting started, and I wasn't really aware of anybody else in the room but me and almost a dozen motionless bodies. The silence was haunting. I tried to remember exactly where on the floor Fabrice had been, but I had somehow lost all physical orientation. I had to open up my field of vision, to take in the whole room, and that's when I started seeing things I had missed, or purposefully avoided: the blood pooled on the floor, and more bodies than I had initially realized. I started picking my way over to the spot where I had first found Fabrice. "Hey!" someone shouted. "What are you doing over there?"

The police officer, strapped in a bulletproof vest, was not happy to see a stranger rooting around on the floor.

"I'm an office neighbor," I said. "One of the victims asked me to look for his wallet."

"Come here!" he commanded. I think he was the lead investigator, already at work.

I had to be careful getting to him. I found myself stepping gingerly over the bodies. I had to take special note of the positioning of the corpses to make sure I didn't step on one of them. It was the first time I remember being fully aware of the enormity of that day, these motion-less human beings twisted and distorted in death—a picture that has proven hard to erase.

As I was slowly making my way over to him, the police investigator asked me if I could help him identify the bodies. "I don't think I can," I said, thinking quickly, because I really didn't want to stay in this room any longer than I had to. "I might be wrong."

"Well, then it's time for you to get out," he said.

The authorities didn't release me right away but decided to send all of us who had been witnesses to the extreme violence of the day to a nearby hospital for sessions with trauma counselors. Before we left Rue Nicolas-Appert, I did manage to give Fabrice's glasses to a friend of his, who promised to get them to Fabrice's wife.

When we got to the hospital, the few survivors who had been present for the actual attack were put in one room, the rest of us in another. While I was in one of those counseling rooms, President Hollande appeared out of nowhere. He was there to look in on the victims who had survived the actual shooting, but he stopped by our little counseling session also. He went around the room, talking to everyone, and when he came to me, I could see a faint glimpse of recognition. "Hello, Mr. President," I said. "We were together a month ago in Kazakhstan."

"Yes, of course," he said, "but what are you doing here?"

MY EXPERIENCE OF this mass murder and its immediate aftermath was very blinkered and very personal, and it was only later, like when President Hollande showed up at the hospital, that it began to dawn on me that I had been a small part of national history in France, a witness to an event that captured the attention of the world. The larger meaning of the event came into focus for me over time. I remember in the first hours afterward, when my colleague Martin Boudot told me that he and everyone else in our office had heard the boom of every bullet that morning, while pointing me to a television screen with a news feed, including video of the shooters on the street, making their escape. "I am the one who filmed that," Martin said.

Our building was on every news channel in Europe for the next few days, and in the rondo of footage playing in the constant loop was the video of Edouard and me carrying Fabrice out of the building. I received dozens of calls from friends and family, some of them afraid for me.

Meanwhile, every day for days, the news accounts spread across the world, with new details about the victims, and the perpetrators, and the twisted motives. The attack was a planned hit, an act of terror, against *Charlie Hebdo*, a leftist magazine best known for its irreverent cartoons.

The publication had angered some fundamentalist Islamic jihadists with drawings depicting the Prophet Muhammad, which was a taboo for some devout Muslims. Two gunmen affiliated with al-Qaeda in Yemen had forced their way into the offices that morning intent on wiping out the editorial team.

"Where is Charb!?!" the assassins had yelled as they burst into the office with their faces covered by balaclavas and their AK-47 rifles loaded with ammunition. They wanted the editor, Stéphane "Charb" Charbonnier, first. And they got him. The men sprayed a hail of fifty or more bullets in just a few minutes, killing Charbonnier, his body-guard (Charb had been threatened many times already), and four other longtime cartoonists, ages 57, 73, 76, and 80. One of them a recipient of the French Legion of Honor. They also killed two columnists, a copy editor, a visiting journalist from another publication, and the mainte-nance supervisor I had seen on the ground floor, Frédéric Boisseau. In the middle of the murder spree inside the office, the gunmen stopped just long enough to claim they would not kill a woman. But they did.

On the way to their getaway car, as captured on tape by Martin Boudot, the attackers fired wildly and yelled into the now emptied street, "Allahu Akbar. We have avenged the Prophet Muhammad. We have killed Charlie Hebdo." I had unknowingly turned the corner to Rue Nicolas-Appert just a few minutes after they sped away and before the neighborhood started to emerge from hiding spots in apartments and offices.

The attack was widely condemned for its viciousness and for its illib-eral aims. The secretary-general of the United Nations called it "a direct assault on a cornerstone of democracy, on the media and on freedom of expression." The remaining staff at the magazine managed to get out the next issue of *Charlie Hebdo*, and the public rallied around that act of heroism. Circulation rocketed from its normal sixty thousand to as many as *eight million*. That was cold comfort to the survivors. "Living or dead, wounded or not," the badly wounded man whose hand I held that day, Simon Fieschi, would later say, "I think none of us escaped what happened."

I struggled in the weeks after the *Charlie Hebdo* attack. I was still

editing the documentary on French ties to Azerbaijan and other Caucasus countries, but I found it hard to concentrate. I wasn't eating well. I
wasn't sleeping well. I wasn't living well. Terrifying details of the experience would sometimes wash over me: the images of the dead flashed in
my mind; the awful pungent odor I had smelled on entering the *Hebdo*
offices would reprise itself without warning. Any time I saw a person
lying limp and motionless—on a couch, on a bench, on the street—I
could feel it cause me physical stress. I also found myself spending a lot
of time mulling a larger question about the attack: What could I do, as
a professional journalist? What was the proper journalistic response to
crimes committed against the press? How could I help to honor and to
peacefully avenge the martyrs at *Charlie Hebdo*?

I was also continuing to track the doleful news of Khadija in those
weeks. The inducement-of-suicide charge fell apart pretty quickly, since
the supposed victim was alive to refute it, but Khadija was still being held
in a jail in Baku. The prosecutors had introduced a new set of allegations, aimed at the popular radio show Khadija had hosted on Radio Free
Europe. Her own radio bureau lacked the proper license, Azeri prosecutors claimed. She was evading taxes by paying employees as contractors
instead of regular employees. She had neglected to register with the Azeri
Ministry of Foreign Affairs to work as a journalist for foreign media.
There was a host of bogus allegations against Khadija, which added up to
a general charge of "Illegal Entrepreneurship."

The Aliyev government was clearly going to railroad her straight into
prison, and I really didn't want to contribute to that or inflame the prosecutors. I wrote to Khadija saying I would gladly keep her out of the film
I was working on if it would help her in court. Several weeks later, on
March 20, 2015, I received a short note, scribbled out on a small scrap
of checked paper, from a jail cell in Baku. The note was just eighty-two
words long, but it was one powerful little missive: "Laurent," Khadija
wrote, "I knew I would be arrested. I am as strong and cool as when we
met. I don't care about these false accusations against me. Is your movie
ready? Remember: it's very important to expose the corruption . . ."

Khadija, at her insistence, was in the final cut of the documentary that
aired on *Cash Investigation* the first week in September, which happened

to be the same week Khadija was moved from pretrial detention to an Azeri prison. Aliyev's judicial factotums had convicted her of a handful of vague economic crimes and sentenced her to a term of seven and a half years. Khadija continued to project a strength bordering on insouciance in the face of this ordeal. "Prison is not the end of life," she had said. "It is in fact an unparalleled opportunity. I take it as a challenge to use the time for translating a book and writing."

Even on her way to prison for the next seven and a half years, Khadija did not cower. She had long ago vowed she would not be silenced: "Anticorruption investigations are the reason of my arrest. The government is not comfortable with what I am doing. I am about to finish three investigations. I will make sure to finish them before anything happens, if not, my editors and colleagues will finish and publish."

THAT WAS IT, that simple and straightforward phrase ("if not, my editors and colleagues will finish and publish"): the seed of the idea that would grow into Forbidden Stories. *If I can't my finish my work, I'm counting on you to finish it for me.* Five years later, here in an office just a kilometer away from my old building on Rue Nicolas-Appert, Forbidden Stories was real. We were already in the middle of our third major investigation.

I was still scanning the room as Sandrine talked, and I was having some doubts. We were a new organization, young in every way. The average age of our core reporting team was about twenty-five. This new investigation we were contemplating had the potential to blow up into a Wikileaks- or an Edward Snowden–sized revelation, much bigger and more sensitive than anything Forbidden Stories had ever tackled—with added layers of danger. NSO would fight us every step of the way. The company had enormous financial resources, as well as the protection of powerful military and intelligence officials in the Israeli government. Among its clients, the Pegasus end users, were regimes notorious for lashing out at anybody who crossed them and that had the ability to do real damage to those people.

But if any one of our team was daunted by the notion of embarking on this investigation into cybersurveillance gone rogue, they didn't show it that day. Paloma was the first in our group to start asking Sandrine questions about the Pegasus investigation, and the rest of the team followed her lead: How soon could the team expect access to the list? What was the timeline? Were we going to start this new work even before we finished the Cartel Project? How long did we expect it to take? When would we try to publish? What were our first steps?

CHAPTER THREE

FIRST STEPS

Sandrine

The magnitude of the job we had before us was dizzying. *Fifty thousand* possible leads, spread across the world. At least I felt dizzied by it. The only thing to do, I knew, was to maintain composure and proceed methodically. One step at a time. The first step was not difficult to identify: we had to begin the process of assessing the list. We trusted the source, but mere trust was a shaky foundation on which to build a major investigation. We would never publish a story that relied only on the data on the list. We had to authenticate the data independent of the source, and we had to understand and interpret the meaning of that enormous list of mobile phone numbers that had been handed over to us. Did an appearance on the list represent an actual spyware infection, or a targeting, or simply a selection for targeting? And was that spyware in question NSO's Pegasus system? We would have to find out, which would take time. We had to put names to as many of the tens of thousands of phone numbers on the list as possible, and we had to convince a handful of those people to allow us to check their mobile devices for any evidence of infection with Pegasus malware.

We had one small advantage at the start, which was our work on the Cartel Project. Mexican entities—government and perhaps otherwise—were reported to have been the most active end users of NSO spyware, and the list bore out this allegation. More than fifteen thousand of the data points represented targets selected by somebody in Mexico. One of the first things we had done on the Cartel Project was to gather a roster of every journalist who had been killed in Mexico in recent years. So we made a new subset—every Mexican journalist murdered after 2016, the earliest time stamps in the leaked list—put those names up on a board, and tasked Paloma and an intern with the job of finding the cell phone numbers each of those victims was using at the time of his or her death. Maybe some would match the new list. Maybe a few had even left behind phones we could run through a forensics analysis.

The rest of the team helped out by gathering Mexican phone books that would be useful in trying to match as many of the numbers on the list as we could. But that was only the first of many, many steps, and my job was to conceive the first step, the last step, and every one in between required to get us to final publication. It was like reckoning how to lay down, one by one, a series of flat stones that allowed us to cross a wide body of water of unknown depths and dangers, with rapids we couldn't yet see, and likely some very angry crocodiles guarding the final shore, too. Along the way we would have to maintain the absolute anonymity of our source, who could be in real danger, at risk of physical injury or even death, if unmasked.

The added tension of designing a plan for this investigation was the plain fact that the project would be the safest and most secure if we simply kept it within our family circle at Forbidden Stories and Amnesty International's Security Lab. Every outside partner we brought into the project would increase the possibility that the investigation into Pegasus would be found out. Intelligence services from Saudi Arabia or Morocco or the UAE or Israel or from any of the dozens of countries who had a serious interest in keeping the spyware hidden were almost certainly monitoring the digital landscape for breaches. One misstep from one partner could blow the cover for everyone. At the same time, because of the extraordinary amount of data, it was impractical, if not impossible, to do this investigation without very strong reporters and editors from many of those countries. Add to that: the mission of Forbidden Stories, at its heart, is collaborative journalism. We were just three years old, still in the process of growing a network of partners and still working to earn their trust. The more partners we could bring on board, the better.

So my task was to minimize that unavoidable tension: to put together what would likely be the biggest collaboration we had ever done, in the safest way possible. We needed to identify the media partners from across the world that we wanted to bring in to the investigation and determine exactly when to invite them in; to convince them to share *all* of their reporting, with *all* of the partners (not so easy among reporters normally driven by competition and exclusivity); to map out a plausible schedule for the project; to coordinate a final publication date and convince the partners to stick to a predetermined order of stories as they broke. We would also have to institute safety protocols for communication among the partners.

The good news was, Claudio and Donncha were more than capable of designing the safety protocols. And on the question of high-stakes, high-profile journalism in secrecy, we had a really good person to whom we could turn for advice. Maybe the best possible person.

"WE'D LIKE TO set up a call with you," Laurent wrote to Bastian Obermayer on a secure message app, "but it can't be on a cell phone. Do you have any kind of device without a SIM card?"

Bastian wrote back immediately. "I do! Because of John Doe." He seemed excited at the chance to put the device back in use. And what a device it was—the one Bastian and his colleague Frederik Obermaier had used to communicate with perhaps the most famous John Doe in the annals of journalism. This John Doe had pinged Bastian Obermayer out of the blue one evening back at the beginning of 2015: "Interested in data? I'm happy to share."

That offer to an investigative reporter at the German newspaper *Süddeutsche Zeitung* mushroomed over the next year into the then biggest data leak in the history of journalism by far—a total of 2.6 terabytes with more than eleven million emails, texts, and corporate documents tied to a single but very, very productive law firm in Panama. The leak revealed the existence of more than two hundred thousand offshore companies birthed by that firm, Mossack Fonseca, for the benefit of world leaders, political figures, billionaires, drug lords, business executives, and art dealers, among others.

The companies were incorporated in tax-friendly and financial transparency–inimical places like Panama, the British Virgin Islands, the Bahamas, Samoa, Hong Kong, and the states of Delaware, Nevada, and Wyoming in the US. The true beauty of the offshore companies, as far as Mossack Fonseca clients were concerned, was that they shielded the actual owners from public view. This made these entities excellent vehicles for tax avoidance, tax evasion, money laundering, general criminal buccaneering, or in the case of folks like Equatorial Guinean minister of forestry and agriculture Teodorin Obiang, Azeri president Ilham Aliyev, and Russian president Vladimir Putin, plundering a nation's natural resources for fun and profit.

Bastian and Frederik had at first been overwhelmed by this Himalaya-size mountain of data to sort, with more coming in all the time. As their editor at *Süddeutsche Zeitung* pointed out at the start, no single news organization on earth had the resources in-house to do this investigation with the thoroughness required for maximum impact. So Bastian, Frederik, and their editor made a really consequential decision: they decided to share the massive leak with the International Consortium of Investigative Journalists (ICIJ), which helped to turn the Panama Papers into the biggest act of collaborative journalism in history.

When the Panama Papers first broke in April 2016, after more than a year of investigation, it was the work product of four hundred–plus reporters at more than a hundred discrete media organizations around the world. The story was front-page news across Europe, Asia, Africa, and the Americas, in some of the most respected media outlets on the planet. Revelations of corruption torpedoed world leaders and business executives, and eventually helped to expose the corruption of the one-time campaign chairman of a winning US presidential candidate; it also put tax evasion by the wealthy at the top of the agenda for a host of governments and international organizations such as the G20. The former

South African president called the Panama Papers "a massive blow to financial secrecy." The investigation received multiple awards for investigative and explanatory journalism, including a Pulitzer Prize.

The Panama Papers also made Bastian Obermayer, at thirty-eight, one of the most recognized and respected investigative reporters on the planet, as well as the face of collaborative journalism. So who better to call for a chin-wag about how to proceed on our own potentially enormous leak? It helped that Bastian and Laurent were friends.

The two had spent the academic year of 2016–17 together at the Knight-Wallace Fellowship program at the University of Michigan. Laurent had arrived in Ann Arbor in the wake of a punishing eighteen months, which included the *Charlie Hebdo* massacre, the arrest and imprisonment of Khadija Ismayilova, a groundless but still threatening libel suit filed against him, and the coup de grâce, a broken spine suffered in a car crash while on a reporting trip in Iraq. Laurent had decided to take a year away from the grind of investigative journalism, and the fellowship gave him the opportunity to hit pause long enough to try to get Forbidden Stories off the ground and funded. He figured Bastian, who had to stand as the most celebrated fellow in Knight-Wallace history, had gone to Michigan mainly for rest and recuperation from his long year working on the Panama Papers.

Laurent later told me that while he had been impatient to approach Bastian about his idea for Forbidden Stories, he was not without worry. If the face of collaborative journalism was cold to the idea, it would be devastating. Bastian was not only encouraging; he turned into the perfect sounding board and sparring partner for Laurent. Over coffee or beers, the hero of the Panama Papers brainstormed with Laurent about how to build a team, where to raise funds, how to make a pitch for money. Bastian also poked and prodded the weak points of Laurent's proposal. *The most successful collaborations were international, right, but how do you convince people in the US to be interested in a story in Cambodia, or Sierra Leone, or Morocco?* Best of all, over time, Bastian became invested in the idea of Forbidden Stories, even devoted to it. He took Laurent to see potential donors, introduced him to key people at the ICIJ, and agreed to serve on the Forbidden Stories board of directors.

▌▌▌▌▌▌▌

WHEN WE REACHED Bastian on his SIM-free device and began to explain the outlines of the cybersurveillance leak to him, the mountain of inchoate data—tens of thousands of potential victims, in dozens of countries—didn't cow him in the least. He was in yes-mode right away and offered some really important tips from his experience on the Panama Papers. The first thing he did was to assure us that we were right in our instinct to make the protection of the source our paramount concern. He had never divulged to even one of the hundreds of reporting partners identifying characteristics about his "John Doe," he explained to us, no matter how many times they asked. Anybody we let into our new collaboration, he told us, would have to trust our word that the source was solid. (Bastian, who understood the pressure we were under better than anyone, never asked us the identity of the source.) He seconded our plan to grow the project in ever-widening circles to ensure security and control. First spend some time with our in-house team vetting the data. Then invite in a small set of four or five partners we could trust, but insist that there be only one reporter and one editor from each. Nobody else in their respective newsrooms could know in that initial phase, even as they helped us run down more potential victims. After we were confident the material was going to lead us to real stories, of real import, we could widen out to a much larger cohort, one best positioned to run down the stories we wanted to focus on, to give them political context, and to elicit personal stories from the victims of Pegasus. Bastian also warned us never to say anything to the first circle that we weren't also ready to say to the wider circle.

With our Forbidden Stories team at work already, and the advice and support from Bastian in the bank, I scheduled a second meeting in Berlin with Claudio, along with his boss at Amnesty International's Security Lab. This was still the very early stages of our partnership, and there were a lot of questions about security and logistics and division of responsibilities to work out between our two very different organizations. We were a small and very new entity. Amnesty International was a venerable institution with thousands of employees, offices in more than 70 countries, and political imperatives to consider. They had ultra-skilled tech geeks; we were tech novices. They were human rights defenders; we were journalists. The only thing we could do was start down the road together and see where it went. We felt ready to present our plan for executing our end of the difficult project and to hear the Security Lab's. When I asked Bastian if he would be willing to travel from his home in Munich to Berlin in the coming weeks to join the meeting, he agreed.

THE TRIP TO Berlin was a reminder that, especially in the age of Covid, the best-laid plans were likely to require recalibration and improvisation. When the time came to travel, Bastian was grounded by a personal issue, so he asked to join our meetings with the Amnesty International team by secure app. There was much to discuss. We all understood that the data, at this point, was little more than a jumble of phone numbers and time stamps. And even after we put as many identities to those numbers as we could, we wouldn't have proved anything. Not even that the data touched on NSO and its Pegasus spyware system. As Bastian had pointed out, our conundrum was very different from the one he had faced with the Panama Papers. The difficulty there was in explaining very complicated and opaque financial shenanigans to a lay audience. But most of the subjects—the Panamanian law firm that structured the offshore companies, the companies, the strawmen directors who signed the official documents, and the actual owners—were named in the data. Blazoned across millions of emails and incorporation documents and the like.

Our difficulty would be in finding the evidence of spyware attack in the phones, allowing us to write that the data actually represented people targeted by or infected with NSO's Pegasus. Marshaling that evidence depended largely on Claudio Guarnieri's professional expertise. Claudio had spent years chasing down NSO and other private for-profit purveyors of cybersurveillance systems. He and Donncha were in the process of developing a forensic tool capable of capturing traces of Pegasus that NSO operators had left behind in the system files of infected mobile phones. Without Claudio and his tools, the list was just so much indecipherable digital hieroglyphics.

We needed the Security Lab, but the Security Lab also needed us. It would be up to us to convince targets to allow Claudio and Donncha to put their phones through invasive digital forensics analyses. But while the Security Lab could show readers *how* the Pegasus cybersurveillance system worked, it would be up to Forbidden Stories and its partners to determine *why* the end users chose their specific targets—and what were the consequences that befell those targets. It would also be up to Forbidden Stories and its partners to provide what Claudio and his team at the Security Lab really wanted: to make sure the product of all their hard work landed on the public doorstop with a thud that could not be ignored or swept away.

They wanted to have impact, and they wanted to have impact in a way that helped human rights defenders fight back against the intimidation so many suffered in their home countries. One of Amnesty International's central missions was to protect the courageous souls who were trying to "expose human rights violations and to hold people to account for those human rights violations," Claudio's boss at Amnesty Tech, Danna Ingleton, had recently said. "We want to make sure that we identify and prevent risk before it happens."

Danna arrived with Claudio and Donncha at a different Airbnb in Berlin in October 2020. Claudio was just the same: taciturn, to the point, without wasted word or motion. The "We are sorry for the inconvenience, but this is a revolution" sticker was still affixed to his laptop. He wore the knit ski cap pulled tight across his skull. His T-shirt read, "Police the Police." He did seem friendlier, more familiar, but still wary. As he later confided, he was at that moment thinking, *What are we getting ourselves into?* "There was a lot of uncertainty. Partly we didn't know just what the data meant. But I think we were also concerned that you're a journalist and might read too much into it and overhype it and say there's something in the data that isn't there."

This was our first face-to-face meeting with Danna, but she made it plain right at the start that she knew that the only way we were going to get across the finish line on this project was together. Arm in arm. Claudio and Donncha were the maestros of forensics, but Danna was vested with decision-making at Amnesty Tech. She had the power to hit the go button. Her overriding concern, and the first order of business, was the safety of the source, from pillar to post. We agreed.

I spent much of the first part of the meeting sketching out our plan of attack, which was basically what we had discussed with Bastian and a little added detail. We explained to Danna and Claudio the two circles of partners—a few colleagues from the media outlets we trusted most at the start, and then the addition of as many reporters as needed, from all over the world, to chase down the most promising leads. We explained that we needed to safely land our current project, the Cartel Project, before diving headlong into Pegasus. That meant we would inform the first circle of partners of the project after the first of the year, in January 2021, and maybe sit down as a group and start to shape the pieces of the investigation in early March. We wanted to do that in person in Paris.

We would work with that small group for a few months, identify as many victims as we could, and deliver their phones for forensic analysis. When we felt confident that the findings truly did implicate NSO and its end user clients in this massive campaign of cyberspying, and we had identified the stories we wanted to tell, we would widen the circle. From there, we expected, it would take six or eight more weeks to get to publication. We understood those final months would be the most vulnerable for all of us—Forbidden Stories, our partners, the Security Lab, and especially the source. The longer the investigation took, the more partners added, and the more victims alerted, the greater were the chances of being found out, which meant we were worried about stretching the timeline to the breaking point. We told Danna and Claudio we hoped to publish in June 2021.

Laurent and I were anxious to know about security protocols, which would be the responsibility of Claudio and his team. They would have to design a way for us to communicate with the Security Lab as well as with all our media partners. They would have to set up a secure website where an increasing number of partners could share their most recent reporting in real time. I learned some interesting lessons listening to Claudio and Donncha talk online security. Less important than understanding when and where you were protected, I gathered, was understanding when and where you were vulnerable. Which was pretty much everywhere in the digital universe. Here's how they put it:

"We operate on the assumption that any device can be hacked."

"And that's why even though we check our phones regularly, we still turn our phones off and leave them in a different room [when we're dis-cussing sensitive topics]. Or we leave the office and go for a walk."

"If I would have to worry about every specific type of attack and whether or not I would find means to detect it or not detect it, it would be completely impossible for me. I would have to check that device, and that device and this device. Swipe the room with our F scanner and some other kind of equipment, and check every power socket. I would have to make sure that there were no antennas pointing towards the window. You know, it's just impossible. So what we need to start thinking is: 'What do I do to minimize these things on an operational level?' And that's where the compartmentalization comes in. Like meet-ing certain places and not others, you know. Or I know that my phone can be hacked, so either I don't have a phone, or I don't use it for any-thing important. I don't have it with me at important times, or I make sure that my phone number is not known to anybody.

"My laptop has measures that I can afford in terms of mitigations and control and whatnot. But I don't use that laptop for personal things, and I don't bring it with me if I have to do meetings [about Pegasus]. If there are things that are sensitive that I don't want to leave exposed because I'm afraid of someone breaking into my house, then I make sure to take those things with me. These kinds of measures are the ones that matter.

"Ultimately, what really makes a difference is the operational secu-rity aspects rather than the digital one. That's what it boils down to."

BASTIAN WAS ABLE to join us on the secure app a few hours into the meet-ing in Berlin, and he was very reassuring to Danna. He had experience in large journalistic collaborations where secrecy was paramount, and he told her, in his usual direct and resolute manner, that there was no reason Laurent and I would ever need to share the source of the leak with any of the media partners. The ability to publish, after all, depended on the Security Lab's forensic tool digging out evidence of Pegasus infections in cell phones from the list. If the forensics were a success, the media partners would have what they needed to go to press; the source of the leak would be beside the point. If the forensics came up empty, there was no story.

We also decided, over the course of the two days of meetings, that it would be best to break this story all at once. We had considered going to press over a number of weeks or even months, in waves, by geography: a package on the Gulf States, say, followed by one on India or Mexico or Morocco. But this felt too risky. The pressure from NSO's demonstrably aggressive legal team might shake some of our partners who were still working on their stories. So we decided the consortium would publish the initial stories on the same day, across the world, and then roll out a series of reports over the next week or so. Our first-day headlines, assuming we got the proof, would be in the sweet spot of this new partnership: the exact point where the missions of Forbidden Stories and Amnesty Tech intersected. The first articles would reveal the astonishing scale of the use of Pegasus to silence and intimidate journalists and human rights defenders all over the world.

Even early in our meetings with Claudio and Danna, it seemed like we had agreed on a clear way forward. I had a pretty good feel for exactly what stepping-stones we had to lay down, and in what order, to get us safely to publication. This was starting to feel doable.

ONE UNEXPECTED PROBLEM did pop up on that trip to Berlin. Since we had last seen them, Claudio and Donncha had been able to find the identities of the owners of a lot more of the phone numbers in the data. One good sign, Claudio mentioned, was that there were many matches with people identified as victims of Pegasus in a lawsuit filed by WhatsApp against NSO in the US in 2019. The Security Lab team had also turned up a lot of government officials, and while Claudio didn't have a great deal of interest in their presence—it was no big surprise that governments were spying on governments, and besides, national officials tended to have plenty of institutional protections in place, so they didn't need help from us—he did want us to have a look at some of the names he and Donncha had discovered.

Right away, Laurent and I started scanning through a section of the data that appeared to be targets selected by a client in Morocco. There were members of the French parliament and ministers in the French government on the list. And then, I saw one name that shortened my breath for just a second. "Laurent," I said, pointing to the screen. "Look at that name." *Macron. Emmanuel Macron.* The sitting president of the Republic of France. A head of state of one of the most respected democracies in Europe. *Our* president was on this list, a potential target. *This was big*, I thought, *and it was also big trouble.*

Laurent saw it the same way. What struck him was the fearlessness—the sense of absolute impunity—it required to believe you could spy on the president of France and get away with it. This was likely to be somebody at an organization that would do whatever it needed to keep the fact hidden. "Macron was the name," Laurent would later tell me, "that made me realize how truly dangerous it was to have access to this list."

We were also both immediately aware of the complications that might arise if we discovered that a lot of other heads of state had been selected for targeting by clients of NSO. News that the personal cell phone of Emmanuel Macron or other prominent world leaders might be "owned" by a foreign intelligence service would likely overshadow the story we were really after, which was the threat to journalists and human rights defenders. Neither the French government, nor any other, was going to turn over the cell phone of any of their officials, let alone a president, to allow Claudio to run his forensics analysis. And what if there was evidence that opposition politicians from suspected NSO client states like India or Mexico or Ghana were in the data? Alerting those selected targets before the story broke risked blowing our cover before we were ready to publish; politicians with an axe to grind were not likely to exercise much circumspection, even when asked. Then, too, would our partners from those countries be willing to embargo a red-hot local story until mass publication? The bottom line was this: Macron's private phone number in the data and what that represented was sure to entice more partners and to raise the visibility of the final publication, but it would have to be handled carefully.

THIS NEW COMPLICATION paled beside the most pressing one—the one that was largely out of our hands at Forbidden Stories: the ability of Claudio's forensic tool to produce the evidence we needed from the cell phones listed in the data. If the Security Lab was unable to turn up hard proof that these phones were infected with Pegasus and permit us to call out the malefactors, then NSO and their licensees—among them the most vicious regimes on Earth—would just go on operating their cyber-surveillance system with the sort of abandon enjoyed by pirates and privateers. Their victims would continue to suffer the consequences.

I lacked the training or the expertise to plumb the technical aspects of the Security Lab's digital forensic tool, but after spending many, many hours with Claudio, my confidence in him was growing. I knew for sure that overhyping on his part would not be a worry. He was calm, straight-forward, and always thoughtful—occasionally maddeningly so. If I asked him a question, especially a technical question, there was invariably a pause before he answered. I could almost imagine the wheels spinning in his brain as he fashioned a response, which was always on point, and precise. Claudio was also modest to a fault. The forensic tool he and Donncha had engineered was not perfect, they kept telling us, but nothing was. The point was to keep improving it as the investigation developed. Their success depended on hard work and patience and diligence; it depended on being better at forensics than NSO was at anti-forensics, at covering their tracks.

While in Berlin during the planning meetings, Laurent and I got a little demo of the tool Claudio and Donncha were developing, and it wasn't an altogether pleasant experience for Laurent. He allowed his own cell phone to be subjected to the Security Lab's forensic analysis. The process didn't require much from him. He simply handed over the phone and watched as Claudio and Donncha made a backup of the entirety of its contents and then ran it through the tool on a Security Lab laptop. The process was surprisingly labor intensive. Donncha would type in a command and watch as what looked like indecipherable code and data scrolled across and down the laptop's monitor. But he didn't just wait and watch. He'd click on a line of code and enter a new com-mand, then another, then another. He typed a variety of commands as he went, and sometimes went back and rechecked an earlier line by typ-ing new commands.

Laurent said it was like watching a scene from a documentary on coders, but a very personal one, because this was his phone, and much of his work life and his private life was sitting on the Security Lab laptop. There was the fear of having been infected with spyware, but there was also the discomfort of giving over to a stranger access to thoughts and messages and photos meant to be private.

As Donncha continued to type commands, I could see Laurent edge in closer and closer, until their shoulders were touching. I could tell he was excited, and anxious, and impatient. I had known him a long time.

Laurent Richard and I had first met fifteen years earlier, in front of a coffee machine at the public television channel where we were both working, France 3. We were contemporaries in age, both in our late twenties, but very different in professional stature. I was a fairly anonymous young political reporter sent out to trawl public events and meetings for "petites phrases"—buzzy little quotes and anecdotes that were closer to gossip than news, material best used to poke fun at the powerful. Like candy that melts in your mouth, these tidbits were good for a sugar high, but unlikely to lead to any serious news. Laurent meanwhile had already made a name for himself as a very serious reporter on the channel's popular monthly investigative program, *Pièces à Conviction*. He was already doing life-and-death journalism.

The day I met him, Laurent was in the process of reporting a story about the mysterious sinking of a fishing boat off the coast of Cornwall. He was trying to run down some leads that a British submarine in the area for international military exercises had accidently pulled the boat under, leaving five men dead. This was, I would come to understand, the kind of investigation Laurent loves: both difficult and threatening to authority. The kind of investigation that can get you in trouble. "They're a secretive lot," a lifeboat coxswain who had never before seen a military submarine in the middle of a "rescue" operation, would later say.

Over the next ten years, I watched Laurent's career with growing interest and growing respect. He launched a new investigative program, *The Infiltrators*, whose reporters went undercover in really dangerous places. Laurent himself infiltrated the most horrific crime network I could imagine—a ring of pedophiles operating on the dark web. When the report aired in 2010, it made headlines all over France and led to the arrests of twenty-two people. I had lunch with Laurent a few days after the report aired, and he admitted to having been deeply shaken by the indescribably awful images and video he had to view in his reporting.

Laurent was also pitching me on yet another television program he was trying to launch, which would become *Cash Investigation*. He asked me to come and work for him. I had tired of political journalism by then and moved on to doing investigations into private corporations for another channel. This was engaging and fulfilling work (with a steady paycheck), and as a young mother, I thought it unwise to leave for a program that did not yet exist and might fizzle before it launched. I turned him down, much to my regret. From the moment it hit the air in 2012, *Cash Investigation* was a fresh and bracing breeze. The series covered tax evasion, the power of corporate lobbyists, governmental conflicts of interests, greenwashing, and neuromarketing in offbeat and engaging ways that drew viewers in and helped them understand these complex political and economic subjects.

The series had Laurent's fingerprints all over it; it made bold to dive into demanding and difficult subjects and did not shy from dangerous investigations. And unlike most everybody I know in television news, Laurent never talked about the ratings. The quality of the work itself was paramount. *Cash Investigation* quickly became the Holy Grail for any television journalist who wanted to do long and thorough investigative pieces. Including me.

By the time I called him up and talked my way onto the *Cash Investigation* team in 2015, Laurent had a foot out the door. He was already thinking about Forbidden Stories. The next thing was, as he described the mission of his new project to me, the most outlandish startup of the three he had pitched to me over the years: farthest from the mainstream of journalism, maybe the most dangerous, and certainly the most difficult. I mean, he was going to convince a host of competitive and often parochial journalists to collaborate with one another to finish somebody else's original reporting (reporting that had gotten the reporter killed, by the way) . . . for the greater good? Experience, however, had taught me not to doubt Laurent Richard.

It took me a while to free myself from *Cash Investigation*, but by the time I accepted Laurent's offer to take the job of managing editor at Forbidden Stories in 2019, I had no doubts about following him into this strange new world of collaborative journalism aimed at giving voice back to reporters who had been silenced. A big part of the draw for me was my own personal history. I was born in Egypt in the late 1970s, daughter of a French father and an Egyptian mother. I grew up in Syria and Turkey and knew what it was to live in a country where freedom of expression was not a right, but a luxury—a potentially dangerous luxury for anyone who tried to exercise it. Schoolchildren in western Europe and Canada and the US might grow up reading *1984* but have little appreciation of the actual, real-world fact that billions of people are caught up in the repressive—and sometimes violent—daily nightmare that George Orwell describes in his novel. I knew it too well, that feeling of the oxygen of freedom being thin to the point of vanishing. I remember too well how my parents sent me out of the house with explicit warnings: do not speak of political issues outside the family circle. The consequences were just too dreadful to chance. I became a journalist because I wanted to be able to make sense of the world, and to use my voice, freely, to explain it to others.

So being here in Berlin in 2020, trying to launch this new Forbidden Stories project with Laurent, felt a little like destiny for me. This was just where I wanted to be.

Laurent's shoulder was still resting against Donncha's, and his head had moved a little closer to the laptop. I could see his eyes scanning as new commands flashed across the screen, until finally, after what seemed like an interminable interval: "You're clean. Everything is cool." Laurent's phone was in the clear, uninfected by Pegasus. "And I will now delete everything," Donncha said. Then, aware of Laurent's distress at having the entire contents of his phone sitting on somebody else's laptop, Donncha made sure Laurent could see it happen. "Here," he said. "Watch."

THE DISCOMFORT—AND I felt it, too, when Donncha checked my phone later—was a reminder that the process of digital forensic analysis was in and of itself invasive. Not that it was anything like being a victim of the NSO's signature spyware, but it did make us realize just how challenging it would be to ask somebody to submit the contents of their cell phone for a relative stranger to see. We knew we would have to carefully consider how best to approach the person we had chosen as our first test case, our reporting partner Jorge Carrasco. We would have to convince him to let Claudio and Donncha do the forensics, while holding back information that was not safe to divulge to him: the existence of the list, its link to NSO, and the possibility that his phone was infected by the most powerful cybersurveillance tool on the market, Pegasus.

Paloma was headed to Mexico in a few weeks to tie up some reporting on the Cartel Project, and she was going to have to get Jorge in a room alone, no phones and no laptops, and convince him. The logistics of this sortie into Mexico were made more difficult by the pandemic. The vaccines were still in trials, a hoped-for panacea but hardly a sure thing. The numbers of daily cases and hospitalizations were creating a harrowing upward slope. Travel restrictions made it unlikely that anyone from the Security Lab could be on-site in Mexico City to test Jorge's phone. So Donncha was going to try to tweak the Security Lab's forensic platform to allow analysis of the cell phone to be done remotely, with the help of somebody with little background in cyber-research. The idea was that Paloma would make a backup of Jorge's iPhone and upload a digital file to Berlin, where Claudio and Donncha could do their magic.

A remote version of the forensic platform was ready in time for Claudio and Donncha to give Paloma a very quick tutorial on what she needed to do for her part of the analysis. Claudio did not make any promises for success in Mexico. The best he could offer was this: *Finding Pegasus using forensics wasn't as impossible as NSO claimed.* So the great hope for exposing NSO was safely loaded onto Paloma's laptop on a late-October day in 2020 when she left Paris for the long flight to Mexico City, right into the teeth of the NSO/Pegasus story.

CHAPTER FOUR

PLAZA DEL MERCADO

The way NSO co-founder and CEO Shalev Hulio liked to tell the story, he was already in bed asleep on Christmas Eve 2011 when he received his first-ever personal call from a world leader: the president of Mexico. Actually, even when Shalev first revealed the story, years later, in an unprecedented and exclusive interview with a reporter of his choosing, he didn't name the country. He was forbidden—by contractual obligation and national security imperatives—to identify his clientele. But anyone with an interest in the world of cybersurveillance knew the man on the other end of the line had to be Felipe Calderón of Mexico. "I was informed in English that the president wanted to talk to me," Shalev explained. "I was sure [my partner] Omri [Lavie] was pulling a prank, so I said, 'Do me a favor and let me sleep,' and hung up.

"After [the president's office] realized they couldn't reach me, they called Tzachi, the project manager, who was more awake and agreed to take the call. The president of the unnamed nation said he wanted to thank us on his behalf and on behalf of his country, and that 'I couldn't have asked for a better Christmas present. With what you gave us, we can finally eradicate the cartels.'"

The story was classic Shalev, self-effacing and self-aggrandizing all at once—a humblebrag of epic proportion. Yes, he had been stupid enough to blow off the president of one of the world's largest democracies. But the message was delivered nonetheless: you, Shalev Hulio, have given us hope. With the help of NSO's novel Pegasus spyware system, the Mexican *Federales* and the Mexican military finally had a chance to bring to heel the violent and powerful drug czars who held sway over much of the country's local government and police force, not to mention much of its national economy.

Shalev first offered this fantabulous tale to reporter Ronen Bergman in 2019, as one of the early plays in a media offensive Shalev claims he undertook, grudgingly, to protect the honor of his unfairly maligned company. Accusations that Pegasus had played a role in the assassination of Saudi journalist Jamal Khashoggi were affecting company morale. "We decided long ago that we would not respond to anything. No matter what happened, we would not respond, and this worked out fine," Shalev told Bergman. "But now for the first time our staff have been coming to my office, and saying, 'Look, we're upset, because we know the truth.'" They wanted him to tell their truth. So Shalev insisted to Bergman (on behalf of his beleaguered staff) that NSO Group was a force for good in a really scary world. "In the past six months alone," he said, "the company's products aided in foiling several very big terror attacks in Europe—both car bombs and suicide bombers. I can say in all modesty that thousands of people in Europe owe their lives to hundreds of our company employees from Herzliya."

The story of the Calderón call, and of NSO's heartsick staff, and of the heroic feats accomplished by Pegasus were of a piece. First of all, these particulars were very hard to check in 2019. The head of Felipe Calderón's war on the cartels was just then being publicly accused of taking bribes from the drug lords he claimed he was trying to eradicate, so the former Mexican president wasn't picking up his phone to talk to reporters. NSO employees were effectively muzzled. No European police official was willing to go on the record admitting that they licensed and operated Pegasus spyware. Then, too, Shalev's recounting of the NSO story was filigreed with fine little narrative gems—and they were exclusive! Which meant that while the stories were often too good to be true, they were also too good to leave entirely untold, or to leave for another writer to tell instead. So even really good and well-informed reporters such as Bergman and a few others would just put them in quotes and add a clause or two of their own to serve as the written equivalent of an arched eyebrow. The already harried NSO press team did have to occasionally do some cleanup in the aftermath of a Shalev interview. The boss was not well versed in the technical specs of the Pegasus system, or the intricacies of high finance, or the fine points of the laws and regulations that governed the cybersurveillance industry in Israel and abroad. But he did exhibit a genius for controlling the narrative. Shalev Hulio, it must be admitted, tells a very good story. His story of the origins of NSO may be his best.

It starts out as a kind of buddy movie: starring him and his best pal, Omri Lavie. They were both born around 1980, into the false hopes that followed the Camp David Accords and the Israel-Egypt Peace Treaty, and raised with the whiff of peril always in the air. (Between 1993 and 1995 alone, there were fourteen separate suicide bombings in Israel, leaving eighty-six dead.) They were similar boys. Smart enough but undisciplined. Shalev and Omri met in the mid-1990s while both were studying arts and theater at a high school in Haifa (after Shalev washed out of a program for gifted students because of congenital misbehavior). Both completed their compulsory service in the Israeli military and then some, though neither had served in the elite counterintelligence force—Unit 8200. Shalev and Omri remained in touch and passed through their late twenties together, the two men spinning hard to make themselves machers in the hottest industry in Israel. Shalev and Omri sometimes described themselves as "serial entrepreneurs" or "early adopters of technologies." Roughly translated, this was two guys in a bar dreaming up ways to cash in on the newest computer tech. They weren't particular about the particulars.

You could almost imagine them in that bar, as the sun was setting over their city, a pair of ambitious but unsettled young men aglow in their own joy and enthusiasm. While having drinks in Haifa, Shalev says, the two hit on an idea for allowing consumers quick and easy access to merchandise they had seen on TV or in movies. A shirt, a watch, a motorcycle, whatever. They even managed to scare up enough cash from venture capitalists to mock up a demo using scenes from *Sex and the City*. Click on Carrie Bradshaw's pumps or her bag or her dress, and

Shalev and Omri's platform identified the designer—Manolo Blahnik! Fendi! Halston Heritage!—and where to buy it for yourself. The idea was excellent. The timing was not. They tried to sell it in the teeth of the 2008 financial meltdown and ended up being squeezed out by VCs. "You can't be an entrepreneur without being very optimistic," Shalev explained to Bergman. "We said, 'Okay, that happened. Let's move on.'"

They moved on to a start-up company called CommuniTake, where they helped scale a new software program created by a couple of their old Haifa schoolmates—one of whom had served in the Israeli army's renowned Unit 8200. The innovation aimed to solve an emerging tech issue, a conundrum with a maddening feedback loop. When CommuniTake was founded back in 2009, the growing capabilities of mobile phones and the growing number of mobile apps available were vexing the growing number of mobile phone users, that is, the regular folk who were trying to benefit from these new technologies. Didn't matter if their phone was running Android or iOS, or was a Nokia N95, an iPhone, or the then popular BlackBerry. The problem with all of them was too many bells and whistles. Too many options. There was a surfeit of smartphones and a dearth of smart users.

Frustrated cell phone owners found themselves waiting in long queues on tech-support call lines. When they finally did get a technician on the line, it was like the two sides were speaking different languages. Which meant the calls were about as satisfying for the tech gurus on the other end of the line. To the horror of the tech-support crew, even simple issues were rarely resolved in just one conversation. Repeat callers swelled the volumes on help lines. The mobile carriers found themselves hiring support staff at alarming speed, from around the world, and chafing at the increasing costs.

CommuniTake offered a simple and elegant fix. They designed a program that allowed the support technicians to take charge of the phone. The phone's owner simply clicked on a link and gave the techies on the other end of the line complete control over the device, by remote. The experts didn't have to talk anybody through the process of, say, changing their ringtone. They just did it themselves. The end users were happy (or at least happy until the next complication arose), and, as time is money, the cost of tech support fell for the carriers. Everybody was happy. CommuniTake thrived—and still thrives today, having expanded its business into services like multilayer encryption for securing all the data we now have on our phones.

But, according to Shalev Hulio, CommuniTake was missing a very big opportunity back in 2009. "A European intelligence service heard what we were doing and approached us," Shalev says. "'We saw that your technology works,' they told us, 'why aren't you using this to collect intelligence?'" Shalev didn't understand at first. He thought they got all they needed from the carriers already. But the government intelligence pro explained that, no, they were losing visibility into the cell phone communications of potential terrorists and criminals because of advances in encryption. Apple's new iPhone had been a disaster for law enforcement. The European officials told Shalev and Omri that "the situation was grave." Here were the exact words they used, according to Shalev: "We are going dark; we are getting blind. Help us."

Shalev and Omri didn't have to be asked twice, not in Shalev's telling. They went straight to the CommuniTake board of directors with a proposition to provide a cybersurveillance tool for legitimate law enforcement agencies. The board said no. CommuniTake wasn't interested in the intelligence gathering business; it would require an entire new team with new skills. But Shalev and Omri didn't let it go, because they just kept fielding calls from anxious European intelligence and law enforcement agencies. "We were approached several times and asked, 'Can you do it without [the user's] permission?'" Omri later explained. "So we lied and we said, 'Sure.' We didn't understand at the time that this was considered one of the holy grails of the industry."

The two buddies—they were "early adopters of technology," weren't they?—decided this chance was too good to pass up, so they parted company with CommuniTake, with the blessing of the board of directors. News that the pair had raised $1.6 million from one of Israel's most successful venture capital firms did not alter the prevailing sentiment at CommuniTake. The development of cybersurveillance tools, CommuniTake's chief executive explained, came with a very real danger of casting "a shadow on our company."

So Shalev and Omri started a whole new start-up a half-hour drive from Tel Aviv, in an abandoned outbuilding. "Apple started in a garage," Shalev sometimes joked. "We started in a chicken coop." The two partners quickly added to their renovated chicken coop a recently retired Israeli military officer who specialized in intelligence, Niv Karmi. They named the company NSO (like America's NSA, with its top-shelf cryptographers, right?) for Niv, Shalev, and Omri, and registered it with the State of Israel in January 2010 as NSO Group Technologies LTD. Niv had the coding chops, and he also had some insight into Israeli counterintelligence operations and bureaucratic processes. The Israeli Ministry of Defense would have to okay the export of the sort of offensive cybersurveillance system they were engineering.

The crucial task when Niv Karmi came on was to find that digital "holy grail," to design ways to gain control over a cell phone surreptitiously, without being invited in by the owner and without the owner's knowledge. The counterintelligence specialist had few qualms about prying open a back door to a private cell phone if it enabled law enforcement officials to track terrorists and criminals. "Look, I'm Israeli," Niv explained in an interview with *Die Zeit* at the end of 2021. "All of the risk that I grew up with first as a child and then in the service was a life threat. And for us, in Israel, everything is about saving life." Niv Karmi lasted only a few months at NSO, and his memory of that time does not always align with Shalev's—particularly the story about all those requests for help from the many unnamed European intelligence officials. "That's not exactly how it happened," he succinctly told *Die Zeit*.

"In the beginning there was a vision to do something good with NSO," Niv explained. "I was quite fresh out of the service. In the service everything was about vision and what you want to do. And then I got in with these two guys that were very business savvy. . . . For me there was a clash of dialogues. They were more business driven, with a different view on how business should be built or handled."

NSO, minus N, was about to die another unheralded start-up death when, according to Shalev, he was in a coffee shop and overheard some young engineers talking about a friend of theirs who had developed the technology to hack cell phones. Shalev butted into the conversation: "Let me buy you a coffee because I have to talk to you." The engineers agreed to introduce him to their friend—a personage Shalev has refused to name. "Scrawny guy, plaid shirt, glasses, a lot of pens," is how Shalev generally describes him. Miraculously, as Shalev would have it, the scrawny hacker in the plaid shirt pulled NSO's chestnuts out of the fire. It took a year, but by the spring of 2011, Shalev and Omri had a product to take to market. They called it Pegasus, Shalev says, "because what we built was actually a Trojan horse we sent flying through the air to devices."

Claudio Guarnieri was just then starting on his own personal trajectory in policing cyberintrusion. Bored with life as a corporate IT drone at twenty-three, he had taken a job as an internet security researcher trying to identify new cybersurveillance tools and to call out their purveyors. The focus of cyberforensic specialists at the time was the hunt for spyware aimed at desktop computers and laptops. While the cyberdefenders bent to the task at hand, Pegasus flew right over their heads. "I think NSO was the first company that was solely focused on one thing and one thing only, which was mobile," says Claudio, looking back a decade later. "At the time that was a bit premature. But I think that they were seeing that that's where the market really was going to be.

"And also, on the defensive side, [the mobile platform] had been left behind—from an investigative point of view, and from a forensic point of view. It allowed NSO to be unchallenged for much longer."

NSO not only stumbled onto the right technology at the right time. They also found the perfect marketplace. Or, shall we say, the perfect *plaza del mercado*.

IF A START-UP spyware company wished to go bowling for dollars in 2011, there was no better place than Mexico. The lights in the alley were on twenty-four hours a day, and there were plenty of open lanes, because President Felipe Calderón was already five years into a ferocious battle with the Mexican drug cartels. Calderón had called for a war on the drug lords during his campaign for presidency, and he acted on that call in his first week in office, in December 2006. The new president of Mexico sent 6,500 troops into the fight and quickly expanded the combatants to include more than 20,000 soldiers and federal police. Calderón did not waver, even as the death toll mounted—almost 7,000 Mexicans were killed in 2008 alone. That was the same year the United States decided to join its neighbor's fight, sending military and law enforcement agents to Mexico to help coordinate. Better than that, the Americans poured money over the border and into the newly minted "Merida Initiative."

The US Congress appropriated $1.5 billion to aid Calderón and his fighters over the next three years, which meant that even after the Mexican military and police forces upgraded their weaponry and hardware, there was plenty left over for the latest in digital technology: malware capable of monitoring and tracking the cartels and their abettors. Procurement officers from Mexican military, law enforcement, and intelligence agencies had real money to spend on cutting-edge spyware tools.

NSO was a little late to the first frame of the contest. A handful of Israeli tech companies had already closed deals for spyware in Mexico, as had Gamma Group, based in the UK or Germany or the British Virgin Islands (it was hard to tell). Hacking Team, the presumed world leader in this blossoming field of cybermercenaries, headquartered in Claudio's hometown of Milan, Italy, also had its sights on this spectacular, and spectacularly complicated, market. For a new and uninitiated private cybersurveillance vendor like NSO, simply deciphering the tangle of Mexican government acronyms could be head spinning.

The Secretariat of Home Affairs (SEGOB) oversaw two enormous and growing agencies in the market for cybersurveillance tools, the Center for Investigation and National Security (CISEN) and the federal police (PF)—as well as subcategories in each, like the PF's Sensitive Investigative Units (SIU), operated in partnership with the US Drug Enforcement Administration. Then there was the office of the Mexican attorney general (PGR). The PGR had a thin budget for cyber but, as the agency that prosecuted all federal crimes, was constantly on the lookout for what one lip-smacking European cybersurveillance developer called "lawful hacking opportunities." And finally, there were the big dogs with the big budgets—the Mexican military's growing intelligence agencies within the army (SEDENA) and the navy (SEMAR). This alphabet soup only accounted for the *Federales*. There were also thirty-one separate states, plus the federal district of Mexico City, so law enforcement agencies in Puebla, Tamaulipas, Yucatán, Durango, Jalisco, Baja California, Guerrero, and the state of Mexico were among those with an interest in licensing spyware.

The NSO team was fortunate to find just the right guide through the maze of *la Plaza del Mercado Vigilancia Cibernética*: a man known as "Mr. Lambo" (he favored expensive Italian roadsters) or "El Chino" (he was of Japanese descent, but close)—Jose Susumo Azano Matsura.

Azano is a Mexican citizen born and raised in Jalisco, where he joined his father's business. Jose Susumo Azano Moritani (the elder) was a civil engineer by trade and a doer by temperament. "Try to be so great that everyone wants to reach you," he would say, "and so humble that everyone wants to be with you." He gradually expanded his business from the manufacture of bathroom tiles and metal fixtures to metal roofing and then to industrial-size construction projects. When Susumo Azano Moritani died in July 2021, obituary writers credited Grupo Azano with having built major factories or retail centers for Nissan, Honda, Ford, Walmart, Kodak, and the electronics firm Solectron. The company had also won lucrative government contracts to manufacture license plates. All this made the Azano family one of the richest in Jalisco by the end of the twentieth century. But what had really swelled the Grupo Azano bank accounts—into the billions, it was rumored—was its entry into the electronic surveillance business in 1998.

Security Tracking Devices, SA de CV, didn't itself develop spyware systems but acted as the middleman for the cybersurveillance companies. These private companies were all foreign based, so their ability to negotiate the cultural intricacies of the *plaza del mercado* really depended on having a Mexican company to act as sales agent. El Chino was an ace.

Security Tracking Devices (STDi) quickly became Susumo Azano Matsura's favored baby, and he had raised it into a plump and happy adolescence by the time NSO came to him about marketing Pegasus in Mexico in 2011. The company's revenues were tending toward astounding, thanks to an expanding pot of "war on the drug lords" money supplied by Mexican and US taxpayers. STDi sold almost $400 million in equipment and services to the Mexican military in a single year, though none of the deals were disclosed to the folks who had paid for them, which is to say those taxpayers. The company was like the technology it sold, a ghost floating silently in the background, "maintaining," as Azano put it, "a constant presence behind the scenes."

Earnings from Mexico allowed STDi the resources to market the newest spyware systems throughout Central and South America, and to open offices in tax-friendly Singapore and in the world's tallest building, the Burj Khalifa, in Dubai. The UAE was fast becoming, as one of Azano's few confidants explained, the new "hub for this type of business." The profits also allowed Azano and his wife to purchase a waterside manse near San Diego. He liked to fly his private jet up and spend a few days a week in his posh American digs, where he was busy scheming ways to make illicit and illegal campaign contributions to a local mayoral candidate. He expected in exchange a little assistance in the oceanside retail and residential development he hoped to build there. Earnings at STDi also gave him the resources to strong-arm one of California's major natural gas suppliers, called Sempra, for the land where he wished to raise that development.

Azano was a very complicated man to bring on as a business partner. According to public reports, law enforcement officials in the US and Mexico had, at various times, suspected Azano of bribery, money laundering, tax fraud, and drug trafficking. He would later spend three years in an American jail for the illegal campaign contributions in San Diego. "Is this a guy who could be trusted with military secrets? I wouldn't trust him with my laundry," said the former US attorney in San Diego who prosecuted that case. "This is a sophisticated businessman, adept at finding ways to circumvent the law."

But in 2011, when Shalev and Omri were doing the vetting, Azano could still point to a clean bill of health from prosecutors on either side of the border, and a go pass from the US Department of Homeland Security and US intelligence officials. Also in his favor, if you were looking at it from Shalev and Omri's point of view, Azano was an avid and unapologetic proselytizer for the cybersurveillance industry at large. He was happy to push back against the voices, especially in the US, who worried about the erosion of civil liberties. "For the average citizen, the cell phone now serves the purpose of both tracker and wireless data collection devices, as well as the less important function of the phone," Azano wrote in his personal blog. "It is the perfect tool for a society that has come to depend more and more on surveillance, whether we like it or not. The government, it should be noted, did not hand out smart-phones to American citizens and demand they keep detailed logs of their every move. Americans did that to themselves. People were excited about doing it, constantly seeking new ways to advertise where they were, what they were doing, and with whom. Can people really blame governments and advertisers for taking advantage of their actions? Or do people accept that these are the repercussions of naivete, and a nation caught up in a love affair with new technology?"

AZANO SAW THE potential of NSO, this new entrant into the "Intrusion as a Service" industry, right away. STDi reportedly paid NSO $500,000 for the exclusive right to resell its Pegasus technology, and Shalev armed Azano and his team with a set of talking points to take to potential customers in the Mexican government.

That document is a perfect little snapshot of the promise of NSO's earliest technology, which was ambitious right from the start. The Pegasus system, according to this document from 2011, provided a "tactical active approach" for breaking through the wall of encryption built into the most common mobile phones on the market, BlackBerrys and Androids. These devices, the NSO talking points lamented, had become "a secure and convenient method for communication for all kinds of criminal activities, which is difficult to monitor today."

The Pegasus system offered a soup-to-nuts solution. The first step was injection: finding a vulnerability in the phone's operating system that opened the door for Pegasus users to surreptitiously plant the spyware on the phone. Step two was configuring the software so it could successfully monitor, collect, and prepare all data for retrieval. This data included all contacts and calendar entries, all email, voicemail, and instant messages, all system files, as well as current and past geolocation. The earliest Pegasus system, according to the talking points anyway, had the ability to remotely turn on the microphone to monitor "environmental voice interception"—which is to say any live conversation within earshot of the phone. It could also remotely activate the mobile phone's camera for capturing snapshots. Step three was data retrieval, wherein Pegasus would exfiltrate the contents of the phone and place them in one of the end user's servers, ready for archiving, mining, and analysis.

The Pegasus system, as offered, included NSO-provided hardware, software, maintenance, and training for the various sorts of operators needed across the platform. There was an array of "infection vectors" to choose from, each tailored to a target's device and operating system; "front-end consoles," where government-paid operatives executed the initial infection and configured the Trojan horse malware for monitoring and the exfiltration; "anonymizers" to hide the end user's real IP address and "camouflage" its activities on the internet; firewalls and virtual private networks (VPN) for added security and convenience; and "rackable servers" for storing the growing mass of data retrieved from the targets. As a rule, NSO figured 2 terabytes was a good starting point, enough to monitor four hundred different mobile phones—at 50 megabytes of data retrieved per target per day—for an entire year. But NSO also encouraged Azano and his team at STDi to assure potential buyers that "this cluster of servers can grow with the Customer future needs seamlessly."

NSO technicians would do the entirety of the initial setup, maintain the hardware, upgrade the software as needed, monitor the system in real time for any malfunction, and be available to troubleshoot. They would also train the ops who worked on the front-end consoles. For the "attack" and "configuration" agents, NSO recommended local people with degrees in criminology, anthropology, or psychology, an "ability to provide unique insight into target psyche" and to "work under pressure, in non-standard hours." End users could count on up to six weeks of dedicated time from NSO talent to get the system up and running and the operators properly schooled.

NSO looked good to Azano, another sluicing river of income for STDi. Azano, meanwhile, looked good to Shalev and Omri. NSO's new reseller provided instant intelligence in Mexican commercial traditions. Mr. Lambo, for instance, was schooled in the operative custom of *mordida* (the bite); knew which officials in the chain had to get a cut of any big sale, what size cut would be deemed acceptable, and how to make sure it was safely and secretly dispersed. Azano also provided connections; he knew the generals who made the final decisions at SEDENA, the admirals at SEMAR, the supervisors at CISEN and the PF, and the top prosecutors at the PGR. Azano's contacts apparently went all the way to the top, to the Office of the President, to Felipe Calderón himself.

On May 25, 2011, just weeks after Azano signed on to market NSO's spyware system, Shalev Hulio got an email from one of his NSO operatives: "Mr. Azano notifies me that the demo to the Secretary of Defense and the President will take place next Friday. They called me after confirmation, and they asked me to do my best to be there on Tuesday, since the Secretary of Defense requested a demonstration the day before (Thursday) and for the President on Friday."

Neither Calderón, nor his SecDef, nor Azano himself has confirmed that the scheduled demo actually happened, but six weeks later, in July, STDi closed a deal with SEDENA—the first major sale in the history of NSO. The contract was reportedly worth a little over $15 million, which more or less launched NSO as a viable company. When Shalev finally told the story of that first deal, not long before Forbidden Stories and the Security Lab got access to the leaked data, he didn't dwell on Azano (who was at the time in a US prison) and STDi. He talked about the general he met in Mexico City, and the assurances the military man gave Shalev and Omri about the way their powerful new cybersurveillance tool would be used and all the good it would do. "The country had decided to establish a separate new body—a branch of the military—to deal with the drug issue," Shalev remembered, in another of his uncheckable stories. "This body would include spotless individuals with no history of corruption who would undergo a polygraph test. Then we met with the general, the head of that branch. He said: 'You fit us like a glove. We will base our entire drug-fighting apparatus on your new technology. This is how the biggest situation room—not just in the region but one of the biggest in the world—will fight crime and drugs.' And to them, we agreed to sell."

Shalev always wants to make it clear that NSO was a company that took seriously its first principles right from the beginning: sell only to government agencies and never get involved in their operations; vet those agencies to make sure they will honor human rights and civil liberties and adhere to the laws and regulations of Israel. NSO does all of that, Shalev Hulio insists to this day, and he sleeps very well. But there is an insider at NSO who recently, and accidentally, gave us an interesting insight while offering sympathy for the kind of new and underfunded spyware enterprise NSO once was. "We've evolved with time. We are a big company. Making enough money, so you know, we can say no to a deal," the insider explains. "But if you're a small company and you are struggling to pay a salary to your employees and you have ten million dollars coming from a state in Mexico, you know, you don't really think about human rights. That's just the reality."

CHAPTER FIVE

TO LIVE AND DIE IN THE FREE MARKET

The beauty of Mexico, where Shalev and Omri were concerned, was not simply that there was a lot of money to be made there, but that it gave NSO a chance to prove its mettle. Plenty of other companies were jockeying for clients in Mexico, most notably the Milan-based Hacking Team (with offices already in Singapore and Washington, DC). This was capitalism at work: competition leads to innovation, which leads to more sales and more satisfied customers and more profits, which draws investment, which affords more innovation, and more profits, and more investment. So whirs the virtuous cycle at the heart of the free market promise, a cycle that fosters creativity and growth, and makes everybody better. Depending on your definition of "better."

A good place to start the story of the virtuous cybersurveillance industry cycle is at an abandoned schoolhouse on the outskirts of Puebla, a metropolis of almost three million people living in the shadow of the menacing Popocatépetl ("Smoking Mountain") volcano, a two-hour drive from Mexico City. A young field application engineer for the Hacking Team—let's call him Antonio—arrived at that remote building on a warm spring day to set up a Remote Control System (RCS) for a new client in the state government of Puebla.

Antonio was new to Hacking Team, but his first three weeks had been an excellent start for the eager young employee. He was fluent in Spanish, had lived in Mexico off and on for almost ten years, and had contacts in high places. Antonio's offer to make introductions to family friends among the local officialdom, like the head of security in one Mexican state and the head of a European consulate in another, drew a personal shout-out from the company CEO back in Milan. "You are on the team!" wrote David Vincenzetti.

This was an especially welcome note because Vincenzetti was something of a legend in the cybercommunity, a hacker's hacker, a self-styled cypherpunk who had helped develop and perfect the cryptography that served as the early bulwark of privacy on the internet. Vincenzetti had been a partner in three successful cybersecurity firms before he was thirty-five, and then turned to cybersurveillance. He started Hacking Team with one client in 2003, a metropolitan police agency in his home country. His timing was impeccable. In March 2004, less than a year after Hacking Team opened its doors, terrorists exploded ten separate bombs on four commuter trains in Madrid, killing two hundred and injuring nearly two thousand. Vincenzetti flew to the city and convinced the understandably abashed Spanish law enforcement officials that he had a tool capable of stopping these sorts of vicious acts before they happened. A way to monitor bad actors on the internet as they coordinated potentially deadly plots. "Privacy is very important," Vincenzetti would say, "but national security is much more important." National security professionals agreed!

Ten years in, Vincenzetti had made Hacking Team the premier private cybersurveillance vendor in the world. David Vincenzetti looked the part of predator, lean and alert, with a hint of wiry sinew beneath his slim-fit designer suits, like a hunter who could stalk for days before striking. Vincenzetti claimed to rise at 3 a.m. most days so he could get in a little exercise before he started his workday. He carried himself with the air of a winner but also of a prodigy, and a seer. One business partner from Mexico who spent a couple of days at the Hacking Team headquarters in Milan came away underwhelmed by the offices themselves but struck by the aura that surrounded the company founder and CEO. Hacking Team was more like a religion than a business, and Vincenzetti a Godhead. These kinds of organizations "don't have employees," the visitor says. "They have followers."

Vincenzetti had won over scores of dedicated acolytes, a sufficient handful of venture capitalists, and clients all over the world. Hacking Team claimed ongoing deals in forty separate countries, including in Europe, Africa, and the Middle East. The company had also provided its RCS surveillance tools to a handful of discerning federal agencies in the US—the FBI, military intelligence units at the Department of Defense, and the DEA. (The DEA had signed a deal worth $2.4 million.) But even as late as 2013, the bulk of the company revenues still came from Mexico.

The sales team was so prolific at that point that it had kind of outrun the company's engineers. Which meant Hacking Team had already asked a lot of Antonio, even before he got to the strange abandoned house in Puebla. Though still a trainee, Antonio found himself operating solo from time to time in his first few weeks, like when he handled one unplanned emergency with a client in Querétaro, whose agents were having trouble operating the system and were anxious for an upgrade. This was an unhappy customer that needed both technical support and general hand-holding, but Antonio assured his bosses he could handle the delicate situation: "I always take the opportunity to have more responsibility as an interesting challenge."

That can-do spirit had won the day. By the end of the session, the Querétaro client was talking about buying increased capacity—to target more criminals and drug lords and kidnappers. The governor of Querétaro, it was noted among the Hacking Team managers, was a friend and ally of the new Mexican president, Enrique Peña Nieto. "The likelihood that he will speak well of Hacking Team to the president is a fact," said one. "The end goal is for the president to support expansion of the system."

So Antonio's future with Hacking Team looked bright . . . right up to the last Monday in May, three weeks into his employment, when he was ushered into the abandoned windowless schoolhouse by one of the key RCS resellers in Mexico. The reseller had already shown itself less than trustworthy by Antonio's lights. The paperwork at Antonio's previous installation in Campeche was not signed by the client of record, a government prosecutor's office. The official who did sign worked in the

Department of Urban Development, which, Antonio knew for a fact, did not have jurisdiction to use lawful interception on anyone. Here in Puebla, the paperwork was signed by a factotum in the governor's personal office, and the Mexican official on scene to run the RCS cybersurveillance show at the otherwise empty dwelling was well known to Antonio. Was well known to anybody who read the newspapers in Mexico.

Antonio cornered the senior member of the Hacking Team crew at the schoolhouse that morning and said they really needed to talk about what was going on here, but he was waved off and told to get started on the training. At the lunch break, Antonio got his colleague alone again. "I can't do it," Antonio says. "You don't know this guy."

"No, I don't know this guy," his co-worker said. But the deal was done, and the papers signed.

"Well, I can't do it. I can't be in the same room with this man."

"Listen, you're here to work."

"I can't do it," Antonio kept repeating. "I can't be in the same room with this man."

The man in question was Joaquin Arenal Romero, and Romero and his close associates were credibly alleged to carry dirty water for the Los Zetas drug cartel, like, for instance, a little illegal cybersurveillance on an opposition governor. Los Zetas, Antonio explained to his new bosses at Hacking Team after that first day, "is the worst cartel that has ever been. They are not simply narcotraffickers but ex-police and ex-military that also traffic children and manage all kinds of dirty business. . . . I think you understand my ethical worries."

Antonio called in sick and stayed in his hotel in Puebla on Day Two of the installation and training session. Hacking Team managers acted without hesitation, in what they clearly saw as the company's best interests. The operations unit scotched Antonio's next assignment, in Ecuador, which was scheduled for the following Monday, June 3. On that day, instead, a memo went out to the Hacking Team announcing Antonio's departure from the company. They wished him "all the best for his future career" but had already put in the works a nondisclosure agreement for his signature. Yeah, you can leave, kiddo, but keep your trap shut.

■■■■■■■

Davidᴅ Vɪɴᴄᴇɴᴢᴇᴛᴛɪ ᴀɴᴅ his management team adhered to the simple and straightforward economic formula that prevails in business these days: a corporation's sole purpose is to maximize shareholder profits. Period. Ethical worries were beside the point. When one of Hacking Team's exploit developers suggested that perhaps they should be more careful about vetting their end users, a company executive shut him down. "What's your concern with that?" he asked. "Why do you care about things that shouldn't concern you?"

Vincenzetti needed good soldiers, who kept their heads down, marched forward, and didn't ask questions. "Business is not sport," he liked to say, quoting his favorite computer industry pioneer. "It's war."

Hacking Team, circa 2013, could rightly boast something nearing domination in the fight for the cybersurveillance market share, largely because it had developed the most effective and comprehensive cyber-intrusion tools to be had. Vincenzetti believed he had already vanquished his strongest foe, Gamma Group, known for its FinFisher cybersurveil-lance system. "FinFisher is so technologically retarded," he wrote in an internal memo, it belongs to the "remote past."

But Vincenzetti was wary by nature, and he instilled this watch-fulness throughout his team. So Hacking Team saw NSO coming and understood the Israeli start-up was delivering just what Mexican clients were clamoring for now—exploits capable of penetrating a variety of mobile phones. NSO had that, Hacking Team executives conceded, but not much else. Pegasus did not, unlike Hacking Team's cyberweaponry, have any exploits to invade desktops or laptops; the NSO system did not offer any way to deliver an attack vector except through SMS messages, which require the user to click on it; and the system software was not yet stable enough to provide twenty-four-hour monitoring and clean exfiltration of data.

Word among resellers was that NSO's first big client in Mexico, SEDENA, was disappointed in Pegasus. SEDENA had forked over somewhere north of $15 million to NSO, and Pegasus looked like an expensive flop. The hardware and software components were set up in a state-of-the-art monitoring station (a station the Mexican army had reportedly paid Azano as much as $80 million to construct) where nothing really happened. "I have been there," a Hacking Team executive reported back to Milan, "and it is a huge new cement two-building bunker that looks deserted, empty, hi-tech and lifeless. I'm not kidding. It is bright white cement and blinding when you walk across the huge patio to get to the entrance. Unlike any other Mexican governmental office I have been to, there are no plants, no decoration, no grass, nothing. Basic waste of money."

Vincenzetti and his acolytes had a good laugh at that, and as this confirmed their suspicions that Pegasus was a horse that didn't hunt, they breathed a little easier. But not entirely easy. Because, first of all, NSO was an Israeli company, and recent press about Stuxnet, the spectacular malware that single-handedly set back Iran's nuclear program by years (if not decades), suggested the exploit was built on the brain power of Israeli techs. Israeli technology, Vincenzetti occasionally lamented, was "invariably overvalued." More worrisome, NSO's real strength was in selling, and at enormously inflated prices. Shalev Hulio and Omri Lavie appeared to have discovered the key to unlocking the market in Mexico, and it had less to do with technological capacity than with access to the right people. Azano, they had heard, had taken Pegasus right into President Felipe Calderón's private office.

Hacking Team had been momentarily buoyed after Enrique Peña Nieto took over the presidency in December 2012. The first months of the new administration spelled trouble for NSO because Azano was in ill odor with Team Peña. There were whispers that US president Barack Obama had warned Peña, in their first bilateral meeting, that Azano posed a serious threat to good relations between the two countries. Azano's harassment of Sempra, whose subsidiary SoCalGas provided natural gas for more than twenty million people in California, was an issue of national security. When Omri Lavie and NSO technicians next arrived in Mexico City to demonstrate Pegasus to the new leaders in the attorney general's office, according to somebody who was in the room, the highest-ranking government official abruptly turned on his heels and walked out when he saw Azano was also there. "Basically, what he said is that this is the last time he wants to see [Azano] there," the insider says, "and the demonstration was canceled. I think after that NSO understood that [Azano] was never going to sell to this government."

NSO simply pivoted to a new reseller, Hacking Team believed, an Israeli businessman named Uri Ansbacher and his partner Avishai Neryia. An esteemed figure in the Jewish community in Mexico, Avishai was about to be named by President Peña as honorary consul to Haifa, Israel. "The guy that sells is Uri, but the guy that opens the door is Avishai," the government insider says. "[Hacking Team] knew that they were going directly to the president. Not to lower levels. Directly to the president."

NSO wasn't just making hay in Mexico. In August 2013, NSO sold Pegasus to the government of the United Arab Emirates, an oil-soaked regime with very deep pockets. The Emiratis could easily pay five or ten times what the Mexicans could, with far fewer middlemen and corrupt government officials who needed a cut of the proceeds. The sale to the UAE was a shot of much-needed cash for NSO, as well as a direct hit on Hacking Team hegemony. The newbie company, much to Vincenzetti's chagrin, was beginning to get fawning press in glossy financial publications. "Most of your typical solutions for interception are inadequate," Omri Lavie told one reporter, "so a new tool had to be built." Omri went on to explain that he could not talk about how his new solution worked or identify any of their customers. "I don't want to be beheaded," he joked. "In some countries we're not even allowed to know where the building is, where [the system] will be installed. Not only are we not allowed in the building, we don't even know where the building is—it could be in another city."

At this point, Vincenzetti began to get a tad more manic than usual. He worried about where NSO might next challenge them—Romania, Morocco, Saudi Arabia? Or, worse yet, in the private equity market, which afforded the sort of money required to buy new infection exploits or develop new technology. So Vincenzetti made a big play. "Here is my vision," he wrote in an email to his followers in November 2013. The global "chessboard," Vincenzetti claimed, had set up perfectly for Hacking Team's next move. He attached a news item from the day before, describing the Kingdom of Saudi Arabia's unease with the new posture in the Middle East taken by the US and its allies in Europe. Obama's secretary of state was on a trip to Riyadh, the article noted, where he "encountered Saudi Arabia's anxieties over the possibility of a rapprochement between the US and Iran after more than three decades of enmity."

Vincenzetti went on to sketch out for his team his own view of the current dynamics of global power. "Saudi is now isolated," he wrote. "Obama has alienated Saudi, Israel, Turkey, and countless other states who now think: 'We can no longer rely on the US for our security.' . . . There are five 'legs' of war: land, air, sea, space, and cyber. Cyber is becoming more and more lethal. Aramco, the main oil company in Saudi, has been blocked for weeks by an Iranian cyberattack."

And what did all this have to do with Hacking Team? Well, Hacking Team provided cybersolutions, didn't they? Vincenzetti's grand plan was to provide a whole suite of cybercapabilities to the Kingdom of Saudi Arabia. All the kingdom had to do was buy the company.

Three days later, a London-based venture capitalist with billions in the bank and close ties to the Saudi intelligence chief, Prince Bandar bin Sultan al Saud, commissioned a Boeing Business Jets 737 to fly Vincenzetti and his key staff to Riyadh. "We will be met at the airport on Wednesday evening and you will be taken to the hotel which has been arranged for you," wrote the billionaire, Wafic Saïd, whose Safinvest would be running this deal. "It is proposed that on Thursday we will meet the relevant Saudi officials led by the Deputy Minister and the team will have the opportunity to make a full presentation including demonstrations."

Vincenzetti had already instructed his Hacking Team followers on the proper wardrobe and dispatched his COO to the Saudi embassy in Rome, on a Sunday, to pick up the necessary travel documents. "Which will be open only for you! Makes you think right? . . . Here we go!"

The meetings in Riyadh were boffo, according to Vincenzetti. He reported to his team that Mr. Said had said afterward that he would "give standing orders to my lawyers to execute the transaction in a few days." Hacking Team's current equity partners, meanwhile, had already affixed their signatures to the letter of intent to sell more than 70 percent of the company to Saudi Arabia, or to some newly formed shell company controlled by the Saudis. Of course, a transaction of this scope takes time—still a lot of due diligence and lawyering and horse-trading to be done. Wafic's team took a hard look at the Hacking Team revenues for 2013, for instance, and chiseled down the top-line price from $61 million to $49.5 million. Then, just as the final details were being worked out, on February 19, 2014, Wafic's dear friend Prince Bandar was unceremoniously removed as the head of Saudi intelligence. Just like that, the deal was dead.

A month later, more bad news: "This is a surprise," a mergers and acquisitions specialist emailed Vincenzetti on March 20. "Everyone said that NSO was in trouble after product issues in Mexico. Apparently, Francisco Partners thought otherwise."

Francisco Partners had bought a controlling share of NSO for triple the Hacking Team asking price in Riyadh, around $120 million. The news reports put NSO's revenue at $40 million in the previous year, dwarfing Hacking Team's earnings. Vincenzetti made frantic efforts to have US-based Francisco Partners roll Hacking Team into their cyberportfolio. The private equity firm strung them along for a few months and patiently listened to explanations of the ways in which Hacking Team's was the superior technology: "We examined [NSO's] solution with our own eyes and we now have clear and incontrovertible evidence that, technologically speaking, they are behind us. . . . We are definitely underselling our product."

Francisco Partners took a pass.

This was the start of a very bad stretch for Hacking Team. Cybersecurity researchers from Citizen Lab, a Canadian tech laboratory inside the University of Toronto's Munk School of Global Affairs & Public Policy, issued a series of damning reports in 2014, with forensic evidence, alleging that Hacking Team had sold its RCS spyware to more than twenty governments, nearly half of which were considered authoritarian regimes. A number of those regimes, such as the UAE and Morocco, appeared to have used RCS to spy on political dissidents and journalists. Young developers who had taken pride in how the spyware had led to the arrests of more than fifty Italian mafia bosses and driven down the number of Mexican women being kidnapped and sold in eastern Europe, were horrified by public reports that Hacking Team cyberweapons had been used against journalists and political dissidents. A few had even started to talk among themselves about the instances of misuse they were beginning to see with their own eyes. "It wasn't until they put an application into the system that allowed you to put data on a computer," says one former Hacking Team contractor, "to put pedophile pictures onto somebody's personal computer and then they arrest him. That's when I was like 'Shit, this is not good.'"

Vincenzetti, meanwhile, was still in his glory. "He's a show-off," says one former Hacking Team employee. "He had to drive a Ferrari. He wanted to show people he was rich and that he had money. And he didn't give a damn what people did with the system. . . . He would make sales anywhere, to anyone."

"Gradually, there were more and more operations that were really borderline," says another.

Employees and business associates at Hacking Team began to get the eerie sense that they, too, were being spied on. Vincenzetti openly mocked anybody in the company who dared to raise the question of ethics. *Why do you care? If a government says a person is a terrorist, he is a terrorist. It's not for us to decide.*

Attacks from outside the company were met with similar derision. A letter from the United Nations Security Council suggesting that Hacking Team might have violated a ban on sales of "military equipment" to Sudan drew remarkably ham-handed responses from the company's outside legal counsel. Selling RCS to Sudan was not unlawful. "If one sells sandwiches to Sudan he is not subject, as far as my knowledge goes, to [this] law," she wrote to Vincenzetti. "HT should be treated like a sandwich vendor."

Vincenzetti was sure he was being unfairly attacked, even persecuted, and Hacking Team said as much. "Citizen Lab has chosen to target a private business operating in full compliance with all relevant law," a company spokesman offered. "We believe the software we provide is essential for law enforcement and for the safety of us all in an age when terrorists, drug dealers, sex traffickers and other criminals routinely use the Internet and mobile communications to carry out their crimes."

That was the public response. When the Italian government called a brief halt on the export of RCS, Vincenzetti exploded in private: "Those who are destroying our company are half men, they are cowards, they are blind, they don't even live a real life. . . . They'll have to physically kill me to stop me."

Despite the hiccups, Vincenzetti remained on the hunt and optimistic. He was still banking big on Mexico, which remained Hacking Team's single largest client country and had already spent more than $7 million on RCS. The company had ongoing contracts with seven different state-level clients in Mexico and the government-owned oil company, Pemex. Revenue from Mexican government agencies was double the amount Hacking Team got from the Kingdom of Saudi Arabia at that point, and nearly four times the amount from the United States. But the Hacking Team salesmen and engineers were expending a lot of energy trying to calm their most important Mexican client, CISEN, whose operators were complaining that RCS wasn't secure. "WE NEED TO PUT THE FIREWALL IN FOR THEM!" a key account manager wrote back to Milan in the late summer of 2014. "I know it is not our job, but it is not my job to just sit back and let a client destroy our reputation only because they are too stupid to install a firewall. We need to fix this because it is blocking our sales in Mexico."

Vincenzetti's troops were also losing ground to the now very well-funded NSO, which had just made an unprecedented sale to the office of the Mexican federal prosecutor (PGR)—$27.6 million before taxes—promising a capability of five hundred simultaneously monitored targets. Vincenzetti was in a swivet after that news, full of nonsensical ideas for besting his rising rival: "So why shouldn't we do like Oracle did with IBM in the past, boasting its technological superiority and its convenience?" he wrote in an email in early 2015. "Do you remember Oracle's massive comparative ads? Exempli gratia, they booked the back cover of *The Economist* for years comparing the Oracle DB with the IBM DB contrasting IBM's lower performances and high prices with Oracle's much better performance and lower prices."

▮▮▮▮▮▮▮

THE FINAL BLOW to Vincenzetti—a live-by-the-sword, die-by-the sword blow—was heralded by an unexpected message posted on Hacking Team's own Twitter account in the first dark hours of July 5, 2015. "Since we have nothing to hide," read the tweet, "we're publishing our emails, files, and source code."

This hijacked tweet was almost two months in the making. A very patient and cautious hacker who called himself "Phineas Fisher" (he had already hacked the rival Gamma Group) would eventually take credit, publishing a technical explanation of how he found a vulnerability in the system software that pried open a back door into Hacking Team's internal network. Once through that door, Phineas lived undetected inside the network for weeks, sniffing out passwords, listening in on audio, viewing webcam images, even watching one of the system administrators spend hours of his workday playing *World of Warcraft*.

When he discovered an under-protected server used by the company's software developers, its sales team, and its key executives, Phineas mounted the server remotely and accessed a mother lode of company backup files. Within those backups were passwords that gave him access to the live server, as well as the domain admin password, which gave him access to the company's internal emails. He downloaded the emails to his own server, a stealth exfiltration executed against the kings of exfiltration. Phineas continued to live and learn on the network, dancing around and through firewalls to spy on key employees—"one of my favorite hobbies is hunting sysadmins"—until one led him to Hacking Team's crucial asset, the source code for its RCS spyware. Which Phineas also downloaded onto one of his own drives.

The day after he got the source code, Phineas Fisher took over Hacking Team's Twitter account and made the unexpected announcement that a data dump was coming. Vincenzetti and his team didn't have to wait long to see the hacker make good on that promise. Phineas Fisher dumped everything, 400 gigabytes' worth of internal emails, memos, and documents from Hacking Team servers—available to all, on a public site.

The millions of pages confirmed many of the worst tendencies in Hacking Team's business practices, including sales to renowned violators of civil rights and human rights, as well as the defense of those sales. "The King of Morocco is a benevolent monarch," Vincenzetti insisted in one email.

The leak also revealed Hacking Team's growing paranoia and concern about NSO. Vincenzetti and his crew were obsessed with the extraordinary fees NSO was charging, and hot to prove that NSO's claims of having produced zero-click network infection vectors were all make-believe. Hacking Team had set out to produce a point-by-point memo describing the advantages of RCS over Pegasus. Vincenzetti's agents plied NSO Group employees with dinner and drinks to try to get them to spill the secrets of Pegasus, according to the company's leaked internal emails. They even tried to infiltrate NSO product demos in Mexico.

The Phineas Fisher exploit tripped Hacking Team, and though it took a few years for the company to actually hit the pavement, the end was a spectacular public face-plant. In the first days of the embarrassing data dump, Vincenzetti pointed the finger at business rivals and jealous foreign governments. Somebody with really deep pockets had to be behind this breach, he insisted. Vincenzetti also tried to frame a handful of disgruntled employees who had left the company a year earlier to start a cybersecurity firm to guard against the sort of cyberweapons Hacking Team trafficked in.

A two-year-long criminal investigation in Italy was unable to determine the real identity of Phineas Fisher or to pin the breach on any of Vincenzetti's rivals or enemies. But investigators did clear the former Hacking Team employees of any crime, and they did discover that the most likely reason the hacker got inside the company network was an outdated firewall and virtual private network system. A few former Hacking Team employees told investigators that the old software was still in the system because one person was still using it—David Vincenzetti. "Literally," said one, "because he couldn't be bothered to install a software update."

Phineas Fisher offered his own statement after the news that the Italian authorities were closing their investigation. "Maybe now the prosecutors will have time to investigate the various crimes committed by Hacking Team," he said. "But I don't have any illusions that prosecutors will look into any of that."

The now legendary hacker had already published, along with his how-to guide, a kind of manifesto reminding his fellow travelers in tech that they were the best guardians against cyberintrusion. "There's plenty of hackers better than me," Phineas Fisher wrote, "but they misuse their talents working for 'defense' contractors, for intelligence agencies, to protect banks and corporations, and to defend the status quo. Hacker culture was born in the US as a counterculture, but that origin only remains in its aesthetics—the rest has been assimilated. At least they can wear a t-shirt, dye their hair blue, use their hacker names, and feel like rebels while they work for the Man.

"You used to have to sneak into offices to leak documents. You used to need a gun to rob a bank. Now you can do both from bed with a laptop in hand. . . . Hacking is a powerful tool, let's learn and fight!"

THE CHIEF BENEFICIARIES of the Hacking Team leak, to Phineas Fisher's chagrin, did not turn out to be human rights defenders or political dissidents or journalists working in repressive regimes. There was a flurry of calls for regulation of the cybersurveillance industry by a handful of UN officials and NGOs, but that was just talk. The real gold in the leaked data was a handy list of potential customers—Egypt, Ethiopia, Bahrain, Kazakhstan, Vietnam, Sudan, and Saudi Arabia, for instance— customers who would continue to want cybersurveillance tools and would maybe want to buy them from a company that was not itself easy pickings for cyberintruders. "You can see all the Hacking Team emails with the list of their clients right online, right?" says an Israeli software engineer who was working in cybersecurity at the time. "And I think that NSO was the big winner. It eliminated the competition."

CHAPTER SIX

TEMPTATION

Only a handful of people actually saw an early-days Pegasus system in operation in Mexico. Fewer still manned the consoles and truly felt the reach and the possibility of NSO's evolving cybersurveillance tool. The operators in particular are shy to come forward to talk about the experience. Their concern is twofold: they signed nondisclosure agreements before they went to work in government or military agencies; and they tend to know secrets about narcos and kidnappers and corrupt police and corrupt politicians who really want these secrets to remain secret. There are good reasons to keep your head down in Mexico. So when we finally did persuade one of the pilots of a Pegasus operating terminal to talk, he did so with conditions. Jose, we will call him, wouldn't allow us to use his name, wouldn't even tell us his real name. He told us the agency he worked for, but asked us not to name it or to divulge which particular division he worked in, and he would not reveal the location of the facility where the Pegasus system was housed. But he did tell us his story.

Jose was among the very few key people trained to operate a Pegasus system, not long after the agency he worked for spent millions for a license to infect and monitor several hundred separate mobile phones, simultaneously. Pegasus was a welcome new tool in the fight against drug traffickers. Mexican police and prosecutors and military units were almost a decade into the Calderón-initiated war on the cartel-fueled crime, and the results were mixed at best. Kidnappings were down, and so was the trafficking of young Mexican women to Europe and Asia—thanks in part to Hacking Team's Remote Control System—but the murder rate was rising sharply. The drug cartels were doing a bigger business than ever and tightening their grip on many local governments and police agencies. Mounting and maintaining a serious criminal investigation into cartel activity was getting harder by the day. The narcos had a lot of motivation to fund their own countersurveillance programs, and plenty of resources. Even low-level soldiers serving the cartels changed devices and phone numbers constantly or carried as many as five mobile phones so they could execute an elaborate system of hopscotching among those devices, making it virtually impossible to trace calls.

The most notorious of the Mexican narco gangs, run by Joaquín "El Chapo" Guzmán, was also the most sophisticated in covering its tracks on the ground and in the ether. The full story emerged from testimony in El Chapo's 2019 criminal trial in New York. As early as 2008, when he was just about to cross the billion-dollar net worth mark, El Chapo hired an IT whiz kid to create the cartel's own private web of encrypted communication, with a high-speed internet system dedicated to Guzmán and his lieutenants. Guzmán was himself a bit of a Luddite when it came to computers, according to testimony, and he did a lot of his business on his cell phone, so his IT guru made sure all calls were routed through a proprietary central server. Increasingly interested in digital technology, and increasingly paranoid, El Chapo also asked his IT contractor to procure software that would allow him to spy on his many employees. Then he suggested they set up a separate spyware regimen in every internet café in the cartel's headquarter city of Culiacán. (El Chapo was very interested in what the locals were saying about him.)

Jose says he understood from the first moment he saw Pegasus in action, during the weeks-long simulator training he received, that this new cybersurveillance weapon could be a game-changer in the fight against drug cartels like El Chapo's and other criminal enterprises. "When we arrived at [the agency], we did not even know this thing existed, and the head of [a separate agency] was the one who told us, 'Hey, you have a wonderful piece of equipment that does a thousand things,'" he says. "The scope of the tool was explained to us, and at the beginning it did generate a great expectation for results that could be obtained."

The first steps in cybersurveillance Pegasus-style still depended on old-fashioned legal pleadings and gumshoe work. Investigators were supposed to gather enough probable cause evidence for a judge to sign off on targeting a suspect; and then these agents had to go out and find the number of the mobile phone that target was using. The thorniest task was what cyberpros refer to as social engineering, which was still crucial, because at that point, the Pegasus malware could only be installed if the cell phone owner clicked on an SMS message. That act would send them to a domain where Pegasus sat ready to be deployed.

The messages needed to be alluring to the individual in question, bait he or she was sure to take. So investigators would spend a couple weeks gathering open-source information about the target—names of their spouse and their children, their girlfriends, or their pets; their hobbies, interests, and proclivities. "The social engineering had to be done with precision because not many attempts should be made so as not to attract attention," Jose says. "If we succeeded in getting them to click on the SMS message, that automatically installed the software on the mobile device, and from then on, we could access all the information on the phone." If they failed on the first attempt, the social engineers went back to the drawing board, came up with another, better lure, and tried again after a two- or three-day hiatus. The federal ops rarely went back for a third turn at the tumblers.

The other frustration was that an NSO license was good only for operating systems spelled out in the contract; it might be guaranteed to work on recent versions of operating software running Androids, iPhones, BlackBerrys, or Symbian cell phones. Similarly, a Pegasus license was good only for the latest mobile devices on the market. But Apple alone was putting out a new iPhone every year at that point, and even twice a year, as well as new operating systems or iOS upgrades to patch newfound vulnerabilities. Each new iteration of any device or operating system might require new exploits to successfully complete installation of the spyware. "It was complicated because you have to keep updating the licenses every time the companies release a new version of the software or new equipment," Jose explains. "It's very expensive. Like permanent rent."

When the Pegasus system was up and running at full steam, though, with hundreds of potential criminal actors under surveillance on a given day, this was heady stuff. As long as a mobile device was connected to Wi-Fi, Pegasus could exfiltrate hundreds of megabytes' worth of data at a time without raising the tiniest of red flags that might alert a target. The room Jose worked in every day was a hotbed of high-tech friction, literally; the office had to show they had two separate rooms constantly cooled to 65°F, along with fire alarms and marked emergency exits, before NSO engineers would execute any new installation. In Jose's chilled room there were always at least two six-and-a-half-foot-high racks stacked, from the bottom up, with the requisite Pegasus hardware delivered by NSO's reseller: an uninterrupted power system, gateway modems to send the SMS messages, at least four different servers, and two routers with solid firewalls.

The agency had provided a fiber optic network, a cable-based Ethernet, the ability to connect to mobile phones through two separate carriers, and about twenty different IP addresses. A second room held a 10-terabyte server to store the daily wash of Pegasus-exfiltrated data until it could be sifted and categorized (or discarded as useless) by one of the backroom analysts. These specialists would write up reports almost daily, warning of a crime about to happen, developing new avenues of investigation, or identifying potential new targets.

Jose and his fellow operators were limited to monitoring several hundred mobile phones at a time, but there was constant churn. Supervisors were always picking and choosing the highest-priority targets in a target-rich environment, so Jose or the other operators might be asked to disconnect one infected phone and go get another. The operator would get the chosen mobile phone number from the department of social engineering, along with suggestions for devising the SMS message bait. "In our case it was very simple," Jose admits, "because [my] targets were members of organized crime, and we didn't have to look very hard. The [SMS messages] were pornography topics, where it was practically certain that they were going to click on it."

After Jose typed up the missive and hit Send, Pegasus did the rest. The system would send the SMS message through a series of anonymizers in order to veil the end user. "These messages would go through different servers around the world," says one Mexican IT specialist who saw the system in action. "It can go through China, from China to Australia, from Australia to Amsterdam, from Amsterdam to Panama, and from Panama to the target."

Jose did all his postinfection work at one of the few operator terminals at his facility, each with a 320-gigabyte hard drive, with 3 gigs of RAM memory, and an oversize monitor, where the magic appeared. All Jose had to do was get comfortable in his swivel chair and punch in the number of a target under surveillance. The Pegasus system then generated on his screen a set of modules mapping the infected mobile phone. These modules were a series of small boxes on the right half of the screen, each representing a separate application at work on the phone. There might be a box for WhatsApp, or for Signal, or for any other messaging app (encrypted or not) that contained every message archived on the phone and every message in or out since infection. Messages deleted after infection became faint on Jose's screen, almost ghostly, but still readable. There was a box for email; one for calls, call history, and voice messages; one for real-time geolocation and geolocation history; one for the device's microphone; and one for the device's camera. Jose could then choose any app he wanted to check or monitor, and it would expand into an easily readable box on the left of the screen. "If I wanted, for example, the front-facing camera, I would tap on the front-facing camera, and it would magnify the front-facing camera image for me. If I wanted geolocation, I clicked on geolocation, and what was projected in this main module was the map." He could click on the call list, for example, and find out who were the most frequent contacts and if any were local police who might be part of the crime syndicate. Or he could, even from his seat, turn on the remote microphone and listen to any real-time conversation within earshot of the phone.

Jose remains proud of the work he did with Pegasus, and he insists that his team used the spyware only within the parameters of Mexican law and only where truly needed. "This is not ordinary crime that happens in the streets; it is a crime with a very strong economic apparatus, with infiltration at all levels of government," Jose says. "It needs tools with a more invasive nature than normal."

The analysts he worked with, he says, discarded a target's embarrassing personal details and habits if they had nothing to do with criminal activity. But the longer Jose worked at a Pegasus terminal, the more he understood the peril. He came to regard Pegasus as a kind of cyberdevil. Not because Pegasus in itself was an evildoer but because it was, like the devil, seductive. "This is where the human factor plays a key role," Jose says. "We knew how invasive it was in the lives of the targets, and we knew that we could not give in to temptation.

"For any person who sits in the chair where decisions have to be made in the use of this type of tool, it is attractive—with a certain morbid curiosity to get into people's lives. . . . These kinds of tools generate in [public servants] who have them within their reach a feeling of supremacy, of power, of control. And its use becomes perverse; it can become a means of personal satisfaction and not for the benefit of the public interest."

JUST AS JOSE'S Pegasus operation was going online, things were going sideways for the most powerful public servants in Mexico. President Enrique Peña Nieto had expanded Felipe Calderón's efforts to hobble the drug cartels, which amounted to pouring more of Calderón's gasoline on a fire. When authorities took down a drug chieftain, it often unleashed new battles over old turf, fought by factions inside the original gang or interlopers who saw opportunity. The murder rate tripled over the course of those two administrations. International headlines from the fall of 2014, less than two years into Peña Nieto's term, seemed emblematic of the chaos: buses commandeered by a group of college students who were headed to protest administration policies had been stopped by police in the state of Guerrero. The students from a local teachers' college were not treated as the perpetrators of some ill-advised lark. Six people were killed and forty wounded in the melee with police. Forty-three of the student-teachers had gone missing.

The administration promised answers, but those answers were weeks in coming, while the forty-three remained unaccounted for, sparking a wave of demonstrations that swept from Guerrero to Mexico City to Acapulco. The protesters often numbered in the thousands, carrying placards with photographs of the missing students.

Six weeks after the ambush, on November 7, 2014, the Peña Nieto administration finally released an official but meager account. Members from a local drug gang had confessed to the mass killings, attorney general Jesus Murillo Karam explained at his press conference that day. The men had admitted to investigators that they had tortured and killed the student-teachers. They said they dismembered the bodies, burned the remains on a massive pyre, and then ground any visible teeth and bone into dust before stuffing the evidence into plastic garbage bags and tossing them into a nearby river. The investigators had retrieved some of those garbage bags, which left little doubt that they had found a scene of a mass killing, Karam said that day, but "the high level of degradation caused by the fire in the remains makes it difficult to extract the DNA that will allow an identification."

The attorney general had little to say about earlier news reports that the police who had stopped the buses might have actually delivered the victims to the killers. It was hard to tell that day how much the attorney general and his investigators were in the dark and how much they were withholding from the public. (Only years later did the world learn that the students had made the fatal mistake of commandeering a pair of buses that the local cartel had loaded with heroin for a shipment across the US border—in a town where the police and the drug traffickers were closely aligned.) The attorney general had not seemed to be aware of text messages between the local drug kingpin and the deputy police chief in which the two men coordinated the spots where the police officers should deliver the student-teachers to the drug gang. "The massacre of the students," the former head of the US DEA's international operations would say when the full story emerged in 2021, "involves collusion between the police, army, organized crime, and a massive coverup by the Mexican government."

The Mexican citizenry didn't have to be told about collusion and cover-up, by anyone, even back in November 2014. The body politic in Mexico was fed up, which meant Peña Nieto was facing down a growing crisis, made worse when Attorney General Karam shut down his raucous press conference with this unfortunate sign-off: "Ya me cansé"— "Enough, I'm tired."

Within a matter of hours, this ill-considered phrase was a hashtag, and trending. Responses circulated on social media around the world but with the greatest velocity in Mexico. One Mexican filmmaker posted a YouTube manifesto: "Senor Murillo Karam, I, too, am tired," said Natalia Beristain. "I'm tired of vanishing Mexicans, of the killing of women, of the dead, of the decapitated, of the bodies hanging from bridges, of broken families, of mothers without children, of children without fathers. I am tired of the political class that has kidnapped my country, and of the class that corrupts, that lies, that kills. I, too, am tired."

The next day fifteen thousand citizens marched through the center of Mexico City. The protest was generally peaceful, though many in the crowd were seething, and riot police did have to be sent in to secure the National Palace when the angriest in the march spraypainted the façade, broke windows, and threatened to burn through the Mariana Door.

The day after that, in an entirely unrelated episode, a team of reporters headed by the popular and respected journalist Carmen Aristegui broke a story that further embarrassed President Peña Nieto. The report on Casa Blanca (White House), fruit of a multimonth investigation, looked bad. President Peña Nieto and his wife, telenovela star Angélica Rivera, the journalists explained, had the use of a luxurious recently constructed, seven-bedroom, $7 million private mansion with underground parking, an indoor-outdoor living area within a lush garden, a master bath with a spa, and an elevator all the way to the Jacuzzi and bar on the top floor. But the original owner of record of the residence was not the president and his wife, but Grupo Higa, the company that also constructed the house for the couple, to spec.

The investigative reporters also wrote that Grupo Higa, owned by Juan Armando Hinojosa Cantú, had been awarded several large construction contracts from the state of Mexico while Peña Nieto was the governor there from 2005 to 2011. Cantú's Grupo Higa, Aristegui's team further reported, was part of a consortium that won a recent contract from the Peña Nieto administration to build a high-speed train from Mexico City to Querétaro. Aristegui's team had the land deeds and government contracts to back up their reporting. The Casa Blanca story got media play all over the world.

This may have qualified as middling financial corruption, but in combination with the public ire over the missing students—the cover of *Proceso* magazine that week was split in two, featuring the parents of the students on one half and Casa Blanca on the other—it was a hard blow for a Mexican president who had been trying to convince his citizens and the rest of the world that he was a man of integrity. Peña Nieto canceled Grupo Higa's bullet train contract, and First Lady Angélica Rivera went on television to explain that she was in the process of buying Casa Blanca, as always planned, and could easily pay for it with her own money. This did not calm the waters. "Unlike Carmen Aristegui, the journalist who uncovered the Casa Blanca scandal," noted one observer, "Peña Nieto has not released any documents to back up his side of the story."

Two days after the First Lady's television appearance, on November 20, 2014, protesters who had traveled to Mexico's capital city by train, bus, car, and foot staged a massive demonstration. This was, the participants noted, the 104th anniversary of the start of a revolution that overthrew a Mexican dictator. The protests were loud and long, sometimes violent—including an occasional Molotov cocktail and physical clashes with the riot police—but mostly just angry. A culmination of what one Mexican poet and novelist called "fifty-six days of marches, sit-ins, teachers' and students' strikes, looting in shopping centers and supermarkets, ransacking and torching of public buildings, seizing of toll booths, blockading of highways and mass fasting and prayer." The demonstrators in Mexico City that day carried signs reading, "Peña, the people can't stand you" and "Peña, resign!" They burned his photo in the street, and they burned him in effigy in the Zocalo.

These are the times, apparently, that tempt men's souls. On the very day of the massive demonstration in Mexico City, somebody sent Carmen Aristegui an SMS message marked urgent, asking her to click on a link. Aristegui did not recognize the sender, so she let it pass without clicking.

PEÑA NIETO STOOD against the gathering tide as best he could; he promised to dig deeper into the case of the missing students and to reform the Mexican justice system. He announced the existence of a full investigation of the Casa Blanca affair by his secretary of civil service, which cleared the president and his wife of wrongdoing some months later. "Even though I acted according to the law," he offered in a public mea culpa, "this error affected my family, hurt the beginning of the administration, and weakened the public's trust in government. I myself felt the Mexican people's irritation. I understood it perfectly. So I very humbly ask for forgiveness and repeat my most sincere apology for the aggravation and indignation that I caused."

Peña Nieto's own aggravation and indignation, and that of his loyal appointees, did not much abate. When Bastian Obermayer's Panama Project rolled out in the spring of 2016, President Peña Nieto got nicked again, this time by Jorge Carrasco in *Proceso*. A key partner in the Panama Papers consortium, Jorge reported on a small group of wealthy Mexican businessmen who set up offshore trusts to help minimize their tax burden. "In particular, the favored contractor of President Enrique Peña Nieto, Juan Armando Hinojosa Cantú," Jorge wrote on April 3, 2016. "The owner of Grupo Higa appears so far as one of the most important clients in Mexico for the [Panamanian law] firm, according to the files. The supplier of the so-called White House of Peña Nieto and of the residence of the Secretary of the Treasury, Luis Videgaray—the person in charge of tax collection in the country—has been in a hurry to send money out of Mexico.

"In the midst of the storm over the revelation of his close relationship with Peña Nieto, Hinojosa Cantu sought in July of last year to mobilize more than one hundred million dollars in a complex financial network that passed through several countries.

"*Proceso* sought out the Higa Group Communications Department for this investigation to find out about his income and what he has reported to the Treasury, without obtaining a response. The Presidency of the Republic also refused comment."

Stories about the Panama Papers were still dribbling out weeks later when Jorge Carrasco received an SMS message out of the blue: "Hello Jorge. I am sharing this memo that Animal Politico published today. I think it's important to reshare." *Animal Politico* was well known to Jorge, a website also doing a lot of good investigative journalism. But Jorge didn't recognize the sender. "Who is this?" he texted back and got no answer. Jorge did not click on the link, but he did not erase the message either. That turned out to be a critical save for the Pegasus Project.

CHAPTER SEVEN

"CLOSING THE FIRST CIRCLE"

Sandrine

When Paloma de Dinechin asked him if he still had the mobile phone he was using in the spring of 2016, four years earlier, Jorge Carrasco was a bit befuddled. It was October 2020, and Paloma was in Mexico for the final stages of the Cartel Project, now racing to the finish line. She and a small camera crew were spending most of a Saturday doing a follow-up interview with Jorge, to tie up some loose ends about the murder of his *Proceso* colleague Regina Martínez and the aftermath. But Paloma's other assignment that day was to persuade Jorge to agree to have his phone analyzed for possible spyware infection.

Laurent and I had spent a lot of time strategizing with Paloma about how exactly to make the ask of Jorge. We wanted to tell him as much as we could without divulging the fact that we had access to this enormous amount of leaked data about NSO and Pegasus.

Paloma only brought it up to Jorge at the end of the day, with the interview in the can. She was as direct as she could be, explaining that Forbidden Stories was interested in reviewing the contents of his old phone with a new forensic tool that two experts at Amnesty International's Security Lab had developed. Jorge assumed it was part of the reporting on the Cartel Project, but the lack of definite information from Paloma only fed his growing sense of frustration, and his growing sense that he was being left in the dark about important aspects of an investigation in which he was a key partner. A few months earlier, as soon as we had first learned his phone might have been infected with Pegasus, we had asked Jorge to absent himself from the Signal group dedicated to the Cartel Project. Since then, we had been communicating with him almost exclusively through one of the reporters who worked for him at *Proceso*. "I remember talking to Sandrine to ask for more exchange," Jorge later explained. "I had been struck by the fact that communication between us had been reduced."

Jorge Carrasco is a very capable journalist and a very insightful man. He had spent twenty years reporting on issues that raised hackles across private enterprises and public institutions in Mexico: the doings of drug traffickers, as well as the doings of various police, military, and intelligence agencies. He had done significant work on the Hacking Team leak in 2015 and the use of the RCS spyware in his country. He and his fellow reporters and editors at *Proceso* had also done follow-up stories in 2017 after Citizen Lab found evidence that Pegasus had been used to target Carmen Aristegui and other Mexican journalists, and on proponents of a soda tax enacted by the Mexican government, and even on lawyers representing some of the parents of the forty-three students who had gone missing in Guerrero. Jorge had wondered for years if he, too, was a target of cybersurveillance. He did still have his old phone, but alas, he told Paloma when she asked him that Saturday in October 2020, he couldn't remember the PIN number.

Mexico was presenting a series of difficulties for Paloma just then; the country was a hard place for a twenty-three-year-old reporter to learn her trade. She had managed to retain her disarming habit of smiling at the end of every statement she made and every question she asked, which proved very effective in putting people at ease. But a charming mannerism wasn't always enough in Mexico. Paloma had spent days in Veracruz getting to know Regina Martínez's closest friends, but none were willing to go on the record to talk about her unsolved death. It didn't matter to them that the case was long past, more than seven years old; the ghosts of Veracruz keep close and seem always present. After a few days in the city, Paloma's antennae were more sensitive than usual. She was phoning back to our office in Paris to update us every day she was in Mexico, and her calls from Veracruz could be worrisome. I remember her call the day she had visited the street where Regina Martínez had lived and died. Paloma had a bad feeling about that street, she told us, like there was an ill wind blowing through the site. She had also begun to sense that some of the people in the neighborhood were not to be trusted. One of her best sources was so upset he made her get in a cab and go to another location—"Let's get the hell out of here," he told her—where they could talk safely.

What amazed me at the time was how the things that had persuaded Laurent to hire Paloma a year earlier—her curiosity and her fearlessness— seemed unchecked. Her full surname, Dupont de Dinechin, suggested she came from an aristocratic French family with a long history and big castles. Nothing else about her did. Paloma was raised by what she would describe as "hippie parents." Her father was French and her mother Chilean. The first thing that struck us about Paloma, from the very first meeting with her, was her diligence. Before she came in for her job inter- view, she had read every single word published by Forbidden Stories. She could paraphrase and quote interviews Laurent had given years earlier, when he was trying to get Forbidden Stories off the ground. She was also possessed of a natural maturity and a toughness that must have come in handy on her chosen field of sport: rugby.

Fluent in French, English, and Spanish, Paloma had—before she was twenty-two—completed a documentary short about violence against the indigenous citizens of Chile and done a six-month reporting internship at a digital publication in Guerrero, one of the most dangerous areas in Mexico. Once hired, she very quickly become a key point of contact for our best sources on the Cartel Project, the person our partners at other media outlets would turn to when they needed somebody to check a fact or go back to a difficult source. At the end of the project, she was fielding ten separate calls a day, requesting her to provide some confirmation or another. So I had no qualms about sending Paloma to convince Jorge to be the test case on the forensics, the first number in the data we would actually check.

Jorge showed up at Paloma's hotel a few days after the interview carrying his old phone; it took some time, and many different attempts, but he finally did get a PIN number that unlocked the device. He had some hesitation about allowing us to make a backup of the contents of his phone, which would include Jorge's contact list, all the text messages he had sent, and crucial to our project, all the text messages he had received, with time stamps. He wanted to know if the Security Lab would delete all the data when they were finished, and how long they would need to keep the backup. When Paloma explained we would need about two weeks to complete the analysis, he said that seemed like a long time. But he did finally agree to let her make the backup and upload the file to Claudio and Donncha in Berlin.

The process sounds simple, but this was new to Paloma. She only had time for a quick simulated run-through in Paris before she had decamped for Mexico. It required several attempts, over several excruciating hours, to get the backup files off Jorge's phone and successfully uploaded to the Security Lab's forensic platform. Then Claudio and Donncha put their new tool to work, looking for a very specific piece of evidence. "At the time," Donncha says, "we were having all these discussions about 'What does the data mean?' That was the big question. . . . We were a little bit concerned that we wouldn't be able to find the spyware. And maybe it wasn't going to be successful."

The first aha moment came when the Security Lab tool isolated that one strange text message from an unknown sender: "Hello Jorge. I am sharing this memo that Animal Politico published today. I think it's important to reshare." Jorge had received that message with the link just a few hours after his phone number, according to the data in the leaked list, had been selected. Not only did the time stamp of the selection match up with the suspicious text message, but the phone number of the sender was also significant. Because it was the same number, already identified in a published report from Citizen Lab, that sent Carmen Aristegui several SMS messages that linked to a fake website that would then load an exploit designed to install Pegasus spyware.

There was no evidence of actual infection, because Jorge had wisely not clicked on the link that would have launched the attack. But Jorge's iPhone had clearly been targeted, according to the evidence found by the forensic tool, and it was clearly linkable to NSO. Better than that, Jorge was a new find. He had not been among the dozen or so journalists and private citizens in Mexico who had already been identified as targets of Pegasus.

The first number we had been able to check in the leaked data was not only confirmed as a target of an NSO client but a previously unknown target. Even to a technological amateur like me, it seemed very unlikely that Jorge's would be the one and only new victim the Security Lab forensic tool would turn up among the fifty thousand numbers in the data set.

Claudio and Donncha didn't show it when they presented their first report to us, but they later told us they had been buoyed by the findings. The evidence of a Pegasus targeting sitting in Jorge's phone, evidence they now had, was a validation of the data itself. "You see the number in the data, and then you see the message appearing in the data at the right time, just when we expect the message to appear. So it was really a confirmation that we were on the right track."

There was still a long way to go, still a chance they could, as Donncha said, "whiff." But as Claudio put it, exhibiting his characteristic restraint: "This, um, could work."

SHORTLY AFTER PALOMA returned to Paris from Mexico, pressure began building at the Forbidden Stories office. In the first days of December 2020, I would occasionally notice Laurent standing by an open window in the office, smoking a cigarette—an old habit he always fell back into in the tense days just before and just after the publication of a major investigation. The Cartel Project was scheduled to go live across the world in a few days, at 6 p.m. Paris time, December 6, 2020, and our own small team was working long, hard hours. They were writing their own stories, while also fielding calls from our partners all over the world. The partners wanted Paloma to check a fact about Veracruz, or for Audrey to point out specifics from shipping manifests from China or India she had discovered, or for Phineas to reconfirm the number of Berettas and Glocks and other handguns sold into Mexico from Europe, or Israel or the United States. Editors and lawyers from various partners called in to parse the language of specific allegations and suggest last-minute emendations.

This was my first experience coordinating an international investigation, and it felt a bit like herding cats. There were sixty journalists total in the consortium, from twenty-five discrete media outlets in eighteen different countries, contributing to the Cartel Project—and they, too, were working overtime in the final days before publication. Many were adding reporting to the still mysterious circumstances of the murder of Regina Martínez. Others had picked up the threads of stories Regina had left unfinished at the time of her death.

Those threads, as well as the threads left behind from dozens of the 119 Mexican journalists killed in the previous twenty years, started in Veracruz and Guerrero and Sinaloa but spooled out all over the world. The cartels were getting precursor chemicals for mixing fentanyl from Asia, and laundering money through Spain, and buying guns from Austria and Italy and America. Which meant each of the partners had a particular local angle to the story about which they felt proprietary.

I was sympathetic when a journalist from one European outlet called me to say they might not be able to hold a story about methamphetamine labs in their country servicing the Mexican drug traffickers. He worried a rival news outlet in their home country might beat them to the punch. This was not an easy position to be in. Nobody wants to be second on a story they've worked on this hard. But I also knew I had to be firm with our nervous partner. No other single outlet, anywhere, was going to bring the depth and sweep to this story that our international consortium could. More important, there was a deal in place, agreed to by *all* the partners, that the first stories would not drop until the appointed hour, and would then roll out in a predetermined order over the ensuing days. If one of the partners started early, I feared it could lead to a stampede among the other partners. This would not only blunt the force of the revelations, but it would also threaten what the Forbidden Stories' collaborative model depended on most: trust among the partners.

I didn't get much sleep in the days leading up to publication. When I wasn't fielding calls or making final edits, I found myself obsessively refreshing web pages to see if any of our partners had jumped the gun.

I did have to call somebody in the Americas to ask them to take down a screenshot of the Cartel Project documentary they had uploaded. But then, mercifully, the project went live, right at the appointed hour, perfectly synchronized on media sites around the world. The first-day stories focused on the life and death of the *Proceso* reporter we had chosen to put at the center of the project; the headlines were splashed on front pages of newspapers and bannered as lead stories on websites across the globe:

Murder of Regina Martinez: One of Many

*Unanswered Questions Haunt Case of
Mexican Journalist's Murder*

*Slain Journalist's Story a Portrait of a Violent,
Corrupt Era in Mexico*

*This Journalist's Brutal Murder Was Dismissed as
a Robbery. Now Reporters from Around the World
Are Determined to Uncover the Truth*

The pickup from other outlets was immediate and kept growing. The first hours after initial publication felt like a jolt of electricity through our otherwise exhausted office. The idea of a big group of journalists from all over the world cooperating on a single story had been a matter of theory for me up to that point, almost academic. Collaboration is not the natural impulse among those who practice the trade of journalism; most of the challenge and half of the fun of reporting is getting the story *nobody else has*. But that day, when the Cartel Project was rolling out, it finally felt real, and I was struck by the sheer power of a collaborative enterprise; the teamwork had amplified both the reporting, and its impact.

We had something to celebrate, and somebody from Forbidden Stories, probably Cécile, had already carried in the requisite champagne and wine and beer. It wasn't long before we were popping the corks, and I saw Laurent and Paloma standing near an open window, both having a smoke. In the middle of the revelry, we invited all our partners to join a celebratory Zoom call. Laurent's old friend and founding board member, Bastian Obermayer, offered a toast to all the partners. Others chimed in.

Dana Priest, a deft Pulitzer Prize–winning journalist from the *Washington Post*, put a bow on the day for all of us. Dana said she was particularly impressed at how this group had managed to put Regina Martínez's face and her story on front pages across the world. Headlines and front-page news about a journalist were a rare thing. The Cartel Project team had not only told the story of Regina's courage in reporting on drugs and corruption in Veracruz, and followed her old leads to new stories, but the international outcry had also shamed the current president of Mexico to call for reopening the investigation into her death. "I feel like we made her live again," I remember Dana saying.

CARTEL PROJECT STORIES were still rolling out three days later when Laurent and I made a previously arranged call to Dana, who was at her farm outside Washington, DC. "Have you gotten any sleep yet?" was the first thing she wanted to know. "I was tired," she said. "You must have been exhausted."

Laurent didn't spend much time on small talk or on another round of kudos on our recent mutual success. We were turning the page to a new project, and we wanted to get Dana and the *Washington Post* to sign on as one of the key partners. "Basically, to explain briefly," he told Dana, "we have access to a lot of information about a massive surveillance campaign all over the world, in many countries, targeting many, many people. A lot of people and including a lot of very big names: heads of state, Nobel Prize winners, many journalists . . . If you are interested, we really need to be able to meet physically to tell you more. We say that because it's involving many intelligence units, and all of them would be very upset if they knew that one of us has access to that information. If we get hacked, it's over."

Dana was technically on a sabbatical at the time. But she generously agreed to talk to the head of investigations at the *Post* and then to set up an in-person meeting so we could make our pitch as soon as we could get to the States.

IT WAS ALMOST six weeks later, the day before the US presidential inauguration in January 2021, when Laurent and I finally arrived in Washington, DC, to make our case to Dana and the editor from the *Post*. We had by then grown even more anxious to lock in the renowned Washington newspaper. *Die Zeit* and *Süddeutsche Zeitung* and *Le Monde* had agreed to operate as reporting partners with Forbidden Stories on the cybersurveillance project. The *Post* would be the fourth and final member of the first circle of the investigation, the crucial US partner.

As we peered out the car window on the ride into town from the airport, it was hard to feel hopeful. The US capital city was a bleak and embattled landscape at that point, reeling from the four-year reign of Donald Trump, and braced for its last ugly spasms. The daily Covid-19 death toll in the country had passed three thousand and was still rising. The reflecting pool had been ringed with four hundred lanterns, each representing a thousand US citizens already lost. The medical trauma was like the handmaiden of the political. The Trump-led effort to overturn the election had been punctuated, less than two weeks before our arrival, by a deadly riot at the seat of national government. News feeds were still filled with newfound footage of Confederate flag–wielding marauders storming the US Capitol, ransacking the Speaker's office and both chambers of the legislature, chasing representatives and senators and their aides into safe rooms in the bowels of the building, beating police officers bloody, and looting camera equipment from journalists on scene to cover the story. "Enemies of the people," the American president had called reporters, making them (and us) just another in a long list of groups with targets on their backs.

The normally festive run-up to the presidential inauguration had all the charm of a prison-yard lockdown. The Capitol grounds were fenced by seven-foot-high chain link, said to be "unscalable." Armored military vehicles sat at key entrances. The perimeter and streets nearby were patrolled by six thousand uniformed soldiers shouldering assault rifles.

Laurent and I quickly aborted our one attempt to get some exercise with a run on the Mall. Then we ended up staying in our hotel to watch the inauguration on television, while the ceaseless shudder of helicopters rattled our windows. We were cheered only slightly by the performance of twenty-two-year-old poet Amanda Gorman.

I couldn't take my eyes off her effulgent yellow overcoat and the way her hands and fingers cut powerfully through the air, measuring her cadences as she spoke.

> For there is always light, if only we're brave enough to see it.
>
> If only we're brave enough to be it.

The rest of the pallid pared-down ceremony felt like a sad reminder of what the world becomes when autocrats begin to use their chosen weapons to chip away at even the strongest of democracies.

WHEN WE MET Dana at her home the day after the inauguration, she seemed a little perturbed by our request that she turn off her cell phone and laptop and put them in another room before we got started. In fact, I wasn't sure she was sold on this new cybersurveillance project. But we were now able to access the data by remote hookup, so it was easy to show her the scope and scale of the data in the leaked list. The reservations she had about the potential of this story seemed to melt away as she scrolled down that massive list, and we highlighted some of the names we had already identified as targets selected for cybersurveillance.

Two days later Dana was driving us across the city for our sit-down with the head of the *Washington Post*'s investigative units, Jeff Leen. Jeff was working remotely from his home about thirty miles from downtown Washington at the time, but he agreed to meet us at the National Arboretum, a midway point. Laurent and I were both a bit nervous because even though Jeff had been the editor in charge of the Cartel Project at the *Post*, we hadn't actually been in the same room with him yet. Dana didn't exactly calm our nerves as she piloted us to the arranged meeting spot. She put us through our paces, rehearsing our pitch. "This guy doesn't have much time," she explained, and he gets pitched 'the next big scoop' every day. So don't waste time."

There was a lot about the leak we wouldn't be able to explain until the *Post* agreed to become a partner in the project. We were nervous about telling Jeff that the company at the center of the investigation was NSO, but we knew we couldn't hold back that alluring piece of information. NSO was not only the most recognized spyware developer in the world, but there were suspicions that the company's cybertool was somehow linked to the recent murder of a journalist who had contributed to the *Post*'s opinion pages. We agreed with Dana that the main selling point, and the big takeaway of the project if we pulled it off, would be the revelation of the vast scale of cybersurveillance now taking place around the world—thanks in large part to Pegasus.

A strict follower of the Covid-careful six-foot rule, Jeff wasn't interested in taking the meeting in the warmth of Dana's SUV, so the four of us got out of our cars and marched across the parking a lot, down a sloping grade, and through the entrance of the arboretum. Nobody else was in the park, as far as I could see. The sky was a crystalline blue, but it was very cold, and the wind was whipping, so I was glad I had worn a parka and a warm hat and an extra pair of socks. Jeff was a tall guy, swaddled in a thick coat and a bulky pair of insulated trousers. He was wearing what looked like some kind of trapper hat with the flaps hanging down, and a pair of the biggest gloves I have ever seen. The head of one of the most technologically advanced investigative teams in the United States was using a clipboard you might see in a middle-school gym class circa 1980 to take notes. It felt like we were in a scene from a very odd spy movie, where one of the protagonists happens to be the foreman of a lumberjack crew from Saskatchewan.

Laurent and I led with the sheer scale of international cybersurveillance suggested by the list, but we were upfront about what we knew and what we didn't know about the leaked data we were ready to offer to the *Post*. There were some remarkable names on the list, but we had a lot of work to do to determine if the people were simply selected for spyware infection or actually targeted or successfully infected.

"Okay," he said, "understood."

Dana was right. He didn't waste time. He only asked a couple of questions, like if there were any Americans in the data. The whole talk lasted less than twenty minutes. It occurred to me that on any other project we could have wrapped this up in a couple of transatlantic phone calls. But our promise to protect the source at all costs meant we had had to make our way from Paris to this freezing spot in a taxpayer-funded forest in Washington, DC, for what might end up being a failed story pitch.

Jeff never said, *Wow!* Or, *This is fantastic!* Or, *I can't wait to get going!*

"What do you need from me?" was all he said.

We suggested we would need a lot of resources in the coming months, but for now maybe a staff reporter to work with Dana.

"Okay," Jeff said. "Understood."

We took that as a yes.

So by the last week of January 2021, things were lining up. Claudio and Donncha had done a successful test run on Jorge's phone, I had coordinated my first major international reporting collaboration, our young team at Forbidden Stories had proven themselves solid, and Laurent and I had gathered a very experienced group of partners to execute the first phase of the Pegasus investigation.

As Claudio might put it: "This, um, could work."

CHAPTER EIGHT

"LIMITED TIME AND RESOURCES"

Laurent

The first key date we set once the Pegasus Project was up and running was in early March 2021; the plan was for Forbidden Stories and the Security Lab teams to meet in person, in Paris, with a small group of reporters and editors from each of our four partners. Until then, everybody was working independently. Claudio and Donncha had constructed a system of security protocols that allowed everybody on the project to safely access the platform that the two tech experts had created to sort and organize the tens of thousands of phone numbers on the list. The platform categorized the data by NSO client country and then ordered it by the date of selection for targeting. The database was being updated daily because every day a new set of phone numbers was being matched to actual mobile phone owners. Matched to actual names.

Those matches were happening at remarkable speed by the beginning of February because Claudio and Donncha were running their own automated caller ID operation out of the Security Lab. They had begun the process with apps that offered what amounted to international digital phone books. The best and most comprehensive was Truecaller, which had more than two hundred million users worldwide. That enormous client base was what made Truecaller the best and most comprehensive phone directory, because whenever a mobile phone user downloaded its app, Truecaller automatically scraped the entire contents of the new user's contacts file and added it to the database. If each of those users had fifty, or hundreds, or maybe even thousands of contacts, well . . . the numbers grow pretty fast.

But that also meant Claudio and Donncha had to take precautions to make sure their contacts didn't get scraped and added to the public database. They set up an account on an anonymous phone, successfully downloaded the Truecaller code from an Android app, then extracted it so they could see exactly how the app's communications portal interacted with the Truecaller server. Then they reverse engineered the code and used what they learned to write their own Python script that could crawl the Truecaller database in a privacy-preserving way over Tor or a Virtual Private Network. It took Donncha a few long days to perfect the new tool and to make sure there would be no data or privacy leaks. But even then he was rate-limited when performing searches, so the crawler was only able to make about sixty matches a day in the beginning.

That was fine when the project was confined to Forbidden Stories, and the early crawls did turn up a lot of interesting people, like more members of the Macron government in France. And a son of Turkish president Erdoğan. Donncha remembers the process could be addictive. He'd come in every day wondering what grim new surprise had been revealed in the twenty-four-hour-a-day digital treasure hunt.

By the time our other four reporting partners started in earnest in February 2021, and there were suddenly new mouths to feed, Claudio and Donncha had an even more efficient system in place. They had dedicated twenty different anonymous phones to the enterprise and had registered a new Truecaller account for each—which meant they might turn up twelve hundred new matches in a day. They were putting a lot of names and identities and faces to the numbers on the list.

The partners were making the next step of trying to get multiple sources to verify the names and numbers already matched, or doing preliminary research on those people now identified as possible targets of Pegasus spyware, or looking for patterns in the data.

In our own offices at Forbidden Stories, Sandrine had divided up the work by client country and handed out assignments. Paloma was focused on Mexico. She had been able to work through only about a quarter of the more than fifteen thousand Mexican numbers so far but had already identified on the list an array of people around the current president. There were more than twenty journalists already identified, from every major news outlet in Mexico, and Paloma was working hard to find the numbers for every journalist who had been killed in the country in the previous few years. She was especially trying to find the number of Cecilio Pineda, a reporter whose murder we had been investigating since 2017, at the founding of Forbidden Stories.

Phineas Rueckert's old-school paper notebook, meanwhile, was filling up with names of journalists targeted by an NSO client, or clients, in India. He had verified the numbers of reporters from the *Hindustan Times*, the *Hindu*, and the investigative magazine *Tehelka*. There were four from the *Wire* alone, including two of the website's four founders. Phineas had also become interested in the list of numbers selected by end users in Hungary. Hungary was not among the countries already identified in the media as a client of NSO, but hundreds of numbers appearing in the data traced back to Budapest. Phineas had already been able to identify from his own contact files the mobile phone of an investigative reporter in Hungary who had been doing work critical of the right-wing, anti-immigrant prime minister Viktor Orbán.

Audrey was working on Saudi Arabia and other Gulf states; this also drew her to Turkey. We had already noticed some really interesting anomalies in the data around the time Jamal Khashoggi was assassinated in the Saudi consulate in Istanbul. Claudio had seen evidence suggesting that the Turkish government was blocking URL addresses related to the Pegasus spyware. They had blocked all the Pegasus domains that Amnesty International had published in previous reports. More interesting, the Turkish block list now included new Pegasus domains that had not yet been published, suggesting that Turkish cybersecurity experts were themselves spotting new cases of Pegasus infections.

Cécile had two of the most intriguing countries, including another newly identified Pegasus client, Azerbaijan. Khadija Ismayilova was one of the first people in the data we had identified, but Cécile was cataloguing multiple instances of people connected to Khadija being selected for targeting, including her personal attorney. Cécile was also investigating the targets selected by the Moroccan client, which appeared to be the most prolific Pegasus user after Mexico.

The team from *Le Monde* was very interested in the Moroccan-related data set as well, because it appeared that somebody in Morocco had selected President Emmanuel Macron, as well as almost every key minister in the Macron administration. The digital reporter from *Le Monde* had been lining up the chronology and finding clusters of selections made at virtually the same time. The timing could possibly be related to the Moroccan government's attempts to steamroll an independence movement in Western Sahara, or to the rising public protests threatening the Algerian president. But these patterns were, like many others, just beginning to be observable in the data; they suggested places to *start* the reporting. Places to go to confirm the targeting of the selected phones with the Security Lab's cybersurveillance tool. Places to poke and prod for a real and publishable story, and to understand the context of the story.

THAT'S WHERE WE were in early March 2021, the first time the project partners were all in the same room together, at the opening session of a three-day symposium in *Le Monde*'s new but chilly amphitheater. The two dozen men and women invited into the meeting were all masked and had taken care to arrange themselves at safe distances in the stadium seating rising from the dais. There was a 6 p.m. curfew in Paris at that point, due to increasing Covid case numbers, so a lot of the morning chatter was about where and how people could access food for dinner in the evenings. The curfew also meant we would have to break early every day, so these sessions had to be brisk and efficient.

Before we started the formal meeting, people from our Forbidden Stories staff walked up the aisles, gathered every cell phone and non-project-dedicated laptops, put them in a big plastic crate, and stored them in another room. Everybody there was a reporter or an editor, except for Claudio and Donncha, who had come in from Berlin. They were there, among other reasons, to reiterate and update the security protocols each of the partners would have to adhere to when accessing the data or communicating with one another. I knew we could count on Claudio and Donncha to be direct with us and with anybody else who had been given the privilege of accessing the leaked data: any single mistake could be the one to sink the project. One shortcut for the sake of convenience could risk the entire enterprise, not to mention the safety of the source.

I opened the meeting by defining the journalistic imperatives of this investigation into NSO Group and its Pegasus spyware. The data was not our story, I reminded everybody. The leak was not our headline. We had been handed a remarkable trove of information, yes, but it meant nothing until we did our work. The next three days we would decide together what exactly we needed to achieve before we could publish; to discuss the stories that were beginning to surface from the database, and to discuss which might be the most powerful and the most gettable. We had to consider the best time to invite in the wider circle of media partners, and to make some determinations about how to divvy up the reporting tasks so that we didn't end up with ten different investigators on one story strand, with other strands left wanting. Maybe toughest of all, we had to agree on a schedule.

"You've seen the records," Sandrine said when she took the microphone and laid out our preferred timing. "You've seen the data. We could be digging into those records for eight years. Or ten. But we have to make hard choices for security reasons." She reiterated a point she had been making to each of our partners separately: we wanted to publish the investigation in June.

I could sense skepticism in the room about moving that fast. I was skeptical myself. But Sandrine didn't pause long enough for anybody to voice a doubt. "We can't risk exposing the project too long," she said. "We need to limit the risk. . . . The more we wait, the more the data becomes obsolete. The data we have is up to December 2020. And remember, there are other journalists already working on NSO. . . . If we establish a plan and start working right after the meeting, this is totally doable."

Sandrine spoke a bit about how to access and read the data and how to update it for the entire group to see. Phineas pointed out that it was important to use uniform terminology. When we say a phone number is "verified," he explained, that means we have not only identified the owner through a caller ID service, but we have double-checked that fact with at least one other source. And that was only the start. The crucial step was gathering forensic evidence, using the Security Lab's analytical tool, that showed a phone was either targeted or infected with Pegasus. When that was accomplished, we could mark the number "confirmed." Only at that point did we have a possible subject for a story we might be able to publish.

The math was not in our favor at that point. We had cross-checked about thirty phone numbers in the data with Pegasus victims of the WhatsApp exploit revealed as part of a lawsuit in the US in 2019, as well as eleven other victims that Citizen Lab had identified in previous reports. In terms of our own forensics, counting Jorge and all the victims Claudio and Donncha had turned up in previous Security Lab analyses, we had confirmed an actual Pegasus targeting or infection on exactly three of the fifty thousand or so numbers in the data.

EVERYBODY HAD A chance to present what they had already been working on. Our team went first. Phineas talked about what he was learning in India and in Hungary. Paloma updated the group on the latest from Mexico. She had just days earlier verified that one of the numbers in the data belonged to Cecilio Pineda, the thirty-nine-year-old journalist whose 2017 murder in Guerrero remained unsolved. His phone number first appeared in the data two months before he was killed and again just two weeks before his death. Paloma had already called a reporter friend in Mexico and got contact information for Cecilio's wife, who was the best hope for doing the necessary forensics. "It will be hard," Paloma told the group, "but there is a small chance that she has the phone."

Bastian Obermayer and his partner from *Süddeutsche Zeitung*, Frederik Obermaier, were eager to get going on possible stories in Hungary and Azerbaijan; Dana Priest from the *Washington Post* wanted to know more about the horrific stories of journalists being persecuted and imprisoned in Morocco, and she also thought she might have contacts in Turkey who could help with the Saudi piece of the story. That was a story of particular interest for her newspaper. Jamal Khashoggi, murdered and dismembered in the Saudi embassy in Istanbul, had been a contributor to the *Post*'s Global Opinions section. *Le Monde* had their hands full with Morocco and France. And everybody wanted to discuss how we might get a former NSO employee on the record to talk about what happened inside the company.

Sandrine mentioned that we had been auditing Glassdoor, where people could write reviews of the companies where they did or still do work. "There are not too many negative against NSO," Cécile pointed out. "A lot were anonymous. There was one who just listed his function. And I don't know if there is a way to ID them. But there are for sure some former employees out there, and I know *Haaretz* is in touch with former employees."

Everybody's ears pricked up a bit at the mention of *Haaretz*, a decidedly left-wing Israeli newspaper but one of the most respected and most read newspapers the country, as well as the oldest still in print. *Haaretz*'s reporters had already done a good bit of work on NSO in particular and the cyber industry in general. We all agreed that the Israeli newspaper should be approached as a possible partner in the second phase of the Pegasus Project. But it would have to be done cautiously.

Kai Biermann of *Die Zeit* made one of the most intriguing presentations of the symposium. Kai is one of the few journalists to have conducted an on-the-record interview with the CEO of NSO group. "I think Shalev Hulio agreed to meet us because they were getting a lot of fire at that moment, and he hoped to get a positive report," Kai told us of his May 2020 interview. He then explained how he had been invited to Tel Aviv to meet with Shalev in a room in the company's PR firm. Kai's request to see the NSO offices was quickly denied, but he found Shalev relaxed and surprisingly open. Among the things the NSO founder told Kai that day was that the company not only did its due diligence (as required by the Israeli Ministry of Defense) before they licensed Pegasus to any client, but they had the ability to find out exactly whom their clients were targeting. Kai knew at the time that this was an extraordinary and novel admission for NSO's head man to make.

Shalev had plenty of opportunity to walk back that statement, both that day in Tel Aviv and later. The ground rules for the interview were what Kai called "the German way." Before the story went to press, Kai explained, *Die Zeit* sent the interview material they had chosen to publish to Shalev and NSO so they could sign off on the accuracy. "We sent all the quotes three weeks before publication and asked if it was okay to use them. They said, 'We'll get back to you.' They didn't.

"Three days before publication, we asked again, 'Can we use them?' 'We'll get back to you.' Never got an answer, so we published. Because of a tech error, the English version was not published at the same time as the German version. But when the English version finally published, they panicked. [NSO] called every day twenty-four/seven, for three days. They kept saying, 'You're hurting us.'

"It came down to one statement: that they can see the targets."

Kai knew exactly what Shalev had said. He had all the tapes from the interview. But *Die Zeit* did agree to publish an addendum to the story, which Kai had passed around for everybody in our group to see: "The company NSO requested a clarification to note that it is only able to view the target of a surveillance operation if an internal investigation into that operation is launched. Otherwise, it is not possible to see who the state purchasers of the Pegasus program are targeting for surveillance."

Kai's final takeaway of the experience with Shalev Hulio was really insightful. "Shalev is a confident guy," he told us. "Easy to like but hard to read." Kai pointed out one of the things Shalev told him about the genius of NSO: "Without mentioning countries, I can tell you that everybody would hug us. We are probably one of the best companies in the world because in the last ten years, hundreds of thousands of people were saved because of NSO technology."

Shalev, as Kai saw it, gave the impression of believing in what he says and what he is doing. Whether it was an act or sincere, Kai wasn't sure. In the end, he said, we needed to be cautious. For all his charm and all his confidence, Shalev Hulio was a very slippery figure. "I tried to fact-check the things he said," Kai concluded, "and he was not absolutely correct on any point."

▪▪▪▪▪▪▪

BY THE END of the three days, there was a galaxy a-sparkle with possible stories, and not a single one we were ready to publish. Until we had solid confirmation that a phone on our list had been targeted by Pegasus or actually infected, we had nothing. Everything depended on getting that evidence. "The idea is to start running some forensics," Sandrine told the group. "See what can be done in the next three weeks. We have to do as much as we can without taking any risk within three weeks." She explained that our team at Forbidden Stories had already reached out to trusted contacts in India and Mexico to get other journalists to agree to let us do forensic analysis of their phones. But India was slow going so far, and Mexico presented a difficulty because so many of the targets used Android phones. The Security Lab's tool hadn't yet been able to detect traces of Pegasus infection on Androids because their backups don't save as much data as an iPhone's.

We also hoped to do the forensics on Khadija Ismayilova's phone right away. But we had to admit that our recent attempt at forensics on the mobile phone of another Azeri journalist who was in the data was cause for concern and for enhanced caution. The journalist's phone, along with his brother's computer, had mysteriously disappeared from their hotel just hours before a Forbidden Stories team member was supposed to meet them.

Bastian and Frederik said they were still willing to go to Budapest to ask a few of the targeted Hungarian reporters to submit their phones for analysis. Others in the group brought up the possibility of approaching journalists selected by Moroccans. Saudi Arabia was tough, we all agreed, but crucial. There was no way to safely get inside Saudi Arabia, but the diaspora of Saudi dissidents and journalists now in London and Toronto and Istanbul might afford us opportunities to do forensics.

Claudio Guarnieri remained poker-faced, as always, throughout these discussions. There were times in the meeting, he admitted, when he was really optimistic. More than anybody else sitting in that amphitheater in Paris, I suspected, Claudio wanted this project to be successful; he had been hunting the purveyors trading in cybersurveil-

lance malware for a lot longer than the rest of us. But there were also times when the discussion spiraled off in unexpected new directions that I sensed our lead forensic specialist was not altogether sanguine. He didn't need more on his already full plate.

The data, the list, the project, and the forensic tool itself were tightly held secrets even inside his organization. There were only three people at Amnesty International's Security Lab who were read into the Pegasus Project: Claudio, Donncha, and Danna Ingleton. Only two of them were capable of doing the forensics or understood what it required. Conducting and writing up a comprehensive analysis on a single case, Claudio and Donncha knew, could eat up a lot of man-hours. In a decade of conducting serious research on spyware, Claudio had run successful forensics on two, three, maybe four cell phones a year, he later told me. Five "if it was a prolific year." There in that amphitheater in Paris, it must have sounded to him like we were asking the Security Lab to do five cases every few days, for days on end.

At one point in the meeting, when the group was tossing out new candidates for forensic analysis, Claudio did ask for the microphone. "I don't want to be an annoying commentator," he said, "but I would try to remind you that we have limited time and resources."

His other real concern—his biggest concern—Claudio kept to himself. He doesn't lack for self-confidence, but he is an empiricist at his core. At that point, the beginning of March 2021, he simply hadn't yet seen enough to convince him that the tool would deliver what we needed. Claudio Guarnieri and Donncha Ó Cearbhaill understood they still had a long way to go on a road the two of them had been traveling for a very long time.

CHAPTER NINE

"IN A POSITIVE DIRECTION"

The unlikely story of Pegasus Project forensics begins on a small farm in the flatlands of central Ireland, in the waning months of the twentieth century, with a five-year-old boy alone in his bedroom, playing for hours on end with his first computer. The farm itself was a modest dairy operation with forty cows; nothing Donncha Ó Cearbhaill's father couldn't handle by himself, as long as he was up every morning at dawn to do the milking and willing to put in a solid twelve hours most days. But the sixty-acre property was also home to legend and lore and purpose. It was known as the Ring, for the distinctive circular hedgerow, a few hundred meters in diameter, that surrounded the farm. Buried somewhere within that circle, it was believed, were the ruins of Loretto Castle, the ancient seat of one of the storied clans in Irish history.

The Ó Cearbhaills counted themselves descendants of Olioll Olum, king of Munster in the third century AD. The clan enjoyed a good long regal run, followed by a thousand years of foreign invasion, foreign rule, and general woe—a millennium that sharpened the Ó Cearbhaills into an instrument of fierce and stubborn resistance. They fought the Vikings, the Normans, and a variety of English overlords; the clan won plenty of battles but few wars and lived in the main under what they considered alien rule. The Ó Cearbhaills (or the Carrolls when anglicized) suffered centuries of indignity and casualty but would not concede defeat. When Oliver Cromwell confiscated their estates for the benefit of the English crown, Donncha's forebears took their losses and stood their ground. When Cromwell's troops burned Loretto Castle down to its foundation, Donncha's forebears stood their ground; when the inhumane policies of the English overlords turned a potato blight into a famine that killed the Irish or sent them fleeing to other lands by the millions, Donncha's people stood their ground.

Donncha's own father had been a soldier in the last great resistance, back in the 1970s and 1980s, as a member of the Irish Republican Army, sworn to defend the minority Catholic population in the violent back-and-forth with the Protestant majority of Northern Ireland. These deadly conflagrations in Armagh and Londonderry and Belfast might have been the dying twitches of the five-hundred-year fight between the English and the Irish, but they were deeply felt. Donncha's father came of age in a boiling stew of what one trenchant observer called "grim lingering rage, a quiet, determined, smoldering spite, resentment." By the time he was thirty, John Carroll had paid a dear price for his resistance. He spent a year on the run, moving from safe house to safe house, and then five years in prison on a weapons charge. John Carroll had been a part of dramatic prison hunger strikes (47 days in his case) that made martyrs of the IRA members who didn't survive them.

But that was all a long time ago by the end of the twentieth century. Just two years before he bought his son the Gateway PC Windows 98 desktop computer, John Carroll had formally and demonstrably put his long-ago past behind him. He pleaded guilty in an Irish court—after eleven separate interrogations at the local police station—to past membership in the Irish Republican Army. He received a suspended sentence, noted the local newspaper, after signing a promise "not to associate with any subversive organisations or individuals connected with subversive organisations." John Carroll had become a respected leader in his local community by then. Aside from running his dairy farm, Donncha's father was a fifteen-year member of the Birr town council and headed for a seat on the Offaly County Council. The issues closest to his heart to this day are universal preschool and equity. He also champions humane treatment of the much maligned Irish travellers, regarded by most as a Gaelic version of the unwanted gypsies. "He always sought to look after the marginalized in the county," one of his fellow board members says of him.

An inclination to resist those who abuse their power and sympathy for the underdog, these were Donncha's chief inheritances from his father and from the long, unbroken line of Ó Cearbhaills that preceded them both. Funny thing about Donncha, though: "the grim lingering rage, the smoldering spite, the resentments" that attended so much of his family history are not the animating force in his own life. Like those mythic castle ruins buried somewhere in the Ring, they might be there, and they might not. It'd take some careful digging to find out. What animates Donncha, without question, is curiosity. Curiosity has been the fount of almost all of his triumphs, and almost all of his considerable tribulations. Curiosity was what kept that little boy up later than he should have been on school nights, tapping away at a keyboard, with the glow of a computer monitor lighting his otherwise dark room.

Rural Ireland at the turn of the late 1990s didn't offer much in the way of internet connectivity; this was the dial-up era, with interminable wait times and a pretty thin menu of gruel to fetch once you finally entered the World Wide Web. Much more interesting than the public-facing websites themselves, Donncha found, was what was happening in the background, where he found a whole new just-being-written computer language to master. He even convinced his parents to drive him to computer certification courses. "I was seven," he says. "I remember there were a bunch of adults in their forties and fifties on the computer and I was this seven-year-old kid who is kind of seeing everything."

His parents didn't really understand what he was up to, but they gave him the time and space he needed to pursue his uncommon interests. They didn't push him out to play with his friends or make heavy demands on his time with chores around the farm. In fact, by the time Donncha was ten or eleven, his father had sold the milk cows; it was clear to him he was unlikely to have a next-generation partner in his agricultural endeavor. "The reason I'm good is that I could do this even before I was a teenager, before there are a lot more demands on your time. I had a lot of free time, and I was interested in computers," Donncha says. "I saw people make mistakes on their websites and how you can take the code and gain knowledge and gain information. It was a puzzle. A challenge."

His parents did get a payoff of sorts when Donncha was in high school. He medaled in computer programming at the Irish Science Olympiads two years in a row, and represented Ireland in the international contests that followed. By then, 2011, Donncha had fallen in with a lot of other computer geeks who shared his general curiosity and his particular interest in the vast and always expanding digital puzzle. He made a whole set of interesting new friends out in the ether and was in thrall to the growing community of hackers. This was the first golden age of the hacker, and the best had a nose for recognizing the best. Donncha was invited into a shape-shifting platoon of hacker collectivists known as Anonymous or LulzSec (translation: Laugh Out Loud Security). LulzSec had about as much shared culture and community as the geek world offers; hackers tend to think of themselves first and foremost as lone wolves, sui generis, with their own distinct specialties, their own chosen targets, their own motivations.

For Donncha, this was just a little good, clean fun; he could participate in online sit-ins and protests or launch spitballs at the high and mighty, all from the safety of his own home, inside the Ring. There was something unreal about it, and a sense that nobody was really watching. His teenage "hacktivism" wasn't serious, but it was undoubtedly political. He was a merry prankster who found it amusing to mess with people who lorded over others. His chosen user name alias, a hacker must, was "Palladium," which is both a chemical element (atomic number 46) often used as catalyst—Donncha had just been accepted into the medicinal chemistry program at Trinity College Dublin—and a religious icon or relic with protective powers. The name also had a hint of the underdog. St. Palladius was the first bishop of Ireland, who actually beat St. Patrick to the Emerald Isle but never got the credit, or the parades.

Donncha's first real hack was a prank on Fine Gael, the mushy, center-right Irish political party that had ballyhooed its intent to take campaigning into the digital age for the election of 2011. The party hired a hotshot American consultant who had embellished his role in the digital campaign revolution that helped elect Barack Obama president. Donncha and a friend shut down the political technician's sparkly new Fine Gael site for a full twenty-four hours in the run-up to the election. And showed out the American campaign guru for the huckster he was.

Donncha's next prank was a good bit more fulfilling, but it also turned out to be a whole lot more perilous. Like the rest of the British Isles, and much of the rest of the sentient English-speaking world, Donncha had been following the public inquiry into the latest happenings in press baron Rupert Murdoch's malodorous media abattoir. Reporters from Murdoch's *News of the World* tabloid had stolen voicemails from the phones of thousands of private individuals; the contents of many of these messages were then leaked for clicks and eyeballs. Among the alleged victims were former prime ministers Tony Blair and Gordon Brown, Spice Girl Victoria Beckham, Eric Clapton, Prince Charles, and most monstrously, a thirteen-year-old schoolgirl who had been abducted and murdered.

The ugly scandal drew only minor corporate comeuppance. *News of the World* was shuttered, and a few of Murdoch's lower-level employees eventually ended up in prison, but it seemed clear that Murdoch was going to walk away, as he always did, without suffering any real consequences. So a few members of LulzSec decided to take matters in hand. On July 18, 2011, a few months after his high school graduation, Donncha and friends hacked the website of Murdoch's flagship London newspaper, the *Sun*, and redirected all traffic to a fake home page they had created. "I thought it would be fine," Donncha says. "The *Sun* was racist. Anti-immigrant. I told my friends that we could do a joke, and nobody would really care."

It was a pretty good joke. Bannered across the fake *Sun* home page was the news of Rupert Murdoch's apparent suicide. The story itself was an obvious lampoon, with little attempt at subtlety: "Murdoch, age 80, was said to have ingested a large quantity of palladium before stumbling into his famous topiary garden late last night, passing out in the early hours of the morning. . . .

"One detective elaborates. 'Officers on the scene report a broken glass, a box of vintage wine, and what seems to be a family album strewn across the floor, containing images of days gone by; some containing hand-painted portraits of Murdoch in his early days, donning a top hat and monocles.'

"Another officer reveals that Murdoch was found slumped over a particularly large garden hedge fashioned into a galloping horse. 'His favourite,' a butler, Davidson, reports."

Rupert Murdoch was not amused.

Seven weeks later, at seven o'clock on a late summer morning, six-teen Irish law enforcement officers stormed the Ó Cearbhaill household, dragged Donncha out of bed, handcuffed him, and demanded that he confess to various cybercrimes. The police kept Donncha's parents cor-doned off in another room of the house. His mother was confused and understandably terrified, but his father did manage to get his head out the door long enough to shout some advice to his son. "Whatever you do, say nothing," he said. "Don't say anything to the police."

The investigators on scene gathered up all the computers they could find and hauled Donncha into the local police station. He must have seemed a very unlikely suspect in that precinct—a skinny teen, with a slightly rounded and whiskerless face; quick to smile and easy to like. The cops pressed their interrogation, nonetheless, and tried to rattle him by explaining that the American election guru hired by Fine Gael had gotten the FBI involved, and the FBI was busy gathering a lot of digital evidence concerning "Palladium."

Donncha took his father's advice and kept his mouth shut. The police were forced to release him after twenty-four hours, the longest they could hold him without a charge, which they were ill-prepared to make. But the story of his arrest was all over the newspapers, and the police made sure the eighteen-year-old computer whiz who was headed off to university in a few weeks understood this wasn't over. "That got real," Donncha remembers of his first arrest. "Oh, people do care what goes on in a computer. That was kind of eye-opening." And yet, he stood his ground, maybe even fought back a little.

By the time Donncha completed his first year at Trinity College Dub-lin, in the spring of 2012, he was notorious. It looked like he was headed for trial in the Fine Gael prank; he had been identified by the FBI, but not yet charged, in the Murdoch prank; and most spectacularly, he was under suspicion of hacking the police themselves. A criminal complaint filed by the FBI in the Southern District of New York asserted that after his initial arrest in September 2011, Donncha O'Cearrbhaill [the FBI special agent who authored the complaint misspelled his name] had infiltrated the digital world of the several police forces who had him under investigation. "Just got into the iCloud for the head of a national cybercrime unit," Donncha had allegedly written to an unnamed FBI informant. "I have all his contacts and can track his location twenty-four/seven." The FBI claimed in its legal filing that Donncha had then accessed the Gmail accounts of the cybercrime commander and one of his detectives and stolen the password needed to access a conference call scheduled for the FBI, the Irish constabulary, and the Serious Organized Crime Agency in London.

The criminal complaint further alleged that Donncha not only dialed into and listened in on the conversation, which touched very briefly on developments in his own case, but actually recorded the call in its entirety, posted it on a public site, and invited listeners. The discussion on the recording suggested a certain fecklessness among the investigators; the crack cyberinvestigators in Ireland apparently neglected to dial in at all.

The case against Donncha went nowhere—even after the Irish police held him for questioning for thirty hours—because the FBI didn't have enough evidence. But the criminal complaint in a US federal court, and the accompanying press release issued by the FBI, did put Donncha in the news again. The publicity made him a sudden new hero in the hacker community, a community dedicated to "watching the watchers." But it only increased the fire he was drawing from the very powerful people he had very publicly embarrassed, like Rupert Murdoch, and law enforcement agents from London to Dublin to New York.

His father stuck by his side the whole way, but the legal jeopardy dogged Donncha throughout his university career and beyond. He was eventually ordered by an Irish court to pay €5,000 in damages to Fine Gael. Meanwhile, lawmen fed stories to the newspapers about the chemistry lab the chemistry major had used for experiments in his parents' home. *Couldn't that be used for making ecstasy? Or bombs?* They also revealed information about the items on Donncha's bedroom wall and his Facebook page. *He posted quotes from the Marxist revolutionary Che Guevara and IRA martyr Bobby Sands. He was an avowed Socialist.*

By March 2017, when Donncha Ó Cearbhaill was finally brought to court, where he admitted his role in the Murdoch hack in exchange for a nine-month suspended sentence, he had learned a valuable lesson about the pursuit of justice: whoever has the ability to write the code, has the ability to control the system. "I wouldn't recommend it," Donncha says of his six-year ordeal, "but it was definitely an interesting life experience to see how the world works and how states operate and how powerful people get pissed off by these things that are just pranks and have a lot of resources to try and do something about it.

"And it was also interesting to see how the criminal justice system works. You're in court and you see all of these people, a whole industry supported by people being charged with mundane stuff, hacking or other kinds of crime: lawyers and judges and police and everyone involved in a kind of assembly line of justice. It's a whole industry. Seeing how all that works was fascinating.

"Fortunately, it worked out [without me going to prison]. . . . But this was kind of an unsustainable way of doing activism. I was trying to figure out how do I use some of these skills in a positive direction."

A SELF-TAUGHT COMPUTER scientist but a formally trained, university-educated chemist, Donncha had been torn between pursuing a career in computers or a career in chemistry. Each of the disciplines played to his preternatural curiosity, which manifested in a desire to find out how things work, right down to the root. The method in both his chosen fields of research is to break down the operating systems into their smallest component parts, their code, and then recombine those parts for novel, hopefully better, purposes. "I like trying to get computers to do things not intended and putting things together in a way that's creating something new," he says. "And what is chemistry? It's understanding what nature designed. It's kind of like hacking the molecules of chemistry to make something new." The life of a chemist in a laboratory had one distinct advantage—fewer police raids and interrogations and indictments—but all roads seemed to lead back to computers.

When he arrived in Berlin as a twenty-one-year-old college student to begin a three-month chemistry research project, Donncha found himself in a promised land of hackers and computer security geeks, complete with its own Moses. "In the year since goateed ex-National Security Agency contractor Edward Snowden catapulted to fame, he has been portrayed in street art, installations, pop songs and performances," the *Wall Street Journal* reported/lamented, "not to mention stickers, posters and fridge magnets. In Germany in particular revelations of the NSA's eavesdropping activities have tapped into the deep-seated aversion to an omniscient, all-powerful state—giving birth to a Snowden cult among creative types here." Two weeks in Berlin and Donncha knew thirty different cybergeeks locked in battle against the rising tide of cybersurveillance.

Donncha ended up back in Berlin after graduation, in the summer of 2015, a few weeks after the unveiling in Alexanderplatz of the life-size bronze statues of Edward Snowden, Julian Assange, and Chelsea Manning, the US whistleblower who had released hundreds of thousands of documents to Wikileaks, a number of them classified or sensitive, and a lot more of them simply embarrassing. Donncha was in Berlin for a Summer of Privacy internship at Tor, a nonprofit cybersecurity venture. "We believe everyone should be able to explore the internet with privacy," read the Tor mission statement. "We advance human rights and defend your privacy online through free software and open networks." He liked the work, and the sense of purpose, and decided to make Berlin home. His first full-time job was with an NGO that created digital tools to help journalists, human rights defenders, and under-resourced civil society organizations to fight back against cyberattacks and state-run censorship.

Among the Berlin cyberluminaries Donncha got to know was the white hat hacker running the cybersecurity department at Amnesty International. Actually, Claudio Guarnieri *was* the cybersecurity department at Amnesty, playing a lonely game of whack-a-mole to provide some small measure of protection for human rights defenders, political dissidents, and journalists, who were increasingly under cyberthreat from repressive and murderous governments around the world. In early 2018, Claudio told Donncha that Amnesty Tech had freed up the money to hire a second threat researcher. "I thought about it for a bit," Donncha says, "and then I was like, okay; this was exactly fitting my skills."

Part of the appeal of the job at Amnesty Tech was the chance to work closely with Claudio. Donncha had first started reading his new boss's blog posts and technical papers back in 2012 and 2013, when he was still a chemistry student at Trinity College Dublin. Claudio not only had the brainpower but, according to a story that appeared in a glossy popular American magazine, he also had the stamina required to track the private vendors of cybersurveillance across the vast landscape of the World Wide Web. Claudio had once used a single digital clue to help link Gamma Group and its FinFisher spyware to some unsavory customers. "He saw that when he pinged the I.P. address of a collection server it replied with an unusual response: 'Hallo Steffi,'" *Vanity Fair*'s Bryan Burrough explained in a 6,500-word article about a posse of computer geeks on the hunt for cyberweapons. "Guarnieri then used a program to survey every server on the Internet—roughly 75 million of them—to see if others responded the same. It took a couple of long weeks, but in the end the scan turned up 11 IP addresses in ten countries, including Qatar, Ethiopia, and the UAE, that were known to monitor dissidents."

Claudio was a rare bird in a community whose members took pride in being outside politics. Even before he was thirty, he had developed a distinct worldview that defined his work. He would sometimes sum it up with a quote by an early computer technologist and founding executive editor of *Wired*, Kevin Kelly: "There is no powerfully constructive technology that is not also powerfully destructive in another direction. Just as there is no great idea that cannot be greatly perverted for great harm. The greater the promise of a new technology, the greater its potential for harm as well." For Claudio, this was just stating the obvious. "Everything we built over the decades and we consider a technology of liberation and self-determination," he told a conference of hackers in 2016, "we discovered had been turned into a tool for repression as well. And it was inevitable. . . ."

He had come by this personal philosophy honestly because he had witnessed the phenomenon firsthand. Drawn to computer tech, like Donncha, by the challenge of deciphering code—of puzzling out how the cyberworld works and why—Claudio's political awakening came in his close observation of the Arab Spring and its aftermath. The initial success of the political uprisings in places like Egypt and Morocco and Bahrain was fueled by social media and instant electronic communication. The same technology had also been used to roll back the gains. Those cybersurveillance weapons that French companies had developed and then sold to state actors in Egypt and Libya, for instance, helped to vaporize dissent. A lot of people fighting for freedom and democracy in the Arab world ended up in exile, or in prison, or dead. Claudio was profoundly changed by watching it happen.

One of his office mates liked to tell people about Claudio's singular work routine back in those days. She would see him surfing through the Twitterverse, growing angrier and angrier, until he finally hit his trigger point. Then he would turn to the drum set next to his workstation, pick up his sticks, and flail away at a raucous death metal solo. Forty-five minutes later, and finally cooled off, he would put down his drumsticks and get back to business.

"There is a technological imbalance between states and their citizens," Claudio would remind his fellow hackers. "Billions of dollars are poured into systems of surveillance both passive and active and not just by the United States but really by any government that is wealthy enough to do so. Credible defenses really lag behind or remain inaccessible, and generally are only available to corporations and businesses with deep enough pockets. The few ambitious public projects attempting to change things radically are often faced with rather unsustainable funding models, which rarely will last long enough to grow these projects to maturity. And nation-states are very aware of this technological imbalance and use it to their own advantage."

Claudio could tend toward fatalism; even when he was making an impassioned public plea, his otherwise sharp features would sometimes sag into a hangdog look. People who knew him best could sense the energy it required of him to battle that fatalism . . . every . . . single . . .

day. But he stayed in the fight. While other accomplished hackers signed on as highly compensated cybersecurity specialists protecting the interests of the major corporations who wrote the checks, Claudio Guarnieri made it his mission to democratize cybersecurity and spread it far and wide. "Security can no longer be a privilege in the hands of those few who can afford it," he would say. "Security has to become a right; it has to be exercised and protected. It is the precondition for privacy, which is the key enabler for freedom of expression, which is a requirement for a healthy democracy."

In 2014, he developed and released a tool to help political dissidents and journalists and human rights defenders identify spyware infections on their personal devices. His idea was to give people the tools to empower themselves to do the detection. The tool itself was "hacky" (in the pejorative sense), according to Claudio. Not quite fully baked, and not the success he had hoped for. "I wasn't really the best engineer back then," he admits.

Claudio went back to the drawing board technically and politically, recognizing that he needed a lot more skilled researchers and coders and engineers on his team. As he was signing on as senior (and only) technologist at Amnesty International, he also co-founded a hackers' collective called Security Without Borders and made a call for his fellow geeks to volunteer their spare time to correcting the imbalance in the state versus citizen cybersecurity battles. "We need to recognize the privilege we have as educated individuals and technicians," he said in announcing the new collective. "Dedicating your time and your abilities to the benefit of society is concretely a political choice, and you should embrace that with consciousness and pride."

Security Without Borders did not really catch fire, and by the time Donncha went to work at Amnesty Tech a year later, Claudio seemed to be edging near burnout. The cybersurveillance developers were turning record profits in 2018, while spreading their intrusive weapons all over the world. The never-ending battle against an enemy that was well funded and well protected by rich and powerful countries was a grind. The whack-a-mole game was growing old and unsatisfying. "He had been doing this work a lot longer than I had," Donncha says, "and he

was a bit cynical that we could have an impact with stuff and really kind
of change the narrative.

"Basically, Claudio said, you can work on whatever. It was good to
have that flexibility, but at the same time it was like, 'What are we going
to do?'"

THE ANSWER TO that question kind of fell into their laps a few months
into Donncha's tenure. An Amnesty International staffer from Saudi
Arabia contacted them about a WhatsApp message she had just received
from somebody she didn't recognize; it was an urgent alert about a protest that was about to take place in front of the Saudi embassy in Washington. "We need your support please," it read, and asked her to click
on a link for more information. The AI staffer had already been warned
about new cybersurveillance weapons aimed at cell phones, and she was
worried somebody was trying this kind of attack on her. Claudio and
Donncha agreed she had reason to be worried, and they investigated.

Looking inside the message and the link, they were able to isolate a
signature quirk in the way the domain and server were configured. This
WhatsApp message and link were painstakingly engineered to hide any
information about the attack and any information about the identity of
the attacker. The link and the final server were configured in a particularly locked-down manner. Any attempt to open a nonexistent page on
the server did not return the typical "Not Found" message; the server
simply did not reply to the request at all, so as not to alert the victim.
This already suggested to Claudio and Donncha that they were not dealing with a common spam or cybercrime attack.

But there was more to it still.

The encryption algorithm on the server had been carefully tuned for
added security. Paradoxically, all this extra care taken by the operators
helped Claudio and Donncha isolate and identify these servers, because
they stood out as unique. Different from any other servers on the internet.

Once Claudio and Donncha mapped that configuration, they possessed a kind of digital fingerprint. They then ran an internet scan in the

summer of 2018, literally connecting to every single server on the web, looking for others that had the same configuration, the same digital fingerprint. They found almost six hundred discrete matching servers acting as launchpads for related spyware attacks.

The chances of discovering the provenance of these servers and the domain names they held would have been slim, but for some earlier forensic investigations run by the University of Toronto's Citizen Lab. Researchers at Citizen Lab had been dogging one particular cybersurveillance provider for a few years. In 2016, they not only found evidence that its spyware had successfully infected the cell phone of a human rights defender in the United Arab Emirates; they had been able to piece together the company's entire network infrastructure. Among other things, they had discovered hundreds of domain names linked to the company's servers. Citizen Lab published many of them for everybody to see.

The company had reacted in a trice, rebuilding the entire system that made up its "anonymizing transmission network" and changing the domain names. But the company made a crucial error; it had reused two domain names from its earlier version: pine-sales[.]com, and ecommerce-ads[.]org.

That's how Claudio and Donncha caught them out. They found those domain names in the new infrastructure, and that told them who was running the system. This was NSO Group. This was Pegasus. "Each Pegasus Installation server or Command-and-Control (C&C) server hosted a web server on port 443 with a unique domain and TLS certificate," they would write. "These edge servers would then proxy connections through a chain of servers, referred to by NSO Group as the 'Pegasus Anonymizing Transmission Network.'"

The search for new Pegasus domains matching the fingerprint also led Claudio and Donncha to a second victim. Yahya Assiri was a former officer in the Royal Saudi Air Force who had made himself an unwelcome thorn in the side of the Saudi royal family. Assiri had fled his home country under threat of physical harm but still managed to operate a network of human rights activists in Saudi Arabia and continued his pointed criticism of the ruling monarchy. He publicly questioned the

Saudi royal family's religiosity, its governance, its maltreatment of its impoverished subjects, and its penchant for meting out barbaric punishments such as stoning, flogging, amputation, and beheading. In other words, Assiri said the sorts of things that invited these punishments for himself. "It is an absolute monarchy which does not allow its citizens to participate in the way their own country is run," Assiri told one Western publication. "They use Islam as an excuse to exploit their own people. This is in contradiction to fundamental Islamic teachings." He called on the royal family to write a national constitution that stood up for democratic institutions and ensured a just and fair and less lethal rule of law. Or he wanted them to cede power. The royal family reacted by making it plain they wanted Yahya Assiri's scalp.

When Claudio and Donncha checked Assiri's cell phone they found an SMS message from May 2018 with a link that invited him into the malicious infrastructure built by NSO. This discovery gave the pair two separate pieces of evidence that suggested somebody in the Kingdom of Saudi Arabia was operating NSO's Pegasus system—and they made this find several months before the assassination of the dissident Saudi journalist Jamal Khashoggi.

Amnesty International published the findings, and later a list of all the domain names linked to NSO attacks. Danna Ingleton scorched the company: "Amnesty International will not stand idly by as companies such as NSO Group profit from selling their invasive Pegasus software to repressive states around the world." Citizen Lab backed Claudio and Donncha with its own findings. And it all had very little impact.

NSO company engineers did have to spend the time and money to rebuild all that infrastructure again, which included retiring another six hundred domain names. Goodbye to alldaycooking and bargain-service and br-travels and buypresent4me and centrasia-news and classic-furnitures and easybett and freshsaladtoday and islam-today and mapupdatezone and movie-tickets and novosti247 and pine-sales and rockmusic4u and turismo-aqui and waffleswithnutella. Hello to hundreds of new banal-looking domain names capable of launching one of the most potent cyberweapons on the market. NSO, meanwhile, did not even bother to contest any specifics in the Amnesty Tech report.

The company simply released a mealy statement about how their technology is licensed to government agencies only, and only to help them thwart terrorists and criminals. Any misuse, NSO claimed, was "counter to . . . the values we stand for."

The Israeli Ministry of Defense dismissed Amnesty International's demand that it revoke NSO's export license because of the blatant abuse of AI staffers. The case for revocation made in a lawsuit filed by Amnesty and others was rejected by a court in Tel Aviv. When the court found for NSO, an unnamed company spokesperson used the victory to preen: "The regulatory framework in which we operate is of the highest international standard." And to scold: "Our detractors, who have made baseless accusations to fit their own agendas, have no answer to the security challenges of the twenty-first century."

But the experience did have real and serious effects inside the Berlin office of Amnesty Tech, newly christened the "Security Lab." Claudio and Donncha had learned one very valuable lesson in their first joint research project. The Pegasus system was not invisible, and NSO's technologists were not invincible. They made mistakes.

One consequential misstep NSO Group had made was in riling Claudio Guarnieri and his new partner, Donncha Ó Cearbhaill. "I guess I got quite pissed off about the attack on the Amnesty staff member," Donncha says, looking back on that moment. "I was annoyed and offended that NSO would sell [Pegasus] to somebody who would go after one of our own staff members. So I guess I had a bit of a grudge."

CHAPTER TEN

THREE DAYS IN MARCH

Sandrine

"So, you're asking me because of suspicion, rather than specific information, that my phone has maybe been compromised?" asked Siddharth Varadarajan. "Correct?"

This was the first of what would be many a delicate dance Laurent and I (along with a handful of other journalists on this still secret project) would have to perform in the coming months. Siddharth and his colleague, co-founders of India's premier investigative reporting website, the *Wire*, had already expressed an interest in joining what we had described to them, in very general terms, as an investigation into cyberthreats against journalists in India. We had just explained to them that before we went ahead with the partnership, we wanted to do a forensic analysis on each of their iPhones to see if either had been compromised by spyware. This was a little more than two weeks after the meeting with our key members in Paris, and so far, we had convinced only one of the selected targets from the list to submit his phone for analysis. That had happened only a few hours earlier, and we had no actual results. We were doing our best not to telegraph any impatience or anxiousness to Siddharth. "The first step of what we're talking about," Laurent had calmly explained at the beginning of our remote call, "is doing those forensics."

Siddharth was obviously intrigued. The *Wire* had done serious report-ing on cybersurveillance after the public revelation in 2019 that more than one hundred Indian citizens had been alerted by WhatsApp that their phones had likely been targeted by operators of Pegasus. Many of the alleged victims were human rights defenders or anti-caste activ-ists or political opponents of sitting Prime Minister Narendra Modi; four were journalists who had been critics of Modi's anti-democratic, strongman tendencies. But neither Siddharth nor his co-editor, M. K. Venu, had been among those identified by WhatsApp. The *Wire* had practiced good electronic communication hygiene. Editors and report-ers there were careful to use Signal and other highly encrypted messag-ing services when working on sensitive stories. They also swore by their iPhones, because Apple had successfully engineered its reputation as the safest mobile device on the market. The two men appeared skeptical at the suggestion that their iPhones had been compromised; they were also maybe a little perturbed that Laurent and I were not more forthcoming about the new information that had led us to them.

Our pitch to Siddharth and M. K. that day had to be fairly vague. We were still wary about expanding our circle of trust too early in the process. We didn't reveal to them that we had an entirely new list of possible targets well beyond the WhatsApp targets; that the leak we had received implicated NSO; that the list of targets numbered in the tens of thousands and spread throughout the world; that there were about two thousand possible new targets in India alone; or that Siddharth and M. K. and a few other journalists at the *Wire* were among those on the list of potential targets.

Siddharth and M. K. had fifty years of experience in journalism between them, a closetful of professional awards, and the nerve and guile to go out and start their own independent journalism website from scratch. They were a pretty savvy pair, in the habit of shaking the change out of a source's pocket, so it wasn't a surprise when Siddharth pressed us about whether or not we had any actual proof that his phone had been targeted with a cybersurveillance weapon.

"We have information," Laurent explained, "but it's not that precise. We really need to fact-check this."

"Frankly, I'd feel much more comfortable agreeing to this if you saw my number on some list," Siddharth pressed. "And if you can say something about the provenance of that list. And then I would happily agree to this exercise. But if it's information of a very general nature that you feel some journalists may be compromised, and you're doing this as a kind of public service, I can still consider your offer. But I need to have more information."

"We have some sources and some information that lets us think that your phone, precisely, might have been compromised," I told him, walking right up to the line we couldn't cross.

"And also my colleague Venu?" Siddharth pressed again. "His phone?"

There was a little more back and forth before Siddharth agreed to submit his iPhone to the Security Lab's forensic analysis. M. K. still had some reservations. "I hope you understand I can't part with all the material on the phone," he explained. "I'm not in the habit like Siddharth of regularly deleting messages. He is very meticulous. I'm not meticulous. So therefore I'm a bit apprehensive. Purely on that front."

Having been through the forensics ourselves, Laurent and I were sympathetic to M. K.'s fear of relinquishing all of his private electronic communications. I explained to him that nobody was going to be combing through the personal exchanges still sitting on his phone: "There are not any human interventions while analyzing those data. Nobody will see the data. . . . The data will be automatically deleted so nobody can access any of your data, and we will not have access to anything— messages or photos. This doesn't go to us. It goes to a very automatized system and a tech team that is looking only for evidence of malware used against your phone."

I'm not sure M. K. was completely reassured, but he did relent. Siddharth, meanwhile, took one final opportunity to pry out more information. "And you're looking for Pegasus, is it?"

"Among the software, yeah," I admitted, again walking right up to the line. "Pegasus is one of the software we analyze."

∎∎∎∎∎∎∎

THERE WAS NOTHING particularly dramatic about the scene that followed in Siddharth's book-lined home study in Delhi. What would turn out to be a momentous full-on remote forensic analysis unfolded more like an international sitcom than a spy thriller. The idea was to do backups of both phones and then upload the files to Claudio and Donncha in Berlin, where they would use their forensic tool to hunt for evidence that the phones had been either targeted by Pegasus or actually infected. I had assured Siddharth and M. K. that the entire process on their end would take about thirty minutes per phone, and that the Security Lab might have some preliminary results within a matter of hours.

I had been overly optimistic.

More than two hours into the remote call, we had yet to complete a backup of even one of the phones. We had meanwhile discovered that Siddharth had swapped out his iPhone a year earlier, so we were trying to get backups of *two* of his phones now—the current and the old one—as well as a backup of M. K.'s. Laurent and I had other meetings scheduled, so we were in and out of the video hookup monitoring the progress from our office in Paris. Phineas Rueckert, the Forbidden Stories India specialist, stayed on the line throughout, doing his level best to keep everybody calm and on task.

The real hero of the day was Sandhya Ravishankar, a freelance reporter who had traveled from her home in Chennai to Delhi to meet in person with Siddharth and M. K. This was a long trip at an inopportune time for Sandhya: two three-hour flights and at least a day's worth of meetings on our behalf, all while she was in the middle of covering her local elections, which were just three weeks away. But when we had told her two weeks earlier that we couldn't do this project without her, and we were counting on her as our go-between with editors at the *Wire*, Sandhya agreed. "You can totally count on me," she promised. We already knew we could.

Sandhya had been one of our most important and dedicated partners in Forbidden Stories' Green Blood series. She had also been part of the recent Cartel Project. Sandhya had a reputation in her home country as a tenacious reporter, having impressed Siddharth and others with a four-part series, published in the *Wire*, about financial corruption and environmental violations in the sand mining industry in her home district. She had been harassed by online trolls and stalked, the fuel line of her car had been mysteriously cut, and she was forced to defend herself (successfully) in a criminal defamation trial. So when Sandhya contacted Siddharth and said she needed to meet with him in person, urgently, he agreed. Siddharth knew Sandhya, but more important, he trusted and respected her. "She said she couldn't say anything about the purpose of the meeting," he later wrote, "but I guessed from her reticence it was about something important."

Before she left for Delhi, Sandhya had taken time from her election reporting to learn how to execute an iPhone backup on her computer and how to upload the file to the Security Lab. Her day in Delhi had started at six o'clock in the morning, when she had persuaded a well-known journalist, author, and academic named Paranjoy Guha Thakurta to let us run the forensics on his phone, and then she ran the backup-and-download operation. The success with Paranjoy's phone may have given us all a false sense of ease. Nothing went as planned at Siddharth's house later that same afternoon.

Sandhya ran into a maddening obstacle in the first minutes of attempting the backup of Siddharth's phone. The default platform for a backup is iTunes, and it turns out many people have already backed up their iPhone there in some distant past, complete with a password, which few people remember. Siddharth was no exception. iTunes would not let him create another backup file without the original password. Phineas managed to patch Claudio into our office from Berlin to see if he could walk us through the technical difficulties. He was patient as ever but not entirely encouraging. "If it's asked for the password, and it's not possible to change it, then there is nothing much to do," he said. "It just needs to be reset or recovered, unfortunately. That's just how it is."

These and similar glitches continued to arise over the succeeding hours, but Sandhya retained her composure and her naturally sunny demeanor throughout the hot afternoon and into early evening. She just kept downing coconut water, while the ceiling fan whirred overhead, and a child of the house raced through the study asking for attention, or

Siddharth's beagle licked at her face, or Siddharth himself, a cigar hang-ing from his lips, peered over her shoulder. Phineas, too, kept up his good cheer. "We were warned," Phineas admitted to the folks in Delhi. "Paloma has done this before, and she said that you have to be prepared for the long haul." Phineas and Sandhya both giggled at that. *Now you tell me.* Siddharth chewed on his cigar. Siddharth's wife came in and offered more drinks. Everybody smiled and pressed on. They even man-aged to find a password that allowed us to execute a backup.

I had just returned to the video call to hear Sandhya report to Phin-eas that her iTunes program was telling her the backup of Siddharth's second phone had thirty minutes remaining and that he was prepared to sign some paperwork we needed to bring the *Wire* into the project. "Actually," Sandhya said just as I settled in, trying to figure out what was happening, "it says forty-seven minutes now. . . . It's really painful. It's crawling."

"Sorry I had to disappear for two hours," I told her. "What did you manage to do so far?"

"So Siddharth's old phone has been backed up and uploaded. And the new phone is being backed up right now." She was moving on to M. K.'s phone, fortifying herself with more coconut water and mollifying Sid-dharth's very playful beagle.

M. K.'s phone, which had about fifty-five thousand undeleted Whats-App messages, took almost four times as long to upload as expected. By the time the Security Lab had M. K.'s backup in hand, Claudio had already delivered us some early results from Siddharth's files.

"So nothing conclusive yet, but the tech team did find some potential infections of your old phone," Phineas explained to Siddharth. "Actually, what they are asking us, if you would consent to it, is to send your old phone to them [in Berlin] to analyze in person. That way they could get more conclusive results."

"You mean the phone itself?" Siddharth asked.

"That way they could jailbreak it, essentially," Phineas explained, "and get more information than what is being given through the online platform."

"Yeah," Siddharth said. "I can do that."

∎∎∎∎∎∎∎

THE FORENSIC TOOL Claudio Guarnieri and Donncha Ó Cearbhaill had developed in the two-and-a-half years since they had investigated the spyware infection of their Amnesty colleague's phone was of an entirely new and singular order. They had discovered in the middle of 2019 that the tried-and-true method—finding the link inside an SMS message and then scanning the entire IP universe to see if it was somehow connected to NSO-created infrastructure—was no longer sufficient to the task. Part of the difficulty was NSO's nimble countermeasures.

When the Security Lab had published reports in the summer and fall of 2018, for instance, NSO had shut down Version 3 of its infrastructure and reconstituted a fourth. The company engineers had also constructed extra barriers to detection on both their new Command-and-Control servers and the servers that launched the spyware infections. Called "port-knocking" or "DNS knocking," these new precautions were the equivalent of a secret signal at the door of a Prohibition-era speakeasy. The would-be entrant had to perform a series of tailored attempts to connect to a C&C server. If made in the correct sequence—"the secret knock"—access would be granted, perhaps to an entirely different server, from which the Pegasus attack could be launched. More important, NSO had perfected a much more insidious method of infection.

Claudio and Donncha first spotted this new weapon in the fall of 2019, when they were approached to analyze the phone of an outspoken critic of Morocco's King Mohammed VI. Maati Monjib's nonstop calls for freedom of expression in his home country had put a target on his back in the aftermath of the Arab Spring, and in 2015 it earned him the criminal charge of "threatening the internal security of the state." Maati was spending much of 2019 in France, largely because he was on trial in Rabat, in absentia, as a treasonous propagandist. He faced the near certainty of a five-year prison term. Maati had not gone silent but, suspicious that Moroccan officialdom had him under constant digital surveillance, he had trimmed his sails considerably. "I need to constantly analyze the consequences of what I say and the risk that this may lead to defamatory accusations against me," he explained of his desire to find out if his mobile phone had been infected with spyware. "This even applies to very practical things like arranging meetings or a dinner downtown."

Claudio and Donncha very quickly identified some links in old SMS messages still on Maati Monjib's iPhone and very quickly tied the links to servers and domains known to be part of the Pegasus system. When they asked him if he would be willing to let them do a deeper dive on his phone to gather additional evidence, Maati agreed to allow the two cybersecurity researchers to execute a jailbreak on his iPhone.

A jailbreak is about what it sounds like, a hack that doesn't conform to all the legal niceties. Here's how it works: Apple Inc. does not allow iPhone purchasers to use the device as they wish but as Apple Inc. intends. Dear and fundamental as our cell phone has become to each of us, almost like an extension of our personhood, we don't so much own our phone as lease it under inflexible company-made restrictions. Avis is not going to let somebody rebuild a car engine during the term of the rental, right? Well, Apple doesn't want its customers so much as *looking* under the hood, let alone tinkering with anything.

An iPhone user can access files needed to run the apps she's permitted to install, for instance, but not for apps of which Apple Inc. disapproves. Apple likewise does not allow access to files in its operating system, iOS. Most especially, the company does not allow access into the "kernel" that controls the entire system. The company engineers have even limited an iPhone user's visibility into the various legitimate processes actively running on the device. Apple doesn't want anybody reengineering the operation of the phone, and it doesn't want anybody to put eyes on that valuable vein of proprietary code within. It requires expert intruders to get inside—cyber specialists like Claudio and Donncha, who have learned how to find or exploit vulnerabilities in the security fencing Apple has erected and then to "elevate one's privileges" on the phone. Experienced cybersecurity techs can get root access to the phone just as Pegasus does and see (or change) just about anything they desire.

That's what the pair set out to do with Maati Monjib's iPhone, and they made two crucial findings along the way, one that applied to iPhones in general, and one that applied to Maati's phone in particular. The first happened when Claudio and Donncha got the full backup and file system image of Maati's phone in iTunes and discovered it had extracted an extraordinary cache of data they hadn't seen before. Unlike an Android phone, where so much relevant data is erased by a reboot or simply evaporates in a matter of months, the iPhone retained years' worth of information in its various backup logs. So the Security Lab techs had access to the standard backup fare like old text messages and their links, as well as the browser history. But they also gained visibility into an iOS log called DataUsage.sqlite, which recorded the distinct name of every process happening on the device, and exactly when, and exactly how much mobile data was used. DataUsage.sqlite opened an entirely new path for tracking Pegasus.

Because Claudio and Donncha had total and unlimited access to Maati's backup files right in their Berlin office, they could take the time to look at every needle in that digital haystack. They could write and update their own code to hunt specific spyware markers already made public or shared privately within the cybersecurity community. One thing they found in Maati's backup logs was a process called "bh." The bh process had first been identified back in the summer of 2016, when Citizen Lab teamed with the private cybersecurity company Lookout and uncovered an attempt to infect an iPhone with Pegasus. The NSO-engineered bh.c was a tool to help in the delivery of "next stage payloads," according to the engineers at Lookout, and "their proper placement on the victim's iPhone." Those payloads, they determined, were early stages of Pegasus web-browser exploits. Lookout also found in the spyware bundle evidence that suggested "bh" was short for "Bridgehead."

What Claudio and Donncha found in Maati's phone three years later was a bh module that, as they reported to the world, "completes the browser exploitation, roots the device and prepares for its infection with the full Pegasus suite."

The Security Lab duo made an even more remarkable discovery in the forensic image of Maati's phone. When Claudio and Donncha combed through the Safari browsing history database and its Session Resource logs, they began to note and then reconstruct certain strange digital detours they were seeing. While trying to determine if Maati's phone had opened any known Pegasus links, they discovered that the phone (having already been subjected to eighteen months of Pegasus's standard SMS message attack) was navigating to strange and previously unknown websites in the spring and summer of 2019. Claudio and Donncha weren't sure just what they were seeing in the databases, but it "looked suspicious," Donncha says, "and the timing was right."

When Maati had tried to make a routine visit to the Yahoo home page one day in July 2019, for instance, he was redirected, in less than three milliseconds, to a suspicious-looking web page named Free247downloads .com at https://bun54l2b67.get1tn0w.free247downloads[.]com:30495/ szev4hz.

Seconds later, Free247downloads dropped a bomb of malicious code into the phone without anything to alert Maati that something out of the ordinary might have happened.

Claudio and Donncha had not only identified an attempted targeting of Maati's iPhone; they had found—inside the phone itself—traces of a successful spyware infection. They had also found evidence of a new and much more dangerous kind of exploit, called a "network injection attack." In layman's terms, this was a "zero-click" exploit. The infection attempt was not triggered when Maati Monjib clicked on a malicious link sent specifically to him in a text message. An outside attack network, maybe a "rogue cell tower or dedicated equipment placed at a mobile operator," Claudio suspected, had hijacked Maati's browser while he was simply surfing the internet.

This was a first for Claudio and Donncha. They had real evidence of a zero-click exploit. They also had a pretty strong suspicion that the spyware in question was Pegasus. But as they prepared their public report, neither was confident enough to actually tie the new 2019 exploits to NSO . . . until they got a little help from NSO. About a week before Claudio and Donncha were set to release the results of their forensic analysis of Maati Monjib's iPhone, they contacted NSO to share the findings and maybe get a comment. The next day, the spyware server that was to be named in the report was taken off-line. "We only privately shared this information with

NSO," Donncha says. "This kind of confirmed for us that NSO really was controlling this infrastructure and was able to shut it down."

Claudio and Donncha further confirmed their groundbreaking findings with a forensic analysis of an iPhone used by a Moroccan journalist named Omar Radi. The Free247downloads site also showed up in the backup of Omar's phone. As did evidence of rogue bh process executions in the moments after the rerouting to a Pegasus installation domain. As did another malicious configuration file buried deep in the phone, CrashReporter[.]plist. This slyly engineered file blocked the phone from doing its programmed duty of automatically reporting any software crash back to the Apple engineers. The CrashReporter file was a simple and effective way for NSO and their customers to cover the Pegasus tracks and make sure they didn't tip off the folks at Apple that there was a security vulnerability that needed patching.

The flurry of digital sleuthing had helped Claudio and Donncha identify domain names and process executions that might allow them to tie other victims back to Pegasus; it also helped them to begin to understand the complicated mechanics of a zero-click exploit. But these discoveries also alerted them to the considerable demands of the task ahead. They needed to engineer a new and better forensic tool, and to keep sharpening that tool. "The big problem with mobile devices is lack of visibility," Donncha says. "On desktop or laptop computers, we have antivirus available, or we have EDR [security] suites available, but there was really nothing similar that was available for mobile devices. These kinds of sophisticated attacks, especially zero-click attacks, were clearly going undetected."

THE SECURITY LAB forensic tool was still evolving in mid-March 2021 when Claudio and Donncha were presented with the backups of iPhones belonging to Siddharth Varadarajan, M. K. Venu, and Paranjoy Guha Thakurta. The two cyber-researchers already had a set of Pegasus markers to search for inside those backup files. They had identified specific servers and domain names of NSO's new Version 4 infrastructure. They were also working hard to catalogue millions of legitimate Apple process names so that they could more easily isolate spyware process names that had been surreptitiously injected into iPhones, the ones that did not belong.

The leaked list, meanwhile, had given Claudio and Donncha important new data points: time stamps suggesting when a phone had been selected for targeting. So once the Security Lab forensic tool had constructed a detailed timeline of all the previous activity on those iPhone backups from India, Claudio and Donncha knew where to focus their detective work.

Most important, they had the handful of Pegasus-based process names found in Maati's phone and Omar's phone to help them identify other possible instances of zero-click infections. Claudio and Donncha could now run a digital search for those processes in the DataUsage .sqlite log and the browser history log. We had reason to hope that the Security Lab's analysis of our Delhi-based iPhones would deliver the first little nuggets of gold from our leaked list.

Claudio called Phineas and me the next day with a report.

"So, nothing came out of M. K.'s phone," was Claudio's lede. "It just seems that it does not overlap at all with our records." But he didn't stop there, or even pause. "The more interesting is Siddharth's old phone, I suppose. And Paranjoy also has some similar artifacts." Siddharth's phone really did give us the first useful bits of evidence that helped build the Pegasus Project. "So basically, what seems to have happened is [Siddharth] started getting selected around April 2018, and it seems like they probably didn't succeed at it, until, ironically, he updated his phone," Claudio explained. "And then the day after, it seems they succeeded."

Claudio wanted us to understand that they had not uncovered any smoking-gun evidence, but it still felt like a good start. Siddharth's logs had recorded the exact same process names of those introduced into the Pegasus-infected iPhones belonging to Maati and Omar. The first two unsuccessful targetings of Siddharth's phone appeared to have happened as a package, in the space of a minute. The third attempt delivered. On April 27, 2018, at 4:41 on a Friday morning, CrashReporter[.] plist was created in the root domain. The infection took.

"We see a few process executions again that are suspicious," Claudio told us. "And I mean very highly suspected to be NSO components.

Then we see another process which uploaded more than three hundred megabytes from Siddharth's phone. We saw that same process also on Maati's phone."

Claudio explained that the exploit might have leveraged a vulnerability in iMessage or FaceTime, but he didn't have enough evidence to know for sure. Claudio, I had come to appreciate, was not one for speculating. Phineas and I were both anxious for more. "So having Siddharth's phone in person," Phineas asked, "how will that allow you to go further to maybe confirm this or get more information?"

"Well, the hope is having physical access we can extract more data," Claudio explained. "We will try to jailbreak the phone and get root access to it. Backups only give a limited amount of data."

"One question," I said. "You said you didn't have a smoking gun. So are you able to prove with the detail you have already that the phone has been infected? But you're not able to link to NSO? Or is there still doubt that the phone has been infected?"

"Well, I think what we have so far is probably strong enough to make the case that something happened, but we need to do some additional verification," Claudio cautioned.

He told us we could try to contact a former or current engineer at Apple who might be able to confirm that they had been seeing the same thing, but he didn't hold out a lot of hope. When Phineas broached the idea of contacting Apple through corporate channels, Claudio waved him off. The company was so concerned with any publicity that might tarnish their reputation for security, he said, that they preferred obstruction to transparency. "If you talk to Apple representatives," he told us, "they're just going to shut you down almost immediately."

There was no fast and tidy solution. The best bet for now was more forensics across a range of iPhones selected for targeting in different countries. "If we find more of these patterns, that's also an additional element," Claudio told us. "Like the fact that there are kind of recurring patterns across different cases. The fact that there are recurring process names and whatnot across different cases, it all sort of contributes to establishing a modus operandi. . . . That's going to be additional confidence and additional consistency. So we will look out for more of these [same patterns] and see if they come back again."

WE DIDN'T HAVE to wait long for another set of results. The very next day, Claudio called to say that the Security Lab had found the same spyware-based processes that had infected Maati and Omar and Siddharth and Paranjoy in the backup files of an investigative reporter based in Budapest. I set up a remote video call with the reporter and his editor at *Direkt36*, a website in Hungary that had been a Forbidden Stories partner in our very first collaborative investigation, the Daphne Project. The Hungarian journalists were not surprised by my request.

Frederik Obermaier had contacted *Direkt36* earlier in March because one of the verified phone numbers in our list belonged to Szabolcs Panyi, a reporter who covered issues related to Hungarian national security and foreign affairs. "[My editor] András [Pethő] casually told me that, you know, Frederik Obermaier asked for your phone number, and I was quite happy that such a famous journalist wants to talk to me. And then András was also telling me to leave our phones in the office and just take a walk around the block where we work. Then he told me that we've been approached by Frederik and Bastian Obermayer. And they say that there is a story that they cannot talk about, but they are pretty sure that we'd be interested in cooperating on."

Szabolcs had not been much fazed when András told him that Frederik had reason to believe he had been targeted by a powerful cybersurveillance weapon and that he wanted Szabolcs to submit his phone to forensic analysis before he could tell the two men from *Direkt36* any more.

We managed to get on the Zoom call as soon as Claudio and Donncha had completed their analysis. When I got on the line with Szabolcs and András and Frederik and started to explain the preliminary results of the forensics, I could see Szabolcs grow increasingly uneasy. "Basically, what we found was that there was what looked like potential traces of infection in Szabolcs's phone," I told the group. "What I'm really asking you right now, because of the security of the project and because of the risks we are taking, is really to keep that information for you and not to release it before we know more about what kind of targeting we're speaking of. There are other people concerned. And if we release that before, they will be in danger. . . . I hope you understand, and I hope you can join us on this project in the coming weeks."

András was the first to speak. "Well, this is, of course, I wouldn't say very surprising, given the sensitivity of the stories Szabolcs has been working on the last few years," he said. "But, you know, it's a lot to digest. In terms of joining the project, of course we are interested."

I could see there at the bottom left of my monitor that Szabolcs seemed to be having a difficult time absorbing the news that he had been personally targeted with this incredibly invasive spyware. He sat quietly, letting others do the talking for the first three or four minutes after the revelation. I only later learned the depths of what he was feeling. Szabolcs had been born into a repressive Communist dictatorship in Hungary in 1986 but had come of age in a relatively democratic society that seemed to honor freedom of expression and personal privacy. That had been the world he knew. It's not that he took these protections for granted, but neither did he fully appreciate the grim fatalism older members of his family couldn't seem to shake. "These are exactly the methods that my parents experienced when they were living in socialist Hungary," he later told me. "The methods that were used against me and the surveillance, this was really reminiscent of the Communist times. It was like being in a time machine, going back to my early youth, experiencing something that was going on in the 1980s."

CHAPTER ELEVEN

"LACKING DUE RESPECT TO THE KING"

Laurent

Our excitement over the initial forensic successes was tempered by news out of the Kingdom of Morocco that same week in March 2021. A judge in Casablanca had just concluded his preliminary investigation and signed off on formal charges in the case of Omar Radi. The investigating judge had essentially rubber-stamped the prosecution's flimsy allegations, while vitiating evidence and witness testimony crucial to the defense. He had even charged the key defense witness as an accomplice in one of the alleged crimes. Omar, who had been jailed for eight months while the Moroccan judge weighed evidence, was now facing trial on two separate counts—"undermining the security of the state" and rape. If convicted, he could be in prison for another five years, or even ten.

This was the latest in a series of sharp blows to the thirty-four-year-old journalist, who had made it a point of personal pride to expose powerful interests in Morocco who jealously hoarded the kingdom's treasure, its political power, its security forces, and its legal system. Omar was "not happy unless he was doing risky investigations and working on topics that disturb those who hold power," one of his friends explained. "He was passionate about understanding and disclosing ongoing processes of theft and robbery of impoverished people and their territories: their lands, water, and sand."

Omar was a trained economist, an experienced investigator, and a clear and fluid writer; he was also fluent in French, English, and Arabic. He could have taken up residence in London or Amsterdam or Paris and done his editorializing against the predations of the Moroccan state at a safe remove. But Omar had done his work at home, in broad daylight, for all to see. "It makes sense for me to stay [in Morocco]," Omar explained to a colleague who asked why he didn't live in exile. "Other people have done this, but, for me, it's not really an option. There are struggles to be made in Morocco, and I want to be part of it: struggles for freedom of expression but also for freedom of organizing and the freedom of people."

That stubborn insistence to remain home, to speak truth to power in the seat of national government, and to advocate for Moroccans who had no voice, had put him in very real peril. He was facing another round of public shaming, and the likelihood of real time in prison.

The development in the Omar case that week in March was also a blow to the Pegasus Project. Morocco was one of the key lines of inquiry that Sandrine and I had settled on with our first circle of partners. The data on the leaked list suggested that the NSO client in Morocco had been the most active user of Pegasus outside of Mexico; there appeared to be thousands of people selected for targeting by somebody in Morocco. Among the targets selected were officials from foreign governments, including at least a dozen in the Macron administration in France, as well as political dissidents, human rights defenders, and scores of working journalists within Morocco and without. The journalists could have been our perfect wedge into the story there, but we were already wary of including a media partner from inside the country. The danger of exposure was just too high, for us and for any journalist working in Casablanca or Rabat. Reporters and editors in Morocco were even more wary of us than we were of them.

Omar's upcoming criminal trial, along with the recent imprisonment of Maati Monjib and a handful of other journalists, was an uncomfortably tight turn of the screw by the Moroccan security services, meant to send a message. In the lead-up to Omar's arrest, his family, friends, and colleagues had all been subject to various forms of intimidation and unwanted publicity. "Every journalist in the country—and there aren't that many left—is scared of being targeted next," one Moroccan reporter said.

The news about Omar, I have to admit, also rattled a lot of folks at Forbidden Stories and the Security Lab. We had recent and pertinent history with him. Omar Radi, or Omar Radi's iPhone, had been crucial to helping the Security Lab build its forensic tool. Well before the Pegasus Project began in earnest, because of Omar's friendship and professional relationship with Maati Monjib, Claudio and Donncha had asked if they could have a look inside his mobile device. The evidence of Pegasus infection inside Omar's phone was strong enough that the Security Lab had decided to release the findings. Forbidden Stories, along with a number of our media partners, had been granted the inside story, by Omar himself. We timed our publications to coincide with the release of the Security Lab's report, on June 22, 2020. The publication had an immediate effect, but not the one we anticipated.

OMAR RADI'S PERSONAL story turned out to be an almost pure distillation of Claudio Guarnieri's warning that any technology bestowed as a tool of liberation could also be turned into a tool of repression. The transformation in Morocco unfolded over a decade, and Omar was at the center of it from beginning to end. He experienced the euphoria of initial discovery, the grinding effort of making new technology work on behalf of freedom, equality, and dignity, and the awful blowback when the state turned that technology against him.

Omar's first glimmers of the power of social media came as early as 2008, when he and his friends discovered they could prank the always watchful Moroccan gendarmerie. Omar was a twenty-two-year-old business reporter at a local radio station, with a growing reputation as an activist agitating for democratic reform. He and his closest compatriots knew they were being watched and used it to their advantage. "We sent each other a text message like, 'Protc   in front of the [police headquarters] at 6 p.m.,'" he told us. The proposed demonstration was a hoax, but the feint caused the local police to expend a lot of unnecessary time and energy. "It was a loop of about eight people who sent this SMS to each other. And at 6 p.m., when the time came, we were just milling around, smoking a cigarette next to the [police headquarters], and there were police vans filling the whole place."

The real potential of this new technology became clear a few years later. When the self-immolation of a street vendor, Mohamed Bouazizi, sparked democracy protests in Tunisia, social media apps fed an unprecedented wildfire of demonstrations across the Arab world. Laptops and cell phones were the preferred weaponry of the movement. People found they could communicate and organize in relative secrecy on Facebook and Twitter. They leveraged this new reality to inform and encourage protesters who were demanding a more democratic society and governance that answered to the needs of the entire citizenry. Freedom of expression was no longer the dream of some unforeseeable future in the Arab street; it was actually happening. The listening circle of anti-regime bloggers and vloggers grew wider and wider. Nobody in power appeared to know how to wriggle this genie back in the bottle.

In the face of the unrelenting protests, and with the world now watching, the Tunisian president ceded power in January 2011, after a quarter century in office. A month later, with men, women, and children occupying Cairo's Tahrir Square and refusing to cede ground, the seemingly inviolable regime of Egyptian president Hosni Mubarak crumbled. Nine days later, the February 20 Movement was birthed in Morocco. Omar was in his glory, in spite of the dangers presented by the police and security officers who carried their batons into the protests and used them to crack heads. The movement in Morocco, Omar explained, was "a rally for all those left outside the public space who wished to reclaim that space, democratize it, and transform it into a genuine avenue of debate."

He kept busy organizing protests, reporting them to the wider world, and spurring fellow movement leaders with what others described as his "contagious optimism." Omar occasionally exhibited the rhetorical excess that comes with youth and ideological ardor. "The only dictators that won't fall are the ones who are already dead," he once exclaimed to a group of protesters and journalists who had gathered to rehash the day's events. But underlying the February 20 Movement was a very sophisticated awareness of political imperatives and political limitations. Omar and his fellow leaders weren't calling for the head of King Mohammed VI; they were calling on him to lead the way to reform, to give up some of his nearly absolute power.

They were asking for a parliament that answered to the people and not the king, for a judiciary independent of the king. They asked for an end to the system of economic privilege that funneled public wealth to the top and encouraged corruption among government officials. They wanted a constitution that enshrined as a matter of law freedom of association, freedom of expression, and closest to Omar's heart, freedom of the press.

King Mohammed VI sounded willing to meet them halfway. The Moroccan sovereign was a clever man, with a keen appreciation for public relations. He had always kept one eye on his standing at home, and another on his standing in the Western world, and had worked hard to cultivate an image of monarchical liberality from the day he took the throne. Back in the first year of his reign, in 2000, he had handled a reporter visiting from *Time* magazine with remarkable deftness: "The front door of the palace opens and out comes King Mohammed VI with a feline bounce in his step," was the almost breathless lede in *Time*. The correspondent fairly gushed over the new leader of Morocco. His English proved to be impeccable and only "slightly accented." The king, noted the reporter, was the same regular guy he had been when he was merely the crown prince. The thirty-six-year-old monarch strapped on his Nikes and went for a jog. He drove himself to the office (even stopped at red lights like everybody else). He smoked Marlboros. He raced jet skis. He "plunged like a pop star into crowds of adoring Moroccans."

This sovereign intended to "meet the people and see how they live," the new king explained. "When I wave at people, I try not to greet the crowd but to greet people individually, to make eye contact."

King Mohammed VI, *Time* reported, had even begun to make amends for the cruelty his father, King Hassan II, had visited upon subjects who crossed him. While Hassan II held sway, dissidents were likely to end up in prison or dead. Mohammed VI—or M6 as he came to be called—had made a public display of releasing some of these accused heretics. "Mohammed VI is modern," said one of the pardoned men. "He does not have an authoritarian disposition."

The magazine ran its 1,700-word profile under the headline: "The King of Cool . . . Mohammed VI is the Beatles of Arabian royalty."

No surprise, eleven years later, M6 handled the uprisings of the Arab Spring with publicity in mind. The men and ministers who served him, the king suggested, were perhaps to blame for the regrettable state of affairs that existed between the monarch and his people. On March 9, 2011, less than three weeks after protests began, the king went on television to tell his subjects he was appointing a committee to draft constitutional reforms that answered to the concerns of the protesters. He began to release political dissidents who had been imprisoned in his own reign. The demonstrations didn't subside, but the beatings by the kingdom's police forces did.

By the time the Moroccan people ratified the proposed constitutional reforms in July, Mohammed VI was being hailed by some for his move toward democratization. There were critics inside Morocco who pointed out that the king's power wasn't much clipped by the updated constitution—the sovereign still chose the prime minister, and he still ruled the highest court in Morocco, and he still appointed most of the judges. But the reforms did look good on paper, especially from afar.

M6 was lauded for his accommodation and his relatively bloodless handling of the crisis. US secretary of state Hillary Clinton called the king's reforms a "model" for the Arab world, as did French foreign minister Alain Juppé. The Kingdom of Morocco continued to enjoy the financial beneficence of the West. In 2013, the EU topped off its annual grant of $250 million in cash assistance with an additional $40 million to help the kingdom with its "democratic transition." That same year, President Barack Obama praised Morocco for its newfound commitment to human rights. The US continued to gift the kingdom more than $100 million a year to help stimulate the Moroccan economy.

Those years immediately following the February 20 Movement turned into the salad days for Omar Radi. He became a key blogger for *Mamfakinch* (roughly translated: No Concession), a citizen-journalist site that debunked state-financed and state-run media. He helped launch the French version of the website specializing in investigative reporting, Lakome.com; he contributed to foreign media outlets like Orient XXI, the BBC, and Al Jazeera English. He was also a founding member of *Le Desk*, a news site that specialized in long-format investigative reporting, multimedia presentations, and data journalism.

The Palace, meanwhile, was becoming even more committed to blunting the impact of any press unfriendly to the state or the sovereign. The Moroccan government shelled out good money to media companies as a neat little quid pro quo. Being a parrot for the kingdom was a much more secure and lucrative business proposition than trying to challenge the government line or report the truth; it also promised juicy scoops from sources inside the security services.

There was a certain amount of harassment that went along with the work of independent journalism in Morocco, and a certain amount of financial hardship, which Omar Radi felt personally. Along with those of other well-known members of Mamfakinch, his computer was infected by Hacking Team's Remote Control System spyware as early as 2012. His computer was so "f-ed up," he remembers, he had to stop using it. The start-up media companies that employed him in Morocco were occasionally censored, or run out of business, or drained of advertising revenue by the command of the state. From time to time, Omar was forced to accept financial help from his parents. But a young man who had watched his father and mother get up at five o'clock every morning to drive to their high school teaching jobs in Casablanca, a waterfront city they could not yet afford to live in, had little fear of hardship and hard work.

From 2012 to 2016, Omar Radi was able to do some really exceptional journalism, specializing in investigations that laid bare the workings of the Makhzen, the powerful state-sponsored cabal that controlled the distribution of Morocco's wealth and natural resources. His first big story was a five-part exposé of Morocco's sand-and-gravel industry, which provided raw materials needed in construction. The quarries were one of the few revenue-generating enterprises in Morocco, but the opportunity to invest in these lucrative businesses was a privilege held tight by the Palace. The kingdom granted cuts of the earnings to the chosen. The profits, Omar found and reported, rarely redounded to the advantage of the citizenry. The money often ended up in banks in Luxembourg and the British Virgin Islands, beyond the reach of the tax collector in Morocco.

Omar's second big investigative piece became known as "The Affair of the Servants of the State." Omar got access to Morocco's public land register, culled sales contracts, tax exemptions, and deeds, and found that the state was selling off some of the most expensive acreage in the capital city of Rabat to friends of the monarchy and loyal bureaucrats who had "served the state well." Omar named names, and he named prices.

These investigations drew some attention to the young reporter, and his first professional accolades, and not much real pushback from the authorities. But there were folks in the Moroccan security services who marked Omar Radi a man, as they would sometimes say of wayward subjects, "lacking due respect to the king."

Omar would always say he meant no disrespect to the king and that he never saw his relationship to the sovereign as one of personal antagonism. He was just out to tell the truth about his native country, in hopes of making it better. "Some of your colleagues find your journalism too investigative and too radical," one friend later said to Omar. "But I remember when we used to laugh, saying that as long as we disturb them—those who really hold power—then it means we are on the right track."

On paper, again, things were still getting better for independent-minded journalists in Morocco as late as 2016. According to the new legal code adopted that year, a reporter could no longer be sent to prison just for writing something that offended the state or the sovereign. But, in Omar's experience, the kingdom was starting to lean in on extralegal tactics when challenged. Omar had contracted with *Le Monde* to investigate a fascinating bit of inter-royalty gifting in the Middle Atlas city of Ifrane. The Kingdom of Morocco had apparently handed over a huge swath of publicly owned land to the emir of Qatar so he could build himself a private mountaintop palace. Construction had already begun by the time Omar got on the story; the land was being deforested, the locals sent packing. Omar was trying to find out how this property deal had been done. Had the dispossessed townsfolk signed off on this? Were they compensated?

Omar could tell he was being followed by government minders from the moment he got to the region, and he noticed how quickly the local leaders and activists cooled on the idea of talking to him. "My conversations with the people, with the activists on the spot, etc., were well monitored," he says.

Omar reported back to *Le Monde* that the story didn't seem doable, that the kingdom was going to keep "putting sticks in my wheels." The editors in Paris weren't willing to give up, and Omar might have pushed ahead, until a sovereign-friendly website jumped on the story. Not the story of the Qatari's new palace but the story of Omar's investigation. "My telephone conversations, especially, ended up on a news site called *Le360*, which was also close to the government, and which told of my intentions in the article," Omar says. "I ended up abandoning the idea of doing that investigation because the threat was direct and clear not to get close to this kind of subject."

The next year, while reporting on land dispossession in the Rif region of Morocco, Omar was arrested and held for forty-eight hours. The Rif was a dangerous place to be in 2017 but also where the best stories were. The people of the region were a forgotten population, poor and poorly educated. But they were proud and showed little willingness to be docile subjects of any king: not of Mohammed V or his son Hassan II or his son Mohammed VI. The ill will was often reciprocated. Hassan II called them "dirty, ignorant, beggars."

After the killing of a local fish vendor in the Rif in 2016—police looked on when he was crushed by a garbage compactor as he attempted to retrieve $10,000 worth of his confiscated swordfish—the region erupted in violent demonstrations that recalled the Arab Spring five years earlier. King Mohammed VI quickly turned the region into a police state, pouring cops into the main cities, one for every two citizens in some places. The police used batons, truncheons, and firearms with impunity, and even, some suspected, with relish. People were jailed by the hundreds over the next few years; leaders of the protest movement were sentenced to twenty-year prison terms. When those sentences were upheld on appeal, Omar's sense of injustice got the better of him. "Let us all remember Appeals Judge Lahcen Tolfi, the enforcer against our brothers," he tweeted in April 2019. "In many regimes, small-time henchmen like him come back begging, later, claiming they were only 'carrying out orders.' No forgetting or forgiveness with such undignified officials!"

Omar was arrested for sending that message, interrogated by the National Brigade of Judicial Police (BNPJ) for five hours, and released. Eight months later, without warning, Omar was arrested again for the same "offense." He was held without bail and in solitary confinement for a week and finally charged with "insulting a magistrate." In March 2020, he was convicted and sentenced to four months in prison, suspended. One of the Moroccan government's well-subsidized media sites called it "light."

SANDRINE AND CÉCILE first interviewed Omar Radi three months later, in June 2020, as the Security Lab was finalizing its report concluding that Omar had likely been a victim of Pegasus cybersurveillance spyware. Omar was in remarkably good spirits. He said he was looking forward to seeing how the Moroccan authorities answered the charge. The "contagious optimism" that his February 20 Movement compatriots had seen a decade earlier was hard to miss; Omar was quick to smile and quick with a joke. Even by remote hookup, you could see the twinkle in his eyes.

Omar seemed amused and slightly bewildered that the Kingdom of Morocco had chosen this moment to give him, twelve years after he had first applied, his official press credentials. He told us he was appealing his four-month prison sentence but was not entirely hopeful. "Given the way they are behaving toward me through the press right now, I think they are a little angry with me," he said. "I guess we'll see." Meanwhile, he couldn't wait to tell us about an ambitious new investigation he was working on, which involved the transfer of millions of acres of land in the course of King Mohammed's twenty-year rule. Omar told us that in one case it appeared the kingdom had bought land from rural Moroccans for as little as €2.5 per square meter and then sold it to real estate developers for about €1,500 per square meter.

His enthusiasm for this new investigation into land dispossession seemed unbounded, probably because it was a culmination of a dozen years of work and study on his part. "This operation aims to take out the land that is considered as 'dormant capital' according to the official language, that is, land used for producing food and so on, and to inject it into the market," he told us. "Millions of dispossessed families who have only agricultural skills ended up on the outskirts of urban centers because they have nowhere else to go. . . . The state drives them out so that, afterward, the state can give this land to the private sector to build golf courses, luxury houses, condominiums, that kind of thing. It's hard to see public utility here. This is about the impoverishment of the population, which suffers both the greed of the private sector under the protection of the authorities, the justice system, the police, and the Ministry of Interior, who are ganging up against a population that has already for decades been the victim of the lack of literacy policy, public schools, health, and general impoverishment due to the general conditions of the country's economic policies."

The investigation was neither fast, nor easy, nor cheap, but Omar was back at Le Desk, and had just received additional funding in the form of a grant from an international foundation specializing in journalism, economic justice, and human rights. Omar was determined to keep at this investigation because he had come to see it as a crime in progress. "The Moroccan state lacks financial resources at the moment," he said. "Land is a financial resource that can easily be taken away from people and is of great value. I think that the phenomenon of land appropriation will multiply in the coming years."

There was one catch to his plan to complete the project, he admitted. He suspected the government had caught wind of it. "Something pretty shocking happened at the beginning of this year," he said. "I finished investigating with a village, and I did some interviews with the members of the village, the people there, the inhabitants, the peasants. And then I received calls from all the members of the village two days later saying, "Please don't talk about us. Don't quote us. I was threatened by the police. You're going to get us in trouble if you ever publish an article."

When Cécile and Sandrine got down to the discussion about his being surveilled by somebody in Morocco using Pegasus, he was philosophical. Cybersurveillance had been a fact of life for journalists in Casablanca and Rabat. "We are in a police state where one of the tools for controlling the public space is to have people under surveillance," Omar explained. "And among those people under surveillance there are people like me, like political activists, like journalists, who are disturbing, who must be systematically monitored."

Omar figured he'd been watched since the Arab Spring. Moroccans were already using the Eagle cybersurveillance system, from the French company Amesys, back in 2011, and later RCS from Hacking Team and FinFisher from the Gamma Group, and now Pegasus from NSO. He was surprised to hear from the Security Lab about the clever new zero-click technology NSO had developed to launch a spyware attack.

"The NSO virus is much more advanced," Omar said. "They're cutting-edge. They know everything. Hats off to them."

In the previous few days, Omar had begun to sense new activity in the campaign against him. It appeared to him that the Moroccan security services were feeding material about him to their paid media mouthpieces, that whoever had gained access to the contents of his cell phone was using that information as a weapon against him. Government-friendly media outlets were beginning to publish details of Omar's personal life that he took pains to keep private. He called the tactic "barbouzerie"—a French slang term that refers to shady spy tactics. "That is to say," Omar explained, "telling exactly what time I was drinking alcohol or with whom I live, who comes to my house, etc. In a barbouzerie press article they are letting you know you're being watched."

Omar had good reason to be concerned about this new development. Barbouzerie in Morocco had taken a dark turn in the previous few years, one that had put the practitioners of independent journalism on edge. The king's prosecutors had used a series of salacious criminal charges to decimate the staff at *Akhbar al-Youm*, a newspaper that refused to toe the government line. The paper's founder and editor in chief, Taoufik Bouachrine, had been arrested in 2018, a few days after he wrote an opinion piece criticizing the king's chosen prime minister for neglecting critical infrastructure in rural Morocco. The public prosecutor of Casablanca charged Bouachrine with multiple counts of sexual assault.

One of Bouachrine's purported victims, also an employee of *Akhbar al-Youm*, refused to corroborate the allegations. "I testified that he was innocent," she said. "The prosecutor did not like that and somehow convinced the judge that I was suffering from Stockholm Syndrome." She fled to Tunisia, with a six-month sentence for perjury and defamation hanging over her head. Bouachrine was convicted and sentenced to fifteen years in prison.

The editor in chief who replaced Bouachrine, Soulaimane Raissouni, was also charged with sexual assault and jailed. Raissouni's niece Hajar, a reporter at *Akhbar al-Youm*, was arrested with her fiancé while leaving her gynecologist's office. The king's prosecutors charged the couple with engaging in premarital sex and terminating a pregnancy, both criminal acts in Morocco. The trial required the twenty-eight-year-old Raissouni to submit to an unwanted and unnecessary gynecological examination. "It was an inhuman experience: imagine a 'doctor' forcibly inserting instruments into your vagina, without your consent," Hajar told reporters from the French publications *Mediapart* and *L'Humanité*. "I was raped by the Moroccan state."

"On top of that," Omar told us, "they falsified documents because in the end, the expert said there was no abortion." Hajar, her fiancé, and the doctor who was falsely accused of performing an abortion were all convicted and sentenced to prison. When the king issued a royal decree of clemency six weeks later—so the couple could "begin a family in accordance with religious precepts and the law"—Hajar fled to Sudan with her fiancé. She felt compelled to write letters of apology to the gynecologist and his staff, who were also convicted of crimes. The newspaper she and her uncle had worked for was on life support by June 2020.

"That's how they operate," Omar told us. "It's breaking people's image, digging up things about them and making them public. There are no ethics, no morals. We're going to expose sexual orientation. We're going to take paparazzi pictures of someone with his mistress or a woman with her lover, and we're going to publish it to say, 'Look, she's cheating on her boyfriend or he's cheating on his girl,' etc. Which is none of their business."

When Sandrine and Cécile had a second talk with Omar the following week, just five days before publication, he was becoming suspicious that Moroccan government authorities were softening the ground for a personal attack to discredit him. The regime-friendly gossip sites had just a few days earlier published details about Omar's roommate, his girlfriend, and even specific details of the money going into and out of his personal bank accounts. The sort of information somebody with access to Omar's iPhone could mine. More worrisome, a popular gossip site called *Chouf TV* had accused Omar of acting as a spy for a foreign government, called him a "cannabis smoker," and asserted he had a reputation among his young activist friends as a "rapist."

ON JUNE 22, 2020, Forbidden Stories posted the story of the Pegasus attack on Omar Radi, along with our partners from *Le Monde*, the *Guardian*, *Süddeutsche Zeitung*, and the *Washington Post*. We were unable to include a comment from the Moroccan government, which refused to answer our queries or even deign to acknowledge receipt. Omar may have been disappointed that there was no official response, but he sent us a message of thanks that day. "Makes a lot of noise here," he said. "It is awesome."

Two days later, Omar was summoned to the BNPJ offices in Casablanca, where the prosecutors were already busy. Somebody there had alerted *Chouf TV* so its cameras could be on hand to record Omar's perp walk, and the king's prosecutor had readied a press release about the reason for the summons. "It's official," Omar wrote to us that afternoon, after suffering through a six-hour interrogation. "They are accusing me of working with foreign intelligence agencies. They are pushing the ridiculousness very far."

Our key partners did follow-up stories on the arrest, with statements from Omar and the Moroccan authorities. The *Washington Post* was able to tag to the end of its report a not-so-veiled official threat from the Moroccan Embassy in DC. "Due to the short notice," a spokeswoman wrote, "we are unable to comment other than to underline that we reserve the right to pursue legal action in case any unverified or false information is published on this particular case." Omar retained his sense of humor—"We'll either see each other again in a few hours," he had told a friend on his way into his interrogation, "or maybe in five years"—and his defiance. "I'm not afraid of anything," he said for publication. "I'm going with my head held high."

Omar was summoned for another interrogation the following week. Investigators grilled him about the grant he had received from the South African foundation to help fund his land appropriation investigation, and then leaked to one of their preferred Moroccan media outlets the identity of Omar's make-believe handler from MI6 in London. Three days later, Omar and a friend were arrested for confronting and taking video of a *Chouf TV* cameraman who had been following him around, recording him and a friend, and taunting them. After the ensuing quarrel, the police arrested Omar and his friend and held them in jail overnight. The prosecutor's office added to Omar's docket new charges of public drunkenness and capturing images without consent.

He sounded weary and maybe a little afraid two days later, on July 8, when he sent Sandrine an audio file to catch us up on the latest harassment. "I'm sorry it's going to make you more work," he said. The tone of his voice was so different from usual; it was the first time I ever heard him sound despairing. "I don't know. Anyway, what I wanted to tell you is that three summonses in two weeks is too much. It's too much. . . . The authorities in Morocco have a grudge against me and they are using all their tools, the police, the media, and the justice system." Omar said he was beginning to believe that NSO was in on it, too. If Morocco branded Omar a spy, NSO and Moroccan officials could both say that Pegasus was being used legitimately, to protect national security.

We kept telling Omar, as we had from the start, that we would help keep his story alive and in the news so at least the prosecutors in

Morocco understood they were being watched. "You can count on us," we told him. But we were helpless, and the mood around the office was tense.

Omar went dark in the middle of July. Sometime between his fifth interrogation and his seventh, he simply stopped responding to our messages. On July 29, 2020, we read the news that Omar had been picked up and remanded to pretrial detention. The investigation had taken on a new dimension. He was now facing charges of accepting money from foreign intelligence services, "undermining state security," and rape. The alleged victim of sexual assault, a freelance employee at *Le Desk*, went public a few days later. Her story of the assault was detailed and compelling. Omar's family and supporters made a point to say that nobody in the Radi camp wanted to silence the alleged victim but that Omar deserved a fair trial—with all the evidence on the table.

NINE MONTHS LATER, with the Pegasus Project beginning to get some traction in Mexico, India, and Hungary, Omar remained unreachable. He was still in jail and headed for trial, but with little hope of being able to mount a real defense. He had occasional visits from his friends and his parents, but we had heard that some of the old twinkle had gone out of Omar's eyes. Each of us at Forbidden Stories and the Security Lab was feeling varying degrees of guilt for having shined a light a bit too brightly on Omar Radi, for having invited the full force of the Moroccan state down on his head.

One of our staffers at Forbidden Stories was so shaken that she spoke about leaving the field of journalism. Sandrine and I tried to explain to her, as we tried to explain to ourselves, that the job of a reporter is not to advocate or to push for a certain outcome; a journalist's job is to tell the truth and let the chips fall where they may. But this was cold comfort where Omar was concerned, for all of us. He had bravely and openly shared his story with us, and when the walls started to close in on him, there was not a lot we could do.

"The case of Omar was an important lesson to understand," Claudio would say. "Things can go wrong, even for the people we tried to help."

CHAPTER TWELVE

"FRAGILE, RARE, AND NECESSARY"

Laurent

I found myself already flagging in early April, maybe even a little tired of the chase. Some days it was hard to believe that this investigation would truly pan out—and I don't think I was alone. After more than six months on Pegasus, four months full-time, the entire Forbidden Stories team was beginning to be ground down. Sandrine and our reporters were fielding queries from partners, or coordinating with Claudio and Donncha, or working new sources across multiple time zones. A day in the office might begin with a series of calls from India before first light and end late at night with calls from Washington, DC, or Mexico City. On some days our rooms felt like a sealed tank, a hothouse bubble where nothing was allowed to leak in or out. Security protocols were at the front of everybody's mind because nobody wanted to be the person who made the mistake that tipped NSO or one of its clients and compromised the investigation. The line between prudence and paranoia was pretty thin.

At home some evenings, when my teenage son would ask me what I was working on, I had to deflect. "Something sensitive, so I can't tell you too much," I'd explain, watching his face fall. I kept thinking about the day at a school fair a few years earlier when the father of one of his friends confided to me that he worked "in the field of telephone interception."

Better to be careful than to risk a small aside to a fellow parent in a play-ground that might expose the project. I felt obliged to be slightly more open with my wife but not much more. If I had to explain my upcoming travel plans, or some strange new safety precaution I wanted her to con-sider, I would shut down both of our cell phones and put them in the refrigerator or the microwave while we talked. "I felt like I was living in a movie scene," Aurélia told me later. "I was prepared for this kind of sit-uation because I remembered the stories Bastian and [his wife] Suzanne told us [about the Panama Papers investigation]. I was afraid of burglar-ies. I also remember the intensity of our talks, where I had to understand quite quickly what you were talking about because it was not going to last long."

Meanwhile, roadblocks were presenting themselves at nearly every turn. I had been anxious for months to find a way to alert Khadija Ismay-ilova in Azerbaijan that she was facing a new danger. I was sorely tempted to warn my friend that her cell phone may have been infected with this incredibly invasive spyware, and I was also keen to do the forensic anal-ysis on her device. That NSO had licensed Pegasus to the Azeri govern-ment would be an important scoop, and evidence was likely sitting in Khadija's phone. But when we reached out to Paul Radu, her colleague and editor at the Organized Crime and Corruption Reporting Project, which had published some of her most recent work, he asked us to stand down for the time being.

Khadija and Paul, a Romanian living in Bucharest, had just wriggled free of two years of harassment in the form of a libel suit brought by an Azeri businessman. Some really powerful figures still had Khadija under thumb in Azerbaijan; she had been released from prison but remained in Baku, trapped by a court-imposed travel ban and closely watched by the Azeri security services. "This is very, very sensitive, especially for her," Paul told us. "She's still basically on probation." We agreed that we should wait to do the forensics until the travel ban was lifted and she could get safely out of the country. But that could be months away, and maybe too late for the Pegasus Project.

Then we found out the phone that Siddharth Varadarajan had prom-ised to send to the Security Lab in Berlin for further forensics had not arrived and probably wouldn't get there anytime soon. There was a ban on shipping electronics to both Paris and Berlin; Covid travel restrictions made it impossible to send somebody to Delhi to retrieve the infected device. So that was another cul-de-sac we had to negotiate.

The situation in Morocco was just one more vexing difficulty. The Security Lab had developed evidence showing that the iPhones of Maati Monjib and Omar Radi had likely both been attacked by Pegasus from within Morocco. But we needed to identify other victims and get more evidence for our new report. There were thousands of names and numbers to choose from in the data out of Morocco—reporters, editors, heads of state, diplomats, human rights attorneys, even officials inside the palace in Rabat—but none presented as an ideal candidate. There was no secure way to contact journalists still in the kingdom; we knew the French government would never turn over official cell phones for inspection by an outside digital lab. The prospect of having allowed a successful spyware attack on some French minister's iPhone—let alone President Macron's—was a public embarrassment that French security services were not going to invite. Neither would governments in Belgium or Algeria, who also had officials on the list of selected targets. Dialing up numbers belonging to apparatchiks within the Moroccan Makhzen was also a nonstarter—surely the fastest way to blow our cover. Even our best bet was still a long shot and kind of risky. But on the first Tuesday of April 2021, Sandrine and I decided we had no choice.

I sent a text message to the head of investigations at a well-known media site whose Paris office was just a five-minute walk from ours: "Fabrice, Hey, how you doing. We have very very important information about Mediapart. It's ultraconfidential. It's quite urgent. Are you by chance at your office? Even if it's only ten minutes."

"Not available at all," Fabrice Arfi answered. "Can you tell me more here?"

I had known and respected Fabrice's work for more than a dozen years. The two of us had been among the leaders of a fight against a proposed French law to criminalize the publication of corporate documents that threatened "strategic interests" of any private company; he was also a member of Forbidden Stories' first informal advisory committee. Among other things, I knew he and the rest of the team at *Mediapart* had the highest of journalistic standards and real backbone. I had read the stories two years earlier about a team of prosecutors and police officers showing up at the *Mediapart* offices to search the newsroom for files pertaining to a recent story they had published. The site's sixty-eight-year-old co-founder and president, Edwy Plenel, had told the lawmen to get the hell out until they had a warrant. And maybe don't bother to come back even if they did get one. "I said it before and I'll say it again: I want to tell our sources they are safe," Plenel told anyone who asked. "We know how to protect them."

Beyond professional respect, I also counted Fabrice a friend. I trusted him, but I did not trust his technology.

"Impossible to tell you here," I texted back to him. "This is very important, Fabrice."

"I can be at Mediapart at 6 p.m.," he answered. "Can you just tell me if it's serious?"

"Yes, it's quite serious. But I cannot tell you on this line."

"Okay. You're freaking me out now. Is it about me personally?"

"Not directly about you," I texted. "But about Edwy. I can come to Mediapart with my editor, Sandrine."

"Okay. Let's say 6:30 to be safe. . . . I can do 6 if it's better for you."

That was great by me. At that point it felt like every half hour made a difference.

WE KNEW OF at least two people from *Mediapart* who had been selected for possible cybersurveillance by an NSO client in Morocco—Edwy Plenel and a reporter named Lénaïg Bredoux. This was no surprise. *Mediapart* had been tracking King Mohammed VI, his only-on-paper reforms, and his chief aides, for more than a decade. The site had given space to protesters who claimed their Moroccan farming village had been befouled by government-regulated silver mines: "In a country like ours everything is for sale," was how *Mediapart* quoted one concerned local back in 2014. "The mine is surrounded by mountains of waste. Heavy metals are used for treating the silver. The amount of irrigated land has fallen dangerously. The winds blow all sorts of toxic substances in the direction of farmland. A considerable quantity of polluted water also seeps into the aquifers because there is no strict control of this dangerous waste."

Mediapart also reported on the regime's brutal police-state tactics that strangled the Rif protest movement in 2016 and 2017, while pointing out the French government's apparently willful ignorance. "It is not up to me to pronounce judgment on a subject relating to internal politics here," President Macron had said on a visit to Rabat.

With help from partners like *Le Desk*, the site made sure its readers were kept abreast of the king's vicious and expanding crackdown on independent journalists in Morocco. "We are witnessing a repression that mercilessly targets dissident voices, journalists, but also any citizen," Omar Radi had told a reporter representing *Mediapart* in January 2020, after being charged with impugning a Moroccan judge. "In terms of freedom of expression, we have never been so repressed. . . . The regime rules by fear."

The site had recently posted a long interview with former *Akhbar al-Youm* reporter Hajar Raissouni, now living in Sudan after her brief stay in a Moroccan prison on invented charges of terminating a pregnancy. "I came here because I'm afraid of the revenge of the Moroccan state," she said. "There is no freedom of the press in Morocco, there is only one voice, that of power, and most of the critical voices are in prison, defamed by newspapers linked to the authorities, or targets of judicial harassment. Independent newspapers are facing financial strangulation."

Maati Monjib surveyed a field littered with Moroccan journalists smeared with charges of espionage, financial fraud, sexual assault, and abortion and offered this assessment to *Mediapart*: "Sticking a bad reputation on opponents is a way of isolating them, of scaring everyone else, of reducing everyone to silence. Defamation is a poison, it is very cynical. Reputation is glass. Once it's broken, you can't put it back together."

Mediapart had also run a long and unflattering profile of King Mohammed VI co-authored by the editor of *Le Desk* in July 2019, on the twentieth anniversary of the sovereign's ascension to the throne. "Little rejoicing," was the headline. "His declared ambition was to champion the country's poor, to be closer to his people. That ambition has failed miserably," was the top-line assessment.

The body of the story was a bulwark of fact in support of that assessment. Rachida El Azzouzi of *Mediapart* and Ali Amar, editor and co-founder of *Le Desk*, ran the numbers on poverty, suicide, unemployment, economic and political inequality, and general discontent. They noted slow economic growth and a dearth of jobs, even for the young and well educated: "More than 600 engineers annually leave the country in the context of the scourge that we today call the brain-drain." Three hundred medical doctors had just resigned to protest poor working conditions and poor pay, and 70 percent of Moroccan adults under thirty wanted to leave the country. Half the country wanted radical political change, the authors noted.

The writers also made bold to reveal a nickname given to the king—His Majet-ski—as well as his recent purchase of an $88 million yacht and the unconfirmed dissolution of his marriage. The king and his court were apparently not amused. By the time that article appeared in July 2019, according to the leaked data, journalists at *Mediapart* were among the thousands of Pegasus targets selected from inside Morocco.

WE ENDED UP running into Fabrice on the street on our way to *Mediapart* that cool April evening, so we took him up to our offices and told him what little we could: we were working on a story about cybersurveillance, and Edwy might be among the victims. Fabrice was frustrated that we wouldn't tell him what sources we had to back this. Or who might be spying on his boss. Or why. But he did agree to go back to *Mediapart* and ask if Edwy would meet with us the next day.

We got a text message a few hours later. Edwy had agreed. He suggested three o'clock. I made a plea for noon, and Edwy grudgingly consented.

Sandrine and I were both a bit apprehensive when we arrived at *Mediapart* the next day. Edwy was an iconic figure among journalists in Paris, with a career marked by erudition and energy. He had been a reporter, a newspaper editor, the author of numerous books, and the editor of others. He didn't exactly court controversy, but he didn't shy from it either. He had started his long career in journalism as a reporter on a Trotskyite newspaper in the mid 1970s, and never disavowed his youthful politics. His investigations for *Le Monde* into the François Mitterrand administration's intelligence services in the 1980s were so thorough and so damning that the Mitterrand government retaliated by illegally wiretapping him and falsely claiming he was a CIA plant.

He had spent a quarter century at *Le Monde*, most of it at the top of the masthead. Plenel's shrewd editorial stewardship of *Le Monde* drove circulation up to the highest point in its fifty-year history, until it finally overtook *Le Figaro* as the most popular daily newspaper in France. Plenel had left his longtime home in journalism after a fight over control of the newspaper's content and went on to start *Mediapart*.

Now a dozen years into that venture, Plenel had proved his point that a subscription-based online news service could be profitable—and that it was necessary. He rejected the standard ad-based revenue model because he believed that the sensational, gossip-driven, celebrity click-bait stories that model encouraged were certain to drown out the infor-mation that actually mattered in a functioning society. "Newspapers are not a commodity like others; they are crucial for democratic vitality," he would say. "We are selling very particular goods that are useful to democracy and public debate. Fragile, rare, and necessary goods. . . . *Mediapart* lives by the motto 'only our readers can buy us.'"

We weren't entirely sure what to expect when Fabrice ushered us in to *Mediapart* to see Edwy Plenel at noon on Wednesday, April 7, 2021. He was nearing seventy but still trim and athletic, with a shock of dark hair and a dark, neatly sculpted mustache. When he smiled, his lips puckered under his mustache and his eyes squinched; he looked like a puckish and unthreatening uncle—surely the most amusing raconteur at any party. But when he set his jaw in consternation, he was an intim-idating figure.

Fabrice and Edwy invited us into a conference room, and neither man appeared much amused when we asked them to turn off their phones and leave them in another room. But they honored our request. Edwy sat down across from us, his jaw set in a hard line and his arms folded defensively across his chest.

Sandrine and I explained again, as Fabrice had already told him, that we were working on a story about cybersurveillance, and we believed his phone had been compromised by spyware. He pressed us for more details.

"But what do you *know*?" he asked. "A few years ago, somebody came in here and said I was on a list of people not paying taxes. Didn't make it true."

We explained again what we could: that his name was on a list of selected targets. We still couldn't say who had targeted him.

"Forbidden Stories?" he said. "Who are you? Who's funding you?"

Part of this felt like hemming and hawing; part of it felt a bit angry.

Fabrice jumped to our rescue. "Laurent's a good friend," he told Edwy. He also vouched for me as a solid journalist.

The boss kept pushing for details, making a point to use the formal "you" when addressing Sandrine and me, like he wanted to make it clear that we were not friends. Who was this spying on me, he wanted to know, maybe NSO?

"I can't tell you any more yet," I said. "After we run the forensics on your phone, we will have more to share."

"Look," he said. "You cannot come here and give me only that kind of information and expect me to give you my phone. I need more."

Fabrice jumped in again. "I can understand this is a bit embarrassing for us to know just ten percent," he said. "But you really can trust Laurent and Sandrine."

"If there is a big issue with *Mediapart*, we should warn people now," Edwy said. He told Fabrice they probably needed to talk to their chief technology officer about safety. Not surprising. "*Mediapart* Hacked" would not be a good headline. I explained that based on what we knew, the problem was not confined to his publication. There were a number of victims, at many different media companies.

I suspect we have a veteran reporter's inherent curiosity to thank, along with Fabrice's willingness to vouch for us, but near the end of the half-hour meeting, Edwy Plenel agreed to submit his phone to forensic analysis.

EDWY WALKED HIS iPhone into our offices at Forbidden Stories the next day. The *Mediapart* editor stuck around to watch as Cécile made the backup of the phone and uploaded it to the Security Lab in Berlin. Claudio texted us to say he had received the file, and he texted back only a few minutes later, with preliminary results. The time stamps in the data lined up perfectly with exact and identifiable moments when Pegasus-system processes were written into Edwy's iPhone operating system. The process names matched ones that Claudio and Donncha found in Maati Monjib's phone, and in Omar Radi's.

"They found traces," I told Edwy. He didn't seem particularly surprised or particularly worried. He was no longer out in the field doing investigative reporting. "They won't find anything," he said. He suggested his life wasn't as exciting as it once was.

Cécile gave him what details she could. There was a lot more to be analyzed but his phone had indeed been infected, and she could give him the specific dates. But the Kingdom of Morocco was almost certainly the perpetrator.

No surprise, as far as Edwy was concerned. He had been in the kingdom's crosshairs since about 1990, he told us, back when he edited a biography of Mohammed VI's father, King Hassan II, a man Charles de Gaulle had described as "unnecessarily cruel."

Edwy had encouraged his friend Gilles Perrault to write that book, and even suggested the title, *Our Friend the King*. The book revealed that Hassan II had not only settled many of his critics into secret prisons, some for a decade or more just for distributing leaflets, but had also subjected those prisoners to deprivation and physical torture. Morocco's minister of the interior tried without success to bribe the publisher to cancel the book, according to Perrault; and lawyers across Paris, working on behalf of the king, made tidy sums suing outlets that printed or aired interviews with the author. *Our Friend the King* remains banned in Morocco to this day, but not forgotten.

Edwy went back through his calendars to see what was happening in July 2019, when the Pegasus attacks on his iPhone began. The link seemed obvious. He had returned from a conference in Morocco, where he had spoken up in support of the democratic movements in the Rif that Mohammed VI had crushed, just days before the initial infection attempt.

"So," Edwy mused, "now I understand why."

THERE WERE A couple of other journalists at *Mediapart* who were also on our list, we explained to Fabrice, and he agreed to ask one of them if she would allow Claudio and Donncha to do a forensic analysis of her iPhone.

Lénaïg Bredoux, according to the data, had been targeted around the same time as Edwy Plenel. She, too, had some history with Morocco, having been a thorn in the side of the King Mohammed VI and one of his trusted lieutenants for nearly a decade. She had written a critical story about Morocco's chief of domestic intelligence back in 2015, for instance, just as he was about to receive the highest honor bestowed by the French government, the Légion d'honneur. This award, Bredoux's reporting suggested, was likely a sop to Abdellatif Hammouchi, who had professed himself deeply and officially wounded when French authorities tried to pick him up in Paris to question him about his complicity in the alleged torture of a Moroccan citizen.

Bredoux quoted experts who pointed out that France had also given the kingdom a green light to bury any charges against Hammouchi. "In the face of Moroccan demands, France has completely caved in," said the honorary president of the International Federation for Human Rights. "[France] is acting in a way that gives priority to its interests over its values! They've just agreed to give impunity to potential major criminals or even torturers."

Lénaïg was nervous but willing to let the Security Lab run the forensics on her phone, and Claudio and Donncha found evidence of a successful zero-click infection. The analysis of Lénaïg's cell phone helped clarify one little bit of the picture by further confirming a pattern our technical partners at the Security Lab had observed. NSO had apparently identified a vulnerability in iMessage, and its clients in Morocco had launched multiple attacks exploiting the weakness.

Informing Lénaïg that she had been targeted with spyware was more difficult than I expected. Sandrine and I explained to her that forensic evidence suggested that she had been under cybersurveillance by somebody in Morocco as early as July 2019 and that she was still being targeted as late as July 2020. The Security Lab couldn't say for sure when it had stopped or if it had stopped. Lénaïg was silent for a beat. We were all masked because of Covid, so I was having a hard time gauging her reaction. She started to tell us she was afraid she'd been targeted as a way to get to her husband, who is Algerian—a country then in the middle of an intensifying diplomatic feud with Morocco. She didn't have to say it, but it was clear she was afraid she had put her husband in danger, maybe even their children. I could see Lénaïg's eyes begin to get moist, and I could feel myself begin to fill up with emotion.

"Do you want a glass of water?" was all I could think of to say.

She regained her composure pretty quickly and started to focus on details in the forensic analysis. Claudio's written report showed that Pegasus had extracted more than 220 megabytes of data from Lénaïg's iPhone in a single month in 2020. She wanted to know what exactly the Moroccans had stolen from her, but Claudio couldn't say for sure. The forensic tool didn't turn up that kind of detail.

She also wanted to know how she could protect herself (and her family) going forward, but we explained there was no absolute fix. She could disable her iMessage, where the back door in the iOS software was pried open for the cyberassault, and maybe FaceTime, another suspected path of attack. She could also upgrade to a new iPhone and change her number, but that was no guarantee she could evade the end users of this cyberweapon if they wanted to target her again.

None of us could be certain of what precisely had provoked the cyberspying on Lénaïg. She mentioned her reporting on Hammouchi, now the head of Morocco's domestic intelligence and the national police, and the man most likely to be in charge of the kingdom's cybersurveillance program. She also told us she was in contact with a group of journalists reporting the latest developments in the Omar Radi criminal case. She couldn't recall writing about Omar recently, but she had had text message exchanges with sources and with other reporters who were working the story.

THERE WERE STILL many questions we needed to answer about Pegasus, NSO, and Morocco, but the *Mediapart* forensics were a big step forward for us, just in terms of confidence in the project. Two phones in our data. Two positive results. A 100 percent success rate. We had evidence of actual infections, tied to the time stamps in the data, on both phones. The digital fingerprints matched those that the Security Lab had found in other phones targeted by Moroccan end users—which meant we were on the right track.

Edwy Plenel ended up being both appreciative and magnanimous, even after we explained that we did not yet feel comfortable revealing to Fabrice or Edwy details of our larger investigation. We never even mentioned NSO and Pegasus. We did reassure them that *Mediapart* was not the main focus of our investigation, that there were many more victims at many different news outlets, but they didn't press us on the size or the scope of the leak. Edwy and Fabrice told us their team at *Mediapart* would be doing its own follow-up reporting, but they gave us their word that their site would hold off until Forbidden Stories and our partners broke our story. Edwy just wanted a heads-up on timing so it didn't look like they were caught unawares.

The Security Lab found traces of Pegasus infections in the iPhone logs of two more Moroccan targets in April—one a human rights lawyer living in France, the other a reporter at *Le Monde*. Another Moroccan target helped Claudio and Donncha identify what looked like a previously unknown attack vector: NSO's hackers had apparently found a way to open a back door in Apple Photos. "The phone of a French human rights lawyer was compromised and the 'bh' process was executed seconds after network traffic for the iOS Photos app (com.apple.mobileslideshow) was recorded for the first time," Claudio and Donncha reported. "Again, after a successful exploitation, crash reporting was disabled by writing a com

.apple.CrashReporter[.]plist file to the device." That attack had happened in October 2019. Lénaïg Bredoux's backup logs showed a May 2020 attack with an almost exact same pattern. The two compromised devices also showed a connection with a Pegasus-created iCloud account, bogaard lisa803[@]gmail.com. These new findings meant Claudio and Donncha had additional markers to feed into their forensic tool.

I can't say any of us at Forbidden Stories or the Security Lab expected these kinds of results; the positivity rate on iPhones on the list tied to Moroccan end users was particularly surprising. We all felt like the NSO/Morocco axis of the investigation was on solid footing now, but it was already starting to seem too little, too late for way too many journalists in Rabat and Casablanca.

The beleaguered Bouachrine/Raissouni newspaper, *Akhbar al-Youm*, had folded a few weeks earlier. Denied Covid relief funds, the paper was unable to dig out of a financial hole dug for them by outside parties. "Under Hassan II, journalists disappeared," the author of *Our Friend the King* explained in a new interview published in France. "Under M6, it was the newspapers. . . . People who advertise in independent newspapers or newspapers critical of Mohammed VI get phone calls: 'His Majesty is very sad to see that you advertise in this newspaper.' The message is obviously received five [times] out of five. The advertising stops, and the newspaper [stops] as well."

More urgent was the ongoing persecution of recent *Akhbar al-Youm* editor in chief Soulaimane Raissouni and Omar Radi. Raissouni had been held in a Moroccan prison for ten months and Omar for eight, much of it in solitary confinement. The men had each been given a few meager opportunities to present testimony and evidence to investigating judges, but neither defendant had been given a formal trial, or anything that approached due process. The Moroccan state, having learned its lesson well in the previous decade, had successfully debased the two men just by making its loud public charges of sexual deviancy and espionage. The trials, if they ever did happen, would be more of the same. "With the Arab Spring and the rise of social networks, young opponents acquired legitimacy and credibility," Maati Monjib explained. "Designating them as traitors, thieves, rapists is the best way to silence them."

Criminal trials for both Soulaimane and Omar had been scheduled to begin that April, then postponed without explanation. Multiple legal efforts to gain their release while the cases were pending failed; petitions from human rights groups, international journalism organizations, and leading Moroccan personalities in the arts, culture, and academia were tossed aside without consideration.

On the day we had confirmed the targeting of Edwy Plenel's phone, April 8, 2021, forty-eight-year-old Soulaimane Raissouni went on a hunger strike. Soulaimane's wife announced that her husband was "facing freedom, justice, or death." Omar Radi, whose Crohn's disease and asthma had worsened during his long prison stay, began his own hunger strike the next day.

For me, the meaning was clear. Every half hour counted, now more than ever.

"SOME THINGS THAT YOU HAVE MISSED BEFORE"

Sandrine

Darkness was falling on Budapest on a brisk evening in the third week of April, when Szabolcs Panyi walked through the gaudy lobby of a downtown hotel on his way to a meeting with a pair of his heroes. The renowned investigative reporters Bastian Obermayer and Frederik Obermaier had just arrived in town from their home base in Munich for a secret conference with Szabolcs and his editor at *Direkt36*, András Pethő. The *Süddeutsche Zeitung* journalists were waiting upstairs in a rented room, with a computer full of fastidiously secured and encrypted data, ready to read Szabolcs and András into the Pegasus Project.

The hotel itself was a little deflating, Szabolcs remembers. "A disgusting interior, like a cheap rip-off of a Trump Hotel, with lots of fake golden decoration and everything," he says. "I was really nervous. And excited at the same time that, finally, will be revealed some big secret."

There were a few maddening hoops for Szabolcs and András to jump through even after they arrived at the appointed room. The two journalists first had to power down their cell phones and other devices and store them in another room, where the electronics would remain throughout the meeting. They also had to take a rapid test to screen for possible Covid infection and then cool their heels inside the bathroom until the results came in. So Szabolcs and András waited out the last fifteen minutes, still in the dark as to the details of the Pegasus Project and their place in it. These were the final frustrating moments of an already long and disquieting wait for Szabolcs Panyi.

A month had passed since I had first told Szabolcs, by remote hookup, that the Security Lab's forensic analysis found evidence that his iPhone had been successfully infected with spyware. I had not been able to give him many details at the time—no mention of NSO or Pegasus. I still remember Szabolcs's immediate reaction; his first instinct had been to reach out to warn his sources. Szabolcs had hundreds of sources, many of them inside Hungary's intelligence, political, and business communities, and his work had touched a lot of sensitive nerves in and around Budapest the previous few years.

Just days before we alerted him of the spyware infection, Szabolcs had dropped a 9,000-word story detailing the growth of the Hungarian government's diplomatic and financial entanglements with China over the course of Prime Minister Viktor Orbán's eleven-year run in office. Szabolcs's report in *Direkt36*, headlined "How Orbán's Eastern Opening Brought Chinese Spy Games to Hungary," represented months of investigation, with reams of documents and data to back it, and some sixty interviews with official and unofficial sources—most of them unnamed for their protection. The report had embarrassed Orbán's ruling Fidesz party.

The takeaway of the story was that China had gamed Orbán and Fidesz with unkept promises of major financing and favorable loans to Hungary's cash-strapped government. Little had come of Orbán's China-friendly "Eastern Opening" policy besides an opening for China to fill Hungary with thousands of proselytizers and citizen-spies and to get a foothold in the EU for profit seeking. "They do everything for money," an unnamed Hungarian diplomat formerly stationed in Beijing explained to Szabolcs.

Szabolcs analyzed the one big Hungary-China collaboration of the past decade, a €1.9 billion reconstruction of a railway line between Belgrade and Budapest, and found it to be a sinkhole of cash with a puny return for Hungarians. "A Chinese-Hungarian consortium won the [construction] contract, with two Chinese state railway builders join-

ing forces with a company of Lőrinc Mészáros, Viktor Orbán's child-hood friend and Hungary's richest businessman," Szabolcs wrote. "As a former senior foreign ministry official put it, this also shows that the 'Eastern Opening' eventually turned out to be just [a] 'ninja smoke-screen designed to conceal Hungarian graft and corruption.' Hungary's national economy hardly benefited from the pro-China turn in foreign policy, only business circles close to the government profited from it."

The day we informed him of the spyware attacks on his iPhone, Szabolcs was finishing up the reporting on a follow-up story detailing a more recent "Eastern Opening" boondoggle, also, as he would write, "based on the model of the Budapest-Belgrade railway investment." He hoped to publish in early April.

The thirty-five-year-old investigative reporter was aware these sto-ries would likely have uncomfortable personal consequences, but he had grown accustomed to being the target of angry recrimination from key players in Fidesz. The prime minister's chief international spokesman had already identified Szabolcs as an enemy of the state, publicly accus-ing him of "Orbánophobia and Hungarophobia." Fidesz apologists in the media occasionally spewed the lie that Szabolcs was a foreign spy, likely CIA.

Szabolcs Panyi had operated his entire journalistic career inside the tightening noose of Orbán's soft authoritarian rule. The prime minister had showed himself a sly tactician since taking office in 2010. He had used electoral reforms to deliver Fidesz a supermajority in the Hun-garian Parliament, and then used those friendly lawmakers to rewrite the constitution. The bloodless legislative coup sabotaged democratic institutions, undermined the rule of law, and accrued power to Orbán himself. "He has disguised his dismemberment of democracy through a package of laws written in impenetrable legalese that only a handful of experts can hope to decipher," says one observer.

The prime minister and his Fidesz minions were also working to suppress media critical of the government. Reporters who tried to get at the truth of the ruling party's corruption and malfeasance didn't rou-tinely get jailed or physically harmed or smeared with salacious crimi-nal charges like they did in Morocco, but they were watched.

"These things have been going on for four years now," Szabolcs told us in 2021. "There was one occasion when I was meeting a source, but in another town. And when I was going to meet him, there was physical surveillance on me, meaning these, you know, classic short-haired, muscular guys in brown leather jackets just standing there and then walking behind me. And after my meeting with this source, when I was traveling back to Budapest on a train, I was sitting in an empty train cabin, and a similar guy just arrived. And he was there throughout the whole train ride, more than an hour, just standing there in the cabin door, not moving. He didn't have any luggage. This is, as we call it, 'demonstrative surveillance.'

"They want you to know that they are following you. It's slightly threatening, but it's more about sending a signal that 'We're watching you. We know what you're doing. We know who you're meeting.' And this physical surveillance did have an effect on the story that I was working on because I couldn't use the information that I obtained because obviously the meeting was compromised. And I didn't want that source to get into trouble."

Szabolcs never considered himself technically proficient, but he had always been careful. He used the latest iPhone because of Apple's reputation for security, and he steered clear of any electronic devices manufactured in China, which almost certainly had back doors in their operating software. He used encrypted messaging services like Signal and Wickr. He used VPNs. When an operative in Hungarian intelligence warned Szabolcs that a competing agency might be using digital means to spy on him, it just didn't seem cause for panic. Szabolcs had never found Orbán's security services particularly competent or energetic.

But when I informed him that somebody was using his own iPhone to surreptitiously spy on him, that he was carrying around their weapon for them, it felt like a quantum leap in capability and intent; it had shaken him. Unlike the demonstrative surveillance, this had been done in stealth, with no signal and no way to know just what the security services were after or what they had learned.

"I was really afraid that my sources could be jeopardized, and they could get into trouble," he says, "so that's why I was really freaking out."

Szabolcs felt obliged to tell some of the sources he used in his China reporting that their communications might have been intercepted, but his editor at *Direkt36* cautioned against it. "Come on, don't do that," András counseled. "We don't have enough information right now. And this story, I mean, the cybersurveillance story is just too sensitive."

Claudio had managed to talk him down a bit also. The cybersurveillance had happened over a specific period of time, from April to December 2019, Claudio had assured him. There was no evidence of recent infection or, as Szabolcs called it, "infestation." So Szabolcs kept the unsettling information to himself, took all the extra security precautions Claudio recommended, and convinced the Security Lab to do a new forensic analysis on his phone every few weeks, just to be sure.

Finally, a month later, in that splashy gilded hotel in Budapest, Szabolcs was about to get the lowdown on what exactly had happened inside his iPhone and how it connected to a much larger story of cybersurveillance.

"AGAIN, SORRY TO not be able to reveal everything because most of it will be revealed, the whole extent of our project, in our meeting in Paris in May," Frederik Obermaier said to Szabolcs and András by way of introduction. "So we would focus on what we know so far from Hungary. We know that several hundred numbers from Hungary were targeted. We have reason to believe they were targeted by a state actor from Hungary."

Part of *Direkt36*'s role, Frederik and Bastian explained, would be to help identify people in our data who might be willing to let us run forensics on their cell phones, Hungarians who could also be trusted to keep mum while we completed the investigation. Frederik and Bastian ran through a few of the selected Hungarian targets already identified by name: one of Orbán's key ministers, now retired, for instance ("He's not even an outspoken critic," András noted), and a member of one of the most important opposition parties in Hungary.

"Are you going to tell him?" András asked of the opposition politician.

"We would rather try to first speak with him," Frederik said. "If we have a super good feeling, and if you also agreed that one can kind of trust him, but we would first of all leave the decision to you."

"I'm skeptical," Bastian said, worried the former minister might not be willing to remain silent until our story broke, "because he is very outspoken."

"I don't know him well," András said. "I spoke with him only a couple of times. But here's the danger: he likes talking. And when you talk to him, he tells you everything."

"Okay, Frederik added, "so that's a no-go."

That's when Frederik opened up his laptop and unveiled to Szabolcs and András the real gem in our possession. He took out an unassuming-looking memory stick, plugged it into a USB port, and accessed our list with the protocols Claudio and Donncha had tailored for the Pegasus Project. The file was encrypted, and Frederik typed in the three long and complicated passwords. Voilà. There it was, finally, for Szabolcs and András to see—hundreds of selected cell phone numbers, catego-rized under the heading of Hungary. Some identified by name and some not. Frederik and Bastian were going to send backups of Szabolcs's and András's separate contact files to the Security Lab in Berlin later that night to see if Claudio and Donncha could match other names to the still-unidentified Hungarian cell numbers on the list.

Frederik scrolled down through the list as Szabolcs and András looked for names they recognized. "Oh, she's a former ambassador to China, and now she's an adviser to Orbán, foreign policy adviser," Szabolcs said, pointing out one familiar name. "I have her number."

"Ooooh, okay," András said. "He's in finance. Investment banker."

"I think it's really interesting to see how many people are not there for criminal reasons but for purely political reasons," Bastian told them. "For me, from Germany, that's a big scandal."

"This will be one in Hungary, I bet," Szabolcs added.

Szabolcs found himself experiencing a déjà vu moment, reliving the strange sensations that had washed over him when he had first learned he'd been targeted by cybersurveillance weapons. "I was very excited that I was presented with this database, and there was this possibility to work from it, but it was also really unnerving," he said later. "I remember especially the name of this guy who worked in Viktor Orbán's own government. He's a retired, old, very respected, very kind economist, respected throughout the political spectrum. And to see his name among the victims of surveillance, that was the biggest shock because . . . there's basically no wrongdoing that he could have been involved in.

"And then seeing the names of very shady people in the same list: Hungarian mobsters who were occupying all the police bulletins and on the evening news back in the nineties. Mobsters involved in organized crime and violence. Some Arabic characters there and Russian names, which, you know, we suspect of being legitimate targets of either counterintelligence or counterterrorism investigations. And then finally seeing my name among terrorism suspects or suspected drug dealers. That's shocking, that there's someone operating the system to whom it just doesn't matter if they surveil a serious criminal or young investigative journalists like myself."

Before they broke up the meeting for the night, Frederik and Bastian presented Szabolcs with much more detailed information from the forensic analysis Claudio and Donncha had completed on his phone. "They basically created a timeline of what they saw on your phone," Frederik explained. The time stamps of the cyberattacks in 2019 were identified down to the day, the hour, the minute.

Szabolcs had his calendar out, matching the timeline. He remembered he had been investigating the growing Trump-Orbán relationship, which involved a lot of talk of weapons sales. "That day I was meeting with an arms dealer," he said, pointing to one of the lines in the chronology from the Security Lab.

"That one?" Frederik asked. "In Hungary?"

"Yes, that story had a US angle and a Russian angle."

"And Hungarian?" said Frederik.

"Hungarian as well," Szabolcs explained. "And also some Israeli angle. The guy I was meeting noticed that there was also someone sitting next to us from a certain embassy, who was known to work for the intelligence agency of that foreign country."

"Oh wow," Frederik said.

And Bastian pressed Szabolcs. "Can you tell us?"

"It was the United States."

Szabolcs wanted some clarity on one last thing concerning forensics. Claudio had told him that whoever had infected his iPhone had only exfiltrated between 50 and 100 megabytes of data. "I assume those were not pictures or videos but rather texts," Szabolcs said, but neither Frederik nor Bastian could say for sure.

"We have to fear for the worst," Frederik explained.

"My assumption is chat logs," Szabolcs said, almost pleading now.

"The assumption is that everything that you saw on your cell phone was accessed and everything that you spoke and wrote," Frederik said. "Even a Signal message that is in theory encrypted could be read using this technology. Because when you are typing it, then basically it would be intercepted there. So it would not be intercepted on the way, when it's already encrypted. But while you type it in."

"But it cannot access the encrypted messages I am receiving and reading?" Szabolcs asked. "Just what I'm typing?"

"They can basically access everything that you see," Frederik told him. "If you're receiving a Signal message that was encrypted on the way, as soon as you read it, and you can see it here [on your phone], then they can access it."

"Okay," Szabolcs said, smiling through obvious pain.

"This is the huge danger," Frederik told him, "because we all as journalists were feeling kind of secure, even after the whole Snowden NSA revelations. That as soon as we use technology like Signal that our communications were kind of secure. This is a huge threat for all of us, and our sources."

WHEN FREDERIK AND Bastian showed up at the *Direkt36* office for a second meeting the next day, Claudio and Donncha had already matched more than a dozen numbers from Szabolcs's contact list with numbers in our data. Szabolcs took one of the matching numbers and typed it into his phone. "Well," he sighed, "that seems to be our colleague working here."

"At the paper?" Bastian asked. "We don't have a name for this number."

Szabolcs identified the number as belonging to András Szabó, who was at work in the next room.

"So, a second colleague from *Direkt36*," Bastian said. "That's annoying."

Szabolcs called András Szabó into the conference room to get his permission for the forensics. Then the team uploaded a backup of András's iPhone to the Security Lab, and the preliminary results came back an hour or so later. Frederik presented the findings to Szabolcs, András Pethő, and András Szabó. This represented fully half of the *Direkt36* editorial staff.

"It looks like he was compromised on June 13, 2019, and again on September 24, same year, 2019," Frederik told them.

"Me?" András Szabó said, looking stunned.

"Yes, you."

"Wow."

"I think it would be good to go through your calendar and your memories basically," Frederik suggested.

"I have a problem," András Szabó explained. "Last year the Hungarian police invited me as a witness in a case, and before these police came to pick me up, I deleted a lot of stuff from my calendar."

Szabolcs was already scanning the *Direkt36* archives to identify the stories his colleague had published back in the relevant months of 2019. Just before the initial cyberattack, András had published an investigation into Orbán's minister of communications. The Fidesz official and his wife had both been gifted luxury cars by a company with ties to Russia. Then he did a story on an opposition pol suspected of financial fraud. Then one on the construction contract for a Hungarian nuclear power plant project that had been given to the Russian corporation Rosatom.

András explained he had important anonymous sources on the nuclear plant story.

"So it could be somebody trying to find out who your sources are," Frederik posited. "Or maybe your sources tipped the government."

"Maybe," András said. He didn't know what to think. But a few things were clear to the *Direkt36* team. This was going to be a big story, and there was a lot of work to be done.

"I think it would be good if you could go through your notes again and think about which sources could be in danger," Frederik suggested.

"Just those two days?" András asked.

"As far as we understand the system now, those were the days the infections took place," Frederik told them. "But that doesn't mean it's only those days. It could be that someone was listening and reading afterward."

András Pethő, ever the editor, reminded Szabolcs and András Szabó that they needed to keep all this information between the three of them. For now, he said, it was best if they told none of their co-workers.

"Don't even put it in your computer that this meeting took place," Frederik cautioned. "Don't speak to anyone about it."

THE CONFIRMATION OF infection on András Szabó's iPhone marked the end of a very productive month at the Security Lab in Berlin. Including the recent confirmation of an iPhone belonging to a reporter in Mexico, Claudio and Donncha had found traces of Pegasus left behind on ten different cell phones in that brief time, across at least four separate countries. The success rate was, in Claudio's experience, off the charts. Even the handful of iPhones that came back clean had been useful in helping Amnesty International's two-man cybersecurity team catalog the millions of legitimate process names in iOS or in apps installed from the Apple store. "There's no documentation for any of it," Claudio told us. "It's not like Apple publishes the details. So there's been a process of understanding and getting more familiar with the [iPhone] operating system as well."

The sudden rush of forensic analyses had swelled the Security Lab's list of legitimate iOS process names, but it had also swelled the list of illegitimate Pegasus-generated process names. Glaringly apparent was the fact that somebody at NSO was cleverly naming the malicious Pegasus processes to help camouflage the attacks, adding or subtracting or moving a letter here, changing a digit there. Apple's legitimate ckkeyrolld, for instance, became NSO's malicious ckkeyrollfd; fseventsd became eventsfssd; nehelper became nehelprd; CommCenterRootHelper became

CommsCenterRootHelper; xpcroleaccountd became roleaccountd. "The more we look at phones," Donncha reported, "the more we gather indicators. We kind of have to build a database of indicators."

The increase in that database was crucial. By feeding this growing list of malicious process names into its brain, the Security Lab forensic tool was learning how to win, as one of our partners later opined, "the world's most complicated game of Spot the Difference."

Claudio and Donncha were clearly gaining confidence in their evolving forensic tool late in April, and with good reason. They had just found traces of a Pegasus attack on Indian journalist M. K. Venu's iPhone, which seemed to be clean when they first analyzed it back in March. But it turned out that at least one Pegasus-generated process name that Claudio and Donncha had discovered in Lénaïg Bredoux's iPhone—otpgrefd—was also sitting in the backup of M. K.'s iPhone stored on a drive at the Security Lab. "Once you feel like you unlock something new you didn't know before, you'd go back and look at previous evidence," Claudio told us. "Perhaps you find some things that you have missed before or interpreted differently."

Patterns and similarities that connected Pegasus end users were beginning to emerge. Multiple malicious NSO-produced spyware processes, Claudio and Donncha had discovered, were operating on multiple infected iPhones, whether the NSO client was in India, Morocco, Mexico, Hungary, or any of the countries in our list.

The recent forensics had also revealed some signature differences among NSO customers, making it possible to track and confirm exactly where specific digital attacks had originated. Each NSO licensee, it appeared from evidence in the cell phones, was using its own particular set of fabricated iCloud accounts to assist in launching attacks. Claudio and Donncha had found multiple instances of iPhones being surreptitiously contacted at a key early stage of the Pegasus exploit by NSO-generated iCloud accounts with specific email addresses. Records of these iCloud or iMessage contacts, all of them using fake names, were then logged in a file deep in the phone. The victims of NSO's Moroccan clients might have been contacted by fakes such as bergers.o79@gmail .com or naomiwerff772@gmail.com or bogaardlisa803@gmail.com or linakeller@gmail.com, the victims of Indian clients by lee.85.holland@gmail.com or bekkerfred@gmail.com or taylorjade0303@gmail.com. M. K. Venu's phone and two others from India had been contacted by herbruud2@gmail.com. Hungarian targets Szabolcs Panyi and András Szabó had both been secretly contacted by the make-believe jessicadavies1345@outlook.com and her make-believe sister emmadavies8266@gmail.com.

The deep and widening forensic analysis was also affording Claudio and Donncha fresh insight into the capabilities of the engineers and coders who were designing and building the Pegasus system. The genius of the technical team at NSO headquarters north of Tel Aviv was not apparent in the malware Pegasus licensees were using to spy on an iPhone and its owner. Kind of "shitty," Claudio calls it, when pressed. "The really sophisticated part of Pegasus isn't actually the Pegasus malware itself," Donncha says. "But the exploit, the actual way of injecting the spyware on the phone, is quite complicated, and it is something that changes all the time."

The sophisticated weaponry that NSO's Pegasus system was deploying to inject its quite ordinary spyware was engineered to exploit vulnerabilities in, say, the Apple software and apps running on an iPhone. The Security Lab had already detected exploits engineered to attack through iMessage and Apple Photos. These weapons are known in the cybersecurity field as "zero-day exploits" because that's exactly how much time a tech company like Apple or Google or Microsoft has known about the issue and that's exactly how much time they have to fix the problem before an attack. Zero days! None. It's already too late.

If an exploit can evade enough security protections and technical mitigations, it can eventually jailbreak the device and write whatever malicious code it desires into the iPhone. But as Claudio and Donncha explained to us, a single exploit is rarely enough to break down modern cyber defenses and get access to the device. Researchers often need a chain of three or more exploits to do the trick. Which means these sorts of weapons require a lot of man-hours and money to develop, and they all start with a really skilled hacker or cyber-researcher discovering a weakness in Apple's software and making sure it's kept a secret until they can sell to the highest bidder.

Claudio and Donncha understood enough about the zero-days market to know that a single reliable exploit chain might go for a million dollars or more. They had also seen and heard enough to believe that NSO was likely expending considerable cash on in-house research to develop its own proprietary zero-day weapons. The scale of NSO's business operations—with paying customers in dozens of countries—almost demanded it. "It's completely worth it for NSO if they have to spend five million a year on an exploit room for iPhone," Claudio told us, "if they can sell [Pegasus] to fifty different customers and they all pay millions."

Claudio was convinced by what he was seeing that the researchers, coders, and engineers at NSO were engaged in a constant game of hide-and-seek with one of the most (reputedly) security-conscious tech companies on the planet, Apple.

"Apple patches when they know about it," Claudio says. "But Apple can only fight who they know is out there. If they don't know about it, they can't patch. Apple's model is to fix what they can fix but then create as much friction as possible.

"Remember, when you say, 'I want one iMessage exploit, it's never one exploit," he explained. "When an iPhone gets compromised with an iMessage exploit, they are using maybe three, four, five different exploits packaged in one.

"There's so many things that [NSO technicians] have to compromise with an iPhone that make it a lot more complicated. They need to compromise a number of [different] security measures that Apple put into place purposely to add layers of complications before you can successfully get complete ownership of the device.

"The difficulty with compromising an iPhone is that you have to have a functioning exploit for all of these different security layers and all of it be reliable and working at once. They have to subvert all these other components of the operating system. One of them might get patched in the night, and they need to find something else to replace that one. So it's just not that straightforward. It's a pretty complex process."

▪▪▪▪▪▪▪

Laurent and I still had some serious concerns—Omar Radi and Khadija Ismayilova right at the top—but the Pegasus Project had moved well down the tracks on both the forensic analysis and the journalism in the month of April. We had identified important new partners; confirmed a number of infections; settled on key story lines. We were already beginning to plan a meeting for a much wider circle of partners to help us pursue those stories. On top of that, I felt like we were also beginning to get a handle on just what drove the rise and growth of NSO. As well as the spectacular overreach that followed. The world's most famous (and infamous) cybersurveillance company—from its founders down to its overworked researchers—had clearly come to understand the power and possibilities of vulnerability. You could say they built their entire business model on vulnerability. They did it in a country that had learned how to live with fear, and how to conquer it.

CHAPTER FOURTEEN

THE FIRST DON'T

When CEO Tim Cook and his gurus were deciding where to situate Apple Inc.'s largest R&D facility outside the United States, they had few limits. The company's annual net profits were around $40 billion a year and climbing, as was the global market share of its mobile phone. Cook and company had the planet to choose from, and they picked a midsize suburb pinched between sea and desert, 7,500 miles from their headquarters in Cupertino, California, in a country with less than nine million inhabitants and a gross domestic product in the vicinity of Norway's and Nigeria's. Apple erected a gleaming twenty-first-century glass box of an eco-friendly building in that faraway spot and reserved 180,000 square feet of office space for seven hundred of its employees—with room to grow. The talk in that building and beyond was that this new facility would be the launchpad for future versions of Apple's signature product, the iPhone.

If anybody at Apple had an inkling that a few dozen NSO cyber-researchers right around the corner from the new digs were spending their days and nights hunting for weaknesses to exploit in the iPhone operating software, they didn't show it. NSO was barely known at the time and not really on Apple's threat radar. So the relatively small spyware company's presence certainly didn't shake the conviction that the business district of Herzliya, just north of Tel Aviv, was the place to be. "Apple is in Israel," Tim Cook said on his visit to inaugurate the new

R&D center in February 2015, "because the engineering talent here is incredible."

Talent in Herzliya was hard to miss; an air of ambition and confidence permeated the restaurants and bars catering to the thousands of cybersecurity specialists and coders and software engineers working at dozens of neighborhood tech firms. The talk at table was often loud and learned and argumentative, whether debating the merits of the latest dating app or the latest job listings—must possess "a deep knowledge of radical Islam"—or the latest elections. This cohort was among the brightest 1 percent in Israel (the government had the test scores to prove it), working in the most lucrative and most glamorous field in the country. These young men and women were, quite literally, the Chosen People—identified as schoolchildren as possessors of uncommon intelligence, then encouraged to pursue math, physics, and computer science and to prepare for their extraordinary personal destinies. The way Europeans seek talent and cultivate skills on the soccer pitch, and Americans seek talent and cultivate skills on the basketball court, Israelis spend their time and energy creating the magicians of cyber.

The best of the best, known as "rosh gadol," or "big brains," are filtered at age seventeen or eighteen and slotted into the Israeli army's cyberintelligence units, where they can do their mandatory military service at a reasonable bodily remove from the dangers of combat. "When the IDF [Israel Defense Forces] really want to get someone, they might send officers to speak to this young person's parents, convincing them it's best for their son or daughter to go and study, and this will give them the best start for their life," says one of the rosh gadol. "That's like the common thing around here. Every Jewish mother wants their son to be a tech engineer these days, not a doctor. Doctor is second place."

The IDF demands a longer term of service for its cyberwarriors but offers in return a combination of training, coursework, real-world experience, and affirmation. *Anything is possible*, was the message members of this elite unit got from their commanders. *You can open any door if you just put your mind to it.*

The thousand or so rosh gadol who finish their service and enter the private sector each year walk away with instant connection to high-paying, high-tech jobs. They often follow their ex–team leaders into new start-up tech companies, lured in part by the very real possibility that they are in on the next big thing. Evidence abounded by 2015. There was plenty of talk in Herzliya and other high-tech hotbeds in Israel about startling new deals for companies led by former IDF cyberspecialists: an Israeli tech start-up reportedly sold to Oracle for $50 million; another to Apple for $300 million; another to Cisco for $500 million. Microsoft bought a data privacy firm for a rumored $320 million. Facebook paid $150 million for a mobile analytics company. PayPal, $60 million for a company that sees hacks coming before they happen. Even if the real purchase prices were half the rumored figure, they were still pretty good. *Anything is possible. You can open any door if you just put your mind to it.*

The Israeli cyberspecialists were the pride of a nation; a tiny country in the Middle East, then prime minister Benjamin Netanyahu often boasted, had made itself the equal of Russia, China, the United Kingdom, and the United States in high-tech. "Israel receives roughly one-fifth of the world's global private investment in cybersecurity," Netanyahu said in 2017. "And given that we are one-tenth of one percent of the world's population, it means we're punching about two hundred times above our weight. Not two times, not ten times, and not even one hundred times. Two hundred times above our weight. Which means there's something here that defies numerical size."

How DOES A tiny nation carved from a desert become, within seventy years of its founding, one of the world's five cybertechnology superpowers? Ask that question of anybody who got their cybertraining in the Israeli military, from foot soldier to top commander, and they will tell you it all boils down to two things—vulnerability and need. The State of Israel was founded to secure for the Jewish people something they had been denied in modern history: a place of their own, where they could live by their own lights and thrive, beyond threat of the next pogrom or the next Holocaust. This has been one hell of a struggle, maddeningly enduring and often bloody because Israel is an island surrounded by

countries that don't really want it there. Governments in the neighborhood range from the cold and unfriendly to the hostile to the irrational
and hateful. A few have attempted to destroy the Jewish safe haven by
force of arms.

The continuing existence of Israel has depended on constant watch-
fulness, on identifying and shoring up their own points of weakness
at any given moment, on the ability to anticipate where the next strike
might happen. The attack could be armored batteries rolling into Israeli
territory or lone suicide bombers intent on murdering a few dozen private citizens in bars, restaurants, or bus stops. "If [the Israelis] are not
good," says a former technical director in the French intelligence services, "they suffer."

The Israelis understood this from the beginning, back when Prime
Minister David Ben-Gurion was constructing the new country's defense
doctrine in the late 1940s. Military intelligence—the ability to "predict
new threats and supply early warning"—was a crucial pillar in Ben-
Gurion's doctrine. "This is the reason we need early warning," says Ehud
Schneorson, a former commander of the IDF's elite intelligence unit. "If
we had [tried to fund] an army as big as our neighbor's, we would have
collapsed economically during the first two or three years, and I don't
know how we could have survived.

"If you look at the Americans, intelligence is not as important—as
you can see from the period from Pearl Harbor to Hiroshima. Americans are big enough that they can take a huge blow at the beginning of
[World War II], and they can, you know, kick your ass after three or four
years. We don't have three or four years. We have forty-eight hours. This
is the way we live. Intelligence is very important."

That imperative was hardened and purified into something like steel
after the Yom Kippur War in 1973, when Egypt and Syria launched a
synchronized two-prong offensive blitz that the IDF did not see coming. By the time Israel's under-resourced Seventh Armored Brigade
halted the Syrian tanks' advance on the Golan Heights and reinforcements helped push them back to the edge of Damascus (and "saved the
State of Israel," according to Defense Minister Moshe Dayan), the IDF

had determined they would never again suffer that kind of intelligence failure.

Over the next five decades, Israel fed the best of its brainpower into its elite military intelligence service, known as Unit 8200, to make sure there would be no repeat disaster. The top-secret unit—its members were not allowed to speak its name or tell their closest family about their assignment—evolved with technology, from analog to digital, from landline to cell phone, and always one step ahead.

Innovation mattered above all in Unit 8200, and innovation could come from anywhere in the ranks. The rosh gadol who landed in 8200 weren't selected merely for their phenomenal test scores in math and physics. The scores were just the first filter. The potential intelligence ops were also screened for a certain suppleness of mind, a distrust of the common wisdom, and a willingness to challenge superiors. Debate was encouraged in 8200. Ideas trumped rank. "You are put into small teams where you study, brainstorm, train, analyze, solve problems, from early in the morning to very late at night," an 8200 veteran told a reporter from *Forbes* in 2016. "It's not a passive approach to information."

The cyberintelligence specialists in 8200 worked long and hard—sometimes full twenty-four-to-forty-eight-hour shifts during special operations. The young techs might spend their days and nights listening in on suspected terrorist cells, disabling an enemy's early-warning system before an Israeli airstrike, helping to engineer the Stuxnet malware that crippled Iran's nuclear program, or providing eyes and ears (by remote) for a secret combat mission. A young cybersoldier could find herself on the phone with a curious cabinet minister or an Israeli general or a commander whose troops were, at that very moment, in a life-and-death firefight.

"It's a hyper-stressed, hyper-worked technical environment where you have to make real choices," says one veteran of 8200. "Always under the gun to make decisions in time to be meaningful to somebody. Nobody tells you exactly what to do. They tell you, 'This is the problem; go figure it out.' With a crazy deadline. So you're inventing, being entrepreneurial, and only understanding what you were doing after the fact. But you have to do it because you don't have any other choice to meet the mission you were given."

"I was nineteen," another ex-8200 soldier told the reporter from *Forbes*. "While my friends in the States are doing their undergraduate work, you're doing that. By far it was the period in my life where I had the most responsibility and the most impact to other people."

"You're also part of this secret thing," says another former member of Unit 8200. "Sometimes you know about special operations or special abilities that nobody knows about outside and you feel you're special and part of this special ring. . . . Maybe the prime minister of Israel and the defense minister and a few others know, but not a lot of others. So it's pretty big."

IN THE FEW years after Apple set up its new R&D facility in the Promised Land and peopled it with the highly trained rosh gadol from Unit 8200, the Israeli cybersecurity industry boomed. The data was all there in the charts that Prime Minister Benjamin Netanyahu liked to flash on the big screen every year during his speeches at Cybertech and Cyber Week in Tel Aviv. The number of cybersecurity firms in Israel had grown from 171 in 2013 to 420 in 2017; private investments had sextupled in those same four years, to more than $800 million. Team8, a seed fund started by a former commander of 8200, was nearing the $100 million mark after new investments from Microsoft, Qualcomm, and Citi. The personal investment fund of Google executive chairman Eric Schmidt had been one of the first to kick money into that fund.

So Tim Cook and Apple were in the flood tide. Amazon, Google, and Microsoft had operations in Israel, along with NEC and IBM and Cisco. "We have special programs for comfortable landing for companies that are coming here," Netanyahu explained.

Netanyahu had become the chief proselytizer for the new industry, which gave him plenty chances to take credit as its chief visionary. The prime minister had taken a good look over the horizon and seen approaching danger. Israel had the stats on that, too: from 20,000 cyberattacks per week to almost 700,000—in just three years. Which meant, as Netanyahu said, "there is a tremendous business opportunity in the never-ending quest for security."

His pitches to international audiences of government defense experts, cybersecurity specialists, and salivating private investors also gave Netanyahu plenty of chances to take credit as the lead architect of his country's biggest growth sector. The Netanyahu government had invested "vast sums of money in our military intelligence, which goes to the army, the Mossad, Shin Bet, to other arms as well," the then prime minister told one cyber gathering in Tel Aviv. "So we create an enormous number of knowledge workers. . . . People who can deal with the internet. Can deal with the ramifications of this revolution. Both as workers and as entrepreneurs. And this is what we did in Israel. We took the sunk costs and created a business environment."

The Netanyahu government was executing a list of dos and don'ts to create this environment, consistent with its long drive to convert Israel's controlled economy ("not quite socialist but semi-socialist") into an oasis of free market capitalism ("Because markets know better than politicians," Netanyahu would say, "even prime ministers."). The dos included tax breaks for cybersecurity entrepreneurs and their financial backers, and public investment. The Netanyahu government built a national security laboratory next to a major university campus. "Be'er Sheva used to be known for camels and palm trees from the days of Abraham," Netanyahu says. "Be'er Sheva means seven wells; now there are wells of human creativity and cybercreativity. Everybody works together there in a small place, government, academia, the private sector. The best young minds we have."

Netanyahu's list of don'ts was much smaller, only one, really. "The first don't," he told the attendees of the Cybertech conference in Tel Aviv in January 2017, "is—don't overregulate."

THAT ONE AND only don't was a crucial driver of the consistently upward growth curve enjoyed by Israel's cyber industry. But NSO Group belonged to a small and sensitive subset of that industry—representing only about 5 percent of that sector, according to an estimate by the chief of Israel's National Cyber Directorate back in 2017—that needed close regulation. Most companies in Israel were marketing strictly defensive technologies that protected governments and businesses against cyberattack. NSO's signature technology, the Pegasus system, was engineered to invade and then take over a mobile phone in order to surveil the owner. This was a military-grade, offensive weapon.

Anybody who had seen stories about the terror attacks at *Charlie Hebdo* or the Bataclan theater in Paris, or a holiday party in San Bernardino, California, or a nightclub in Orlando, Florida, or the synagogue in Copenhagen could not doubt the necessity or the value of cybersurveillance weapons like Pegasus. There were 7,000 people killed in more than 1,400 separate ISIS-led terror attacks around the world in 2016 alone—in Germany, Belgium, Turkey, Kazakhstan, Indonesia, Bangladesh, Pakistan, and Saudi Arabia, just to name a few. Disrupting terror attacks before they happened was the great hope at that moment, and tools like Pegasus were much sought.

As a purveyor of these coveted offensive cyberweapons, NSO did have to operate within a regulatory regimen overseen by Israel's Ministry of Defense. The MOD required two separate licenses spelled out in the country's Defense Export Control Act. NSO and any other Israeli company selling these military-grade cyberweapons needed official permission just to talk to potential clients, and official permission to provide the technology to an end user. The MOD restricted sales to government entities like law enforcement and national security agencies and, in theory, restricted the countries to which Pegasus could be exported. The restrictions had a lot of give in the joints in 2017. Pegasus and the like was a fairly new technology, so the government minders hadn't really caught on to the potential for abuse. Then, too, cybersurveillance enjoyed the "don't overregulate" ethic that protected the rest of the cybersecurity industry in Israel. The Netanyahu government, according to the head of its National Cyber Directorate, was there to clear the way for "the private sector to do its thing."

The only hard-and-fast rule written into the Defense Export Control Act was that these cybersurveillance systems could not be sold to a country that was under an official United Nations Security Council arms embargo. This took North Korea, Lebanon, Libya, and a handful of African countries off the table. But the Israeli MOD had discretion to permit sales of the Pegasus system to any other foreign government, and the prime minister's office had the power to override any MOD denial.

The bulk of NSO's MOD licenses at the time involved law enforcement clients in Europe, which, as one French national security professional explained to us, was gaining the reputation as the "soft underbelly" for potential terrorists. European law enforcement really needed this tool, and they were a relatively uncontroversial client base. (These cops were almost always bound to seek court-approved warrants to use the spyware on an individual.) The bulk of the company's revenue, however, came from big-spending countries with dicey human rights records, most notably the Kingdom of Saudi Arabia. The Israeli defense chieftains trusted NSO with sales to regimes like Saudi Arabia or the UAE or Morocco because they trusted NSO executives to abide by the one unwritten but inviolable rule: they kept their mouth shut about the identities of their end users.

There was talk among the 8200 alums that the company might be walking dangerously close to the ethical line; many preferred to steer clear. A few even made it plain to recruiters at other companies that they didn't care to use their skills on anything but defense, true cybersecurity, and they wouldn't work for any company trafficking in spyware. But with Unit 8200 disgorging a thousand or so hyper-trained cyberbrains every year, Shalev Hulio and Omri Lavie didn't have much trouble filling their growing ranks with capable young men and women. Shalev did have to work a little harder than most because he was an outsider among the rosh gadol, who don't have a lot of trust for outsiders to begin with. "He's like a very nice person, but he gives me a feeling of a car salesman," says one cybersecurity engineer Shalev tried to recruit. "Always has a big smile and talking and trying to sell you. He's a very friendly person, but every time I check a little bit deeper about something he said, nothing adds up."

What Shalev and Omri did have going for them in corporate recruitment, even as outsiders, was that the stated values of NSO were not so different from Unit 8200's. *We're saving lives here.* The work itself was challenging, too: like the chance to go head-to-head with Apple's engineers, reputed to be the best and the best-resourced in the cybersecurity business. And the chance to get the better of them. NSO "became very good about 2017 and 2018," says a former commander of 8200, "because the deals they had with the Gulf infused tons of money into the company and because of working with the Europeans and against real targets. I think it matured their technology." If you were a young rosh gadol just entering the job market, the pay was a serious draw; an NSO hire right out of the army might see his salary jump from $2,500 a month to $25,000 overnight.

Back in 2017, that was certainly enough to make it possible to ignore the sideways glances of the 8200 alums who stuck to the defense side of cyber, or to dismiss malicious talk around Herzliya. "They have the third tier of talent that we have in Israel," an executive at a successful start-up in Tel Aviv would say. "These are the guys that don't have the right sense of smell. We have a saying in Hebrew that money always has a smell. And they don't smell the stinky smells of where that money came from."

WHATEVER THE TALK among the world of 8200, Shalev and Omri and the rest of NSO must have taken heart in the support they got from the Israeli officialdom, like when Citizen Lab produced a series of reports toward the end of 2017 about the abuses of Pegasus technology in Mexico. Researchers in Toronto had documented Pegasus spyware attacks against about twenty people there, including reporters, human rights lawyers, opposition politicians, and even the outspoken parents of one of the student-teachers taken off the bus and murdered by a drug cartel in Ayotzinapa. When Shalev and Omri refused to speak to any specific charges but suggested instead a nefarious anti-Semitic plot afoot within Citizen Lab, Israeli government apparatchiks joined the chorus singing cabal and conspiracy. "I can tell you that's for sure that we see the fingerprints and footprints of anti-Israel and even anti-Semitic elements [at Citizen Lab]," says one of Netanyahu's key advisers from the time, without adducing a whit of evidence.

The Citizen Lab reports did prompt a legal petition in Israel to forbid the sales of Pegasus to governments that regularly violated human rights, but the petition was waved away. The Supreme Court in Israel refused to interfere with MOD decision-making, or to air the suit in public, or to even release the full text of the judgment to the public. The judges agreed with the Netanyahu government that the details of the cyberweapons license needed to be kept under seal. "Our economy, as it happens, rests not a little on that export," Supreme Court President Justice Esther Hayut had once said.

THE PROTECTION AFFORDED by this government-wrought cloak of secrecy had swelled Shalev's confidence to something approaching impunity by 2018. The sense of invincibility was hard to miss in the aftermath of the violent assassination of Saudi journalist Jamal Khashoggi, who was a contributing columnist for the *Washington Post.* News of the shocking murder of this occasional critic of the Saudi royal family made headlines around the world in October 2018. Khashoggi had been lured to the Saudi consulate in Istanbul, Turkey, where a team of fifteen men killed him, sawed him to bits, and disposed of the body. The CIA's official assessment was that the operation was authorized by Saudi Crown Prince Mohammed bin Salman. The kill team, according to the CIA report, included seven members of the Rapid Intervention Force, MBS's personal protective detail: "The RIF exists to defend the Crown Prince, answers only to him, and had directly participated in earlier dissident suppression operations in the Kingdom and abroad at the Crown Prince's direction. We judge that members of the RIF would not have participated in the operation against Khashoggi without Mohammed bin Salman's approval."

The NSO spyware was also implicated in the Saudis' latest "dissident suppression operation." Pegasus had reportedly been used by the kingdom to track Khashoggi and a number of people in his circle. One of them had filed his own lawsuit against NSO in Tel Aviv. Shalev, who was then in the middle of a deal with another private equity firm to restructure the company and pump some more cash into its operation, went on a publicity campaign to defend NSO and its hundreds of dedicated employees.

This campaign culminated in a one-on-one interview with Lesley Stahl of *60 Minutes*, in March 2019.

"It's been reported that you yourself went to Riyadh in Saudi Arabia, you yourself sold Pegasus to the Saudis for fifty-five million dollars," Stahl told Shalev near the top of the broadcast interview.

Shalev just grinned. "Don't believe newspapers," he said.

"Is that a denial?" Stahl pressed.

Shalev remained silent, still grinning.

"No," Stahl said.

Shalev more than held his own after that, though, crediting Pegasus with saving "tens of thousands" of lives. He claimed that he knew of only three "real" cases of misuse in the eight years of NSO's existence: "Out of thousands of cases of saving lives, three was a misuse, and those people or those organizations that misuse the system, they are no longer a customer, and they will never be a customer again."

On the question of the alleged cybersurveillance of Jamal Khashoggi and his close friends and relatives, Shalev was direct and unequivocal. "The Khashoggi murder is horrible, really horrible," he said. "And therefore, when I first heard their accusations that our technology has been used on Jamal Khashoggi or on his relatives, I started an immediate check about it. And I can tell you very clearly, we had nothing to do with this horrible murder. . . . I can tell you that we've checked, and we have a lot of ways to check. And I can guarantee you our technology was not used on Jamal Khashoggi or his relatives."

CHAPTER FIFTEEN

"NEW TECHNIQUES"

Sandrine

Claudio Guarnieri had developed uncommon mental and physical dexterity in a decade of tracking cybersurveillance weapons like Pegasus. Just this moment, on the floor of *Le Monde*'s barely lit auditorium, at the end of a long day in early May 2021, Claudio was putting both to good use. The head of Amnesty International's Security Lab was sitting in a low-slung armchair, his legs akimbo, with his right ankle resting on his left knee to form his own working table. He was typing furiously on a laptop that rested on that makeshift table, while occasionally glancing at the screen of an Android phone, which was connected to the laptop by a short wire and rested precariously on the arch of his right shoe. Claudio was also mindful of the Pulitzer Prize–winning reporter seated just a few feet away and nudging closer, trying to make out the characters dancing across the screen of his laptop. Dana Priest, of the *Washington Post*, had lots of questions.

"Okay, what does that mean?" she asked, pointing at his screen.

"Just one second," Claudio said, patiently, and continued typing in silence for about half a minute. "All right," he finally said, picking up the cell phone to read something on the screen. "I think I found something."

"Oh good," Dana said and then watched as Claudio fell silent again and went back to punching keys on his laptop, and glancing over at the phone on his shoe, and punching more keys. This went on for three excruciating minutes, while Dana cooled her jets. She really wanted the secrets inside that cell phone unlocked. Like right now. Because there was a very real chance that device held evidence of Pegasus spyware used against one of Jamal Khashoggi's relatives around the time of his assassination. For Dana and everybody else from the *Washington Post*, especially after Shalev Hulio's repeated denials, implicating Pegasus in Khashoggi's murder was, as Dana called it, "the golden get."

Each of our growing number of reporting partners understood the potential explosiveness of this story; if we could nail it down, it would likely be the marquee story of the Day One rollout of the Pegasus Project publication. But Dana was especially invested. She had met Jamal Khashoggi on a trip to Bahrain in 2013 and always remembered him as soft-spoken and cautious; he was clear-eyed about the shortcomings of the Saudi regime at the time but also one of its most dependable defenders, as he had been for decades. Jamal had even worked as a media adviser for the Saudi ambassador in Washington and London. But when newly anointed Crown Prince Mohammed bin Salman began purging Saudis he found threatening to his personal rule—by arrest and later by execution—Jamal believed he had to choose a side. "I spent six months silent, reflecting on the state of my country and the stark choices before me," he wrote in his debut column in the *Washington Post*'s Global Opinion section in September 2017. "It was painful to me several years ago when several friends were arrested. I said nothing. I didn't want to lose my job or my freedom. I worried about my family.

"I have made a different choice now. I have left my home, my family and my job, and I am raising my voice. To do otherwise would betray those who languish in prison. I can speak when so many cannot. I want you to know that Saudi Arabia has not always been as it is now. We Saudis deserve better."

Khashoggi warned again and again that the new crown prince, Mohammed bin Salman, known as MBS, was a volatile and retrograde force in the Kingdom of Saudi Arabia. "Replacing old tactics of intolerance with new ways of repression is not the answer," he wrote of MBS in April 2018.

Jamal Khashoggi's willingness to raise his voice cost him. Just over a year after he published the first of his fourteen Global Opinion columns, he was dead, brutally assassinated by the crown prince's chosen hit team in a foreign country. "It was such an outrageous crime," Dana says. "I don't remember ever having a case of a journalist who was so clearly killed by a government without that government even trying to hide it. It broke every norm of humanity of civilized nations and of international law. And it was all just right there in our face."

There were serious allegations, and even scattered bits of evidence, that Jamal or people around him had been targeted by Pegasus, which was then used to track him just before his murder and to track his family and friends just after his death. But nothing solid enough to penetrate NSO's wall of denial. New possibilities, however, were beginning to emerge from the data that Amnesty International, Forbidden Stories, and our early partners had access to.

We had identified cell phone numbers in the data belonging to Jamal's fiancée, Hatice Cengiz, and her attorney; to Jamal's son Abdullah; to Jamal's emergency contact in Istanbul, Yasin Aktay, who also happened to be a close friend of Turkish president Recep Tayyip Erdoğan; even to the prosecutor in Istanbul who was overseeing the investigation into Jamal's murder. All of those selections had taken place in the immediate aftermath of the assassination, but we hadn't yet approached any of these people about allowing the Security Lab to do the forensics on their cell phones.

The cell phone resting on Claudio's foot that evening in May 2021 was of a higher order. The number of this cell phone had also been in the data, and its owner identified less than a month earlier by a different reporter at the *Post,* who had the number in her contact file. The phone belonged to Hanan Elatr, an Egyptian-born stewardess living in the Washington suburb of Alexandria, Virginia, who had quietly wed Jamal in a religious ceremony four months before his death. (Neither Hanan, the wife, nor Hatice, the fiancée, seemed to have been aware of the other.)

Hanan had known Jamal for almost a decade, but they had grown close in 2016, while he was living under quasi–house arrest in Saudi Arabia and often depressed. After Jamal fled to Washington in 2017,

Hanan says, she called him every morning at seven to buck him up. Jamal had promised his terrified ex-wife in Riyadh that he would quietly disappear into the US and refrain from speaking ill of the Saudi regime until things changed. Until it was safe. But Hanan encouraged him to accept the offer from the *Washington Post*, she told us, and to use his column to call attention to what was happening in his home country. The relationship turned romantic in March 2018, Hanan says, and the couple were married that June.

Hanan was hesitant to help when Dana first approached her. She had lost her job with Emirates airline and was living in hiding, afraid she and her family were being watched by the security services of Saudi Arabia and the UAE. But Dana, with the backing of Hanan's attorney, convinced her to help us. Hanan allowed Dana to do a backup of the two Android phones she was using in the months before Jamal's murder, which Dana uploaded to Claudio and Donncha's forensic platform. Some of the lines of code looked interesting on the screens in Berlin, but Claudio had been unable to make any definite findings because, as he had already learned from long experience, Android backups offered so little data to work with. Claudio asked Dana to bring the phones with her to our all-hands-on-deck meeting in Paris in the second week of May 2021. Hanan relented, entrusting Dana with the phones and all the necessary passwords. So there sat one of those cell phones in Paris, perched faceup on Claudio's shoe, while he typed away at his laptop for those three long minutes.

"Okay, so this is one," Claudio finally said to Dana, showing her an SMS message on Hanan's phone. "This is one message."

"Is that coming to her?" Dana asked.

"Yeah."

Dana pointed out that the message was made to look like it was sent by Hanan's sister, who was inviting Hanan to download a new photo from Photobucket.

"Yeah, so this is a tactic we've seen many times," Claudio explained. "They send a message pretty generic like that, and they include a link."

Dana was writing down the domain name of the link sent to Hanan: https://myfiles[.]photo/sVIKHJE.

"This is definitely a message that would have likely triggered the exploitation of the browser," Claudio said.

"So would the person have to click on that link?" Dana asked.

"Yeah. They would have to click on that, and it would open the browser on the phone. And then by opening the browser, they would have attempted to trigger the exploit."

Dana asked if Claudio had a date for the exploit, and he read the time stamp of the message right off the phone: April 15, 2018.

"This I think appears also in the browser history," Claudio explained, pointing to the malicious domain name. "This basically means that she probably clicked on the link at the time."

"Wait, sorry, what shows you that she probably clicked on it?"

"Could be because it appeared also in the [cell phone's] project history," Claudio explained.

"Okay."

"And there's another one," Claudio said, while scrolling through the phone's SMS messages. "This is a bit older."

"So just to point this out," Dana said, still processing the first date she'd heard: April 15, 2018. "This is *before* the murder."

The revelation that evening was like so many in the middle stages of the Pegasus Project—a major leap ahead and still a bit short of the mark. We could say without caveat that an end user of Pegasus had attempted to infect a mobile phone belonging to someone in Khashoggi's most intimate circle, his wife. But Android phones simply didn't retain enough digital information—there was no data usage log to record any of the malicious process executions, for instance—to quickly or easily provide evidence of a successful infection. Or to allow us to say with certainty which Pegasus end user had made the attacks.

Claudio trudged off that night with Hanan's two cell phones tucked in his backpack, promising to take a closer look back at his hotel that night. "I'm going to do some more digging," he said.

THE ONE-ON-ONE DIGITAL forensic session with Dana marked the end of two long and difficult days for Claudio, and for Laurent and me and everybody else on the Pegasus Project. We were in the middle of a three-and-a-half-day conference Laurent and I had convened to reveal our investigation to a wider set of journalists and to settle on a plan going forward. We had made enormous progress in that short stretch but still had a lot of unanswered questions and a lot of nervous new partners deciding how to handle the big hot cybersurveillance potato we had just dropped in their laps.

The first circle of partners—*Le Monde*, *Die Zeit*, *Süddeutsche Zeitung*, and the *Washington Post*—had all sent reporters and editors, some of them new to the team. The newer partners, all of whom had joined the project when they agreed to allow the Security Lab to run the forensics on employee phones, also sent reporters. This included the *Wire* from India, *Direkt36* from Hungary, *Aristegui Noticias* and *Proceso* from Mexico, and the Organized Crime and Corruption Reporting Project (OCCRP), which specialized in Eastern Europe, the Caucasus, and Central Asia. The least settled journalists in Paris were from the media organizations who were learning the details of the Pegasus Project for the first time—folks who knew nothing of the specifics of the leak and nothing of our reporting to date: the Belgian daily *Le Soir* and the Belgian weekly investigative magazine, *Knack*, the Beirut-based media site *Daraj*, and the *Guardian*, headquartered in London.

The *Guardian*, with an editorial staff of more than six hundred and a daily average readership approaching a million, offered the Pegasus Project an opportunity for remarkable reach and a solid team of reporters and editors. We had been eager to inform the *Guardian* about the data leak and get them on board because we knew exactly what their team would bring to the Pegasus Project. The newspaper had enormous resources, and Stephanie Kirchgaessner and a few of the *Guardian*'s other journalists had been doing very good reporting on cyberintelligence for many years. The *Guardian* had also been a trusted partner of Forbidden Stories going back to our very first project. Not including the London-based media outlet in the first circle of the Pegasus Project had been a really tough call, but Laurent and I were so afraid for the security of our source that we made the difficult choice to keep the circle smaller than we had wanted. And as soon as we reached out to Paul Lewis, the

Guardian's investigative editor, in late April, he began gathering a small team to join us for the meeting in Paris. Part of the allure, Paul later admitted, was the chance to get out of London, where he had been stuck during the yearlong Covid pandemic.

Not that our city was great fun at that point. President Emmanuel Macron had just extended France's third Covid lockdown, which meant all bars, restaurants, museums, and theaters remained closed. Streets were eerily quiet during the day and ghostly after 7 p.m., the hour of the officially enforced curfew. All of the partners and potential partners who first gathered on the afternoon of May 11, 2021, had submitted negative results from their recently completed PCR tests. An editor from the *Wire* who was scheduled to attend was unable to leave India because he tested positive.

The initial sessions of the three-and-a-half-day conference, Tuesday afternoon and Wednesday morning, were loose free-for-alls at our office in the Bastille district. We had set up workstations where each of the new partners could get on a secure laptop and take a look at the reporting, fact-checking, and forensics done to this point. This was their first look at the secure platform we had set up to communicate with all the partners, where they could post their most recent reporting for all to see, and where the Security Lab could share the results of its forensic analyses. Claudio and the Forbidden Stories team were there to walk the newly initiated through the steps for entering the platform, then show them how to navigate through various folders, how to update files, and how to do it all in secrecy. "Passwords, lots of them," Paul Lewis remembers of his first session. "Various secure protocols. A lot of them. But then, finally, we were in. And I remember looking at that stream of phone numbers with different country codes all over the world. Tens of thousands of phone numbers.

"Data of this kind had not been leaked before, certainly pertaining to NSO technology used by governments around the world. Not on this scale." Paul was all focus and intensity in those first sessions. ("Later I'd realize that's just Paul," one of his colleagues would say.) The *Guardian*'s lead investigative editor seemed goggle-eyed as he noted people in the data that we had already identified: the sitting presidents of France

and Mexico, the prime minister of Pakistan, the former prime minister of Belgium, Emirati princesses, the inner circle of the Dalai Lama.
The list of identified selections included opposition politicians in the
supposedly democratic nations of India, Mexico, and Hungary; human
rights activists and lawyers from around the world; journalists by the
hundreds, some of them now in prison, or assassinated. This could be
a game-changer, Paul saw immediately, a chance to reveal the growing
dangers of NSO and the rest of the for-profit cybersurveillance industry
run amok.

"What really felt overwhelming," *Guardian* reporter Stephanie Kirchgaessner later said, "was how could we possibly do justice to this treasure trove of information. As excited as I was from the first moment . . .
there's also a real sense of responsibility."

Paul found himself running the mechanics of this investigation over
and over in his head. Verification, fact-checking, confirming targeting
or infection through forensics, selecting the most exemplary stories, and
then scrambling reporters to dig into them. Collaboration was the best
way forward, he understood. The only way forward. "No single news
organization, not Forbidden Stories on its own, not the *Washington
Post* or the *Guardian* or *Le Monde* or *Süddeutsche Zeitung* or *Die Zeit*,
none of us could have done this on our own," he would say. "The only
way it was going to work is if we all worked together." The scale of the
data Paul had seen that first afternoon did little to shake his conviction
that this investigation would require months; the best time for publication, by his reckoning, was October 2021.

Timing wasn't the only hurdle for Paul. He and a number of other
new partners were anxious to hear more about the digital forensics we
had been conducting. Claudio Guarnieri had his work cut out for him
in session three of the meeting, when he was scheduled to present to the
partners, old and new, and all professionally skeptical, the Security Lab's
methodology and its findings to date.

CLAUDIO'S BOSS, DANNA Ingleton, led off the discussion of forensics
in the auditorium at *Le Monde*. This was the first moment representa-

tives of all the Pegasus Project partners had gathered in one room, at the same time, to listen to presentations and ask questions as a group. As at any gathering of journalists, the lectures and prepared speeches quickly gave way to questions. Paul Lewis had a big one, which he asked before Danna could hand off the program to Claudio: "You said you don't know who will peer-review, but can you just explain a bit more about what that means? Is it the report that's peer-reviewed or is it the actual forensics that you're offering to another party to do their own analysis on? How do you envisage that?"

Danna said she'd let Claudio answer the technical aspects of the question, but she wanted to explain one thing. "The layman's term is that the peer review of the report will be a peer review of the forensics, right?" she said. "The problem, and I don't think it's a bad problem. It's a great problem. It's that a lot of this is really new techniques. If everybody knew how to do these forensics, we wouldn't be in the position we're in. This has been a lot of figuring it out as we go. So there isn't necessarily one person that could look at it and be like, 'That's exactly right, according to the textbook.'" Claudio and Donncha, she wanted it understood, were writing a whole new textbook, much of it from scratch.

I wondered if maybe Claudio was chafing a bit already. He understood the necessity for peer review, but it was like his abilities were being called into question before he had had a chance to say a word. He also understood that Citizen Lab, while unspoken, was at the center of this peer review discussion. Citizen Lab was probably the best-known and best-regarded cybersurveillance weapons tracker in the world at that point, particularly concerning NSO and its Pegasus system. But Laurent and I, as well as the entire team at Amnesty International's Security Lab, were a bit reluctant to involve researchers from Citizen Lab in the project this early, when secrecy was crucial. We managed to table the discussion of peer review for later and move on to Claudio's formal talk.

The agenda we had distributed allotted a little more than an hour for Claudio to walk all the partners through the data we had been given access to, the forensic methodology that he and Donncha had put in place, and the results they had achieved so far. Two hours later, Claudio still had the stage. His formal presentation was interrupted by questions from the audience. But the longer he talked, the less those questions felt like challenges, and the more they felt like genuine curiosity. The more Claudio talked, the more inquisitive these journalists became.

Claudio's presentation, stop and go as it became, was detailed and masterful. He explained exactly how the Security Lab's forensic tool had been evolving in the last couple of years, and exactly how the tool was learning to find previously unseen evidence of Pegasus attacks and infections. He was also frank about the limitations; he and Donncha, for example, were unlikely to ever find a copy of the spyware on an infected phone. "[The malware] is not actually stored on the phone," Claudio said in answer to one question. "So if you reboot the phone or your battery runs out, the infection cleans up. But [the Pegasus end users] don't care because they were just going to reattack you again at the next opportunity. And that's just pretty automatic. They can decide on Tuesday, we'll just get all the SMS messages, and then we'll get them again on Thursday. It's as opportunistic as it gets because there is no condition that stops them from being successful. As long as they have the exploit working, they can exploit you like five times a day and just upload whatever they want in that particular moment."

He also offered the journalists in the room a brief history lesson, walking them through the various stages of the evolving and improving Pegasus technology: from the crude, social engineering- and SMS-based one-click exploits, to the multiple reconstitutions of the Pegasus internet infrastructure, to the deviously tweaked process execution names that mimicked legitimate iOS process names, and finally to NSO's mastery of zero-click, zero-day exploits that took advantage of vulnerabilities its researchers had discovered in iMessage and Apple Photos. Even if Apple found a breach and patched it, Claudio explained, NSO was often capable of finding a new vulnerability and engineering a new exploit.

Craig Timberg, who covered tech and tech companies for the *Post*, stopped Claudio for clarification. He seemed a bit surprised that the world's most security-conscious tech company hadn't blocked Pegasus. "If iMessage is the main [attack] vector at this point is there something about the way Apple has engineered iMessage that makes it particularly vulnerable?" he asked. "Is there something that they should be doing to make it harder, to make it less likely?"

Claudio paused for just a bit, as I had seen him do hundreds of times before, and mulled. He meant to be precise in what he said. "So it's not necessarily something that Apple has done wrong with iMessage," he explained. "The reason why it is so popular is the same reason why SMS messages with links were very popular at one time, and then [NSO] abandoned that because they got caught too often. But the reason essentially is that they know that that [iMessage] application will be on every iPhone. So it's a very juicy target from an exploitation perspective because once you have one exploit, you can exploit all of them."

Near the end of his presentation, Claudio told the group that time might be running out on the Security Lab's investigation because Pegasus attacks were becoming more sophisticated and more difficult to detect. He suspected that NSO engineers might even be aware that the Security Lab or somebody else was now stalking Pegasus. The watchers were watching the watchers watching the watchers.

"They definitely have taken notice of people doing forensics, I suppose," Claudio explained. "If the phone is compromised, they can see that someone is doing a backup, for example, or they might be able to. So it's becoming more difficult to do the forensics exactly for that reason. And when I say it's becoming, I mean as of the last four weeks. . . . They are evidently taking steps, so it's becoming harder is the first issue. The second issue is the more we do it, the more they will pay notice. And to me, that's why it's critical that we move as fast as we can. There's nothing we can do to be invisible in this process from a technical point of view."

Nearly two hours in, Paul Lewis raised his hand. "Can I ask three just really quick questions?" he said. "But first of all, I want to say thank you because it's a really impressive body of work." The entire audience burst into applause. The group was plainly dazzled by what they had heard.

THE QUESTION OF peer review kept coming up in other sessions, and one of those exchanges elicited from Claudio maybe the most telling statement of the entire conference. To be frank, it was kind of surprising. Not what Claudio said but that he said it aloud. I had been working closely with Claudio for eight or nine months by then, and he had always been careful not to overstate the results of the forensic analyses that he and Donncha had been conducting. He was almost allergic to "overhype," especially in front of a group of journalists, so he delivered this mini-soliloquy in his inimitable manner. He didn't raise the volume of his voice, or change the tone, or even move forward in his auditorium seat. "I wanted to spend a couple of words, I guess, to contextualize what I believe is the value of the forensic evidence we have got so far," he told the full contingent of partners. "The leads that the data is giving us are extraordinary because the amount of success we're having with the forensics is, to me, unprecedented. And let me tell you that I've been working on the surveillance industry for a decade. I have probably checked hundreds of computers and phones in these years, and if I had a zero-point-five-percent success before this, it would have been good. And now I think we're close to eighty percent. So to me that's a sign that this is pretty strong."

This was the boldest assertion I had ever heard Claudio make about his confidence in the data and in the forensics. At that point, he even allowed himself a quick chuckle, as if he might have surprised himself. "We have all of the documentation that is needed," he continued. "The technical findings are ready to be aggregated and going to be made available as soon as necessary, and we'll make that available to whoever the group decides needs to vet the work."

THE OTHER SESSIONS included presentations by the first circle of partners about the work they had already done and the stories they were already pursuing. We covered Mexico, Hungary, Morocco, India, Azerbaijan, among others. The presentation on Saudi Arabia was the longest because the Khashoggi case was central to this project. "This would be a big deal, you know, because NSO has managed to kind of wiggle out of their responsibility in this," said one presenter. There were discussions about how to divide up the reporting in different countries, who might have ins at NSO, and what kind of response we could expect from the company in the lead-up to publication. We took time to discuss some basic ground rules: never mention NSO to a source; verify every phone number in the data, with double or triple sourcing, before publishing a name; and ask permission from the victims and the selected targets before publishing their names, at least for people who were not public figures.

We also took some time to discuss the proper order of the stories, which would likely roll out over four or five days, the need to have some understandings about what we would *not* be able to assert, and the question of how much editorial leeway the partners would have in shaping their own packages.

Everybody agreed that the great opportunity of this investigation was that we could reveal the shocking scale of the weaponization of cyber-surveillance tools. But scale also had its drawbacks, as was evident from the discussions we had about timing. The group had basically agreed to our suggestions about leading with the stories of human rights activists and journalists and holding the big names for later days. We also agreed on optimal timing for when to approach government officials, politicians, celebrities, spokespeople at Apple and other tech companies, and especially officials from NSO and their client countries. The only truly difficult issue was the publication date. Laurent and I were pushing for the middle of July, which was only about eight weeks away; the *Guardian* had come to Paris hoping to persuade us to push our deadline back to the fall. After almost three days of meetings, it was apparent that the *Guardian* was not alone.

Craig Timberg, of the *Washington Post*, had trouble seeing how we were going to pack all this work into two months. He counted at least eight stories he thought the *Post* would want to tackle, and time to do maybe three of them well. He said, "We are going to enter a world of trade-offs of time versus depth and quality."

I thought we were already close to having solid, publishable stories in Mexico, India, Morocco, and Hungary. With a little luck, we could nail down the Khashoggi story. The more we prolonged this investigation, the greater the chance of burning our source. "Just based on the stories and the work, mid-October is much more reasonable," I heard Laurent tell one of our new partners. "But this is based on the risk assessment for the source."

Bastian Obermayer, of *Süddeutsche Zeitung*, stepped up and defended our choice of July. He reminded everybody that we probably had enough leads in the data to report for six years and not exhaust the stories; and the initial publication was hardly the end of the investigation. "Once we throw a stone in the water there will be the chance that the story develops, that more sources will come up to us and say, 'Listen, I've got more,'" Bastian said. "We're not throwing a small stone in the water. We have this big chunk."

In the end, it was Paul Lewis who really summarized the meetings, and the near future for the entire collaboration, with his own proposed trade-offs. He wanted a measure of editorial flexibility for each of the partners, and something even more crucial. "The whole project obviously rests on the data, the interpretation of the data and the forensics," he told the group. "The work that Claudio and AI have done has been phenomenal. It's really fantastic. I'm in awe. *But* it is just one organization. And we need to be one hundred percent sure. So for me, the peer review is really key here.

"And I think it's in all of our interests. I think it's in your interest, AI's interest, for us to be completely one hundred percent sure on this. And I think if we can fix those two things, if we can be collectively comfortable with the peer review, and if we can all have more flexibility as news organizations, I think late July is possible for us."

CHAPTER SIXTEEN

"A VERY IMPORTANT LINE OF RESEARCH"

Laurent

The lawyer waved us off when Sandrine and I asked him to place his cell phone and his laptop outside his office for our first closed-door meeting. "Look, we all know we're under surveillance," he said. "I know they can hack me." He wasn't specific about *who* exactly could do this hacking, but he had been specializing in press freedom and media issues for years, with many high-profile clients, including our partner *Le Monde*. Of course he had adversaries who would try to run cybersurveillance on him. That's why he was careful about what went into and came out of his mobile phone. So what was the big deal?

The Pegasus Project partners had all agreed on a hard date for publication, less than two months away, and we really needed to put our legal team in place. Our lead attorney had to know everything, but we didn't feel comfortable talking about the most sensitive issues we were facing with electronics in the room. Sandrine and I insisted again—cell phones and laptops outside the meeting. He did agree, but it was apparent he was just humoring us.

This slightly blasé stance of his did not last long into our discussion.

We explained to him that we were investigating NSO and its spyware system. We explained the capabilities of Pegasus, the zero-click exploits, for instance, and how an end user could activate the microphone and camera of a compromised phone by remote to capture live conversations. Veteran though he was, he was plainly shocked by what he was hearing. He didn't ask a lot of questions while we walked him through what we had uncovered up to that day, May 21, 2021: the leaked list of fifty thousand mobile phone numbers selected as potential targets by Pegasus end users around the world; verified identities by the hundreds of those selected numbers, from journalists to human rights defenders to opposition politicians to private citizens who happened to be in contact with the targets. Many attorneys.

We outlined the Security Lab's digital forensics, and how Claudio and Donncha had been able to isolate traces of attack or infection on most of the selected phones we had analyzed; somewhere north of 80 percent for iPhones. This, we felt, was a very strong indication that the list was solid. Jamal Khashoggi's widow was in the data, and we now had evidence of Pegasus attacks *before* his murder. Emmanuel Macron was on the list, along with more than a dozen officials in his administration, all selected by the NSO client in Morocco. The story was going to spread across Europe, Asia, the Middle East, and the Americas, with some serious geopolitical fallout, we told him. We expected that Forbidden Stories and its sixteen reporting partners would draw serious fire, possibly even lawsuits.

We needed his legal advice on our approaches to various victims, I explained, as well as our approach to NSO and the Pegasus system end users. We also wanted help in framing the stories, in vetting the language of the specific allegations we would be making, and in advising just how far we could go with the evidence we collected. Coordination with the legal departments from the various partners to make sure we had consistency would be critical. Above all, we needed his counsel on how best to ensure we kept our promise to protect the source.

Like the best of attorneys, he was already thinking ahead. The immediate post-publication time was sure to be the most intense, he warned, and the potential for lawsuits was not likely to be the biggest problem we faced. Source protection worried him most. The appearance of President Macron and all those French government officials was a big red flag. The Macron administration would almost certainly make the claim that national security trumped the protection of a journalist's source. The French secret services could make the argument that their agents abroad were in danger. They could even demand that we reveal the entire list, he said. French security officials might even show up at Forbidden Stories with a warrant to take possession of the computer drive that contained the data.

The good news, we told him, was that we didn't have any such drive. Forbidden Stories and Amnesty International alone, and none of our other partners, could access the original raw data. That *was* good, he agreed. "The [security services] can try," he said, "but let's make sure that in case the police come to search your offices they won't find anything problematic."

THE COUNTDOWN TO publication was ticking for the first time since we had started the investigation. The Pegasus Project felt real now, but it also felt like something that could grow beyond our control. The partners were adding more reporters to the project and beginning to scramble them into the field all over the world. The chances of a mistake that unmasked the investigation increased by the day. I could see it weigh on Sandrine. Among her many jobs on the project was to keep everybody within our strict security protocol. There had been a disturbing breach even before our Paris meeting broke up. One of the newer partners had called an opposition politician in his country for a background interview about being a potential target of Pegasus spyware. The rule Sandrine had laid down for all the partners was that nobody approaches opposition politicians—who have notoriously loose lips—until the very end of the investigation. And then only when we had discussed it together and cleared it.

"What the fuck!" Sandrine said, in private, when she heard of the call.

She was a tad more diplomatic, but not much less forceful, when she confronted the journalist who made the mistake. "Maybe you missed part of the explanation," she told him, "but it cannot happen again."

THE PEGASUS PROJECT was shuddering up to full throttle, and the pressure was rising on all the partners. I felt especially sympathetic for the

reporters and editors at *Le Monde*, who would be in the same national
security soup as Forbidden Stories. They were investigating multiple stories about Morocco, many of which were sure to have serious geopolitical consequences. *Le Monde* reporters Martin Untersinger and Damien
Leloup, the two tech specialists at the newspaper, had been working
with the list of phone numbers we had supplied them for more than four
months, identifying selected targets and hunting patterns. New surprises hove up from the data every week. NSO's client in Morocco had
not only selected Macron and most of his key ministers but also officials
from other European and African countries, a former US ambassador,
and even members of King Mohammed VI's inner circle and his close
family. Damien had just found the king's father-in-law in the data. The
breadth and reach of these selections (more than five thousand in all)
suggested manic activity in the Moroccan intelligence services, accompanied by an extreme lack of discipline.

Martin and Damien were spending a lot of time trying to discern
motive, which seemed to center on Morocco's concerns in its own near
neighborhood. Macron's phone had been selected around the time he
was traveling in Africa. His main adviser on African issues was selected
by the Moroccan client at the same time. The decades-long battle over
the independence of Western Sahara—which King Mohammed VI
meant to rule, as a matter of Moroccan pride—seemed a strong candidate for motive. But Damien was having a hard time reckoning the path
of the client's mania. "We've thought of several explanations," Damien
told the partners. "None of them is extremely convincing."

Help would have to wait. The risk of asking precise questions of
the French government this far out from publication was too great.
The *Le Monde* reporters even had to be careful in double- and triple-
checking the identity of French officials on the list. The newspaper
didn't yet have enough hard confirmation, for instance, to go to print
with the fact that it was unquestionably Macron's mobile phone in the
data. Approaching French government officials about doing forensics
on their phones was a nonstarter. "Obviously," Damien had explained
to the group, "we have not gone to the Élysée Palace and asked for the
phone of Macron."

They did have reinforcements on this ungainly investigation into Morocco. A reporter from our new partner *Daraj* was reaching out to Hajar Raissouni, the journalist who had fled Rabat for Sudan after being convicted and briefly imprisoned for having premarital sex with her fiancé. Hajar's mobile phone had now been verified, so we had a shot at forensics. *Le Soir* was doing its own reporting on Morocco because a recent Belgian prime minister was also in the data. A Radio France reporter was on the case, too, and within a week of our big meeting in Paris, she had already contacted Joseph Breham, a Paris-based attorney who represented jailed and exiled dissidents in Western Sahara, and convinced him to hand over his phone to Claudio and Donncha. On May 21, 2021, the same day we were meeting with our lawyer, Breham's phone turned up traces of a Pegasus infection. He pronounced himself willing to go on record. "There is no possible justification for a foreign state to listen to a French lawyer," Breham said. "There is no justification on a legal, ethical, or moral basis."

"Things are progressing really quickly," Sandrine was able to report in the first project-wide update four days later, on May 25. Holger Stark, from *Die Zeit*, was planning a trip to Israel to meet with a source, a former employee of NSO, who was willing to speak off the record about the company. He also was trying to get an interview with somebody official at NSO; his colleague Kai Biermann was on his way to Istanbul to meet with Turkish officials who might be able to shed some light on the Khashoggi killing and its aftermath. Dana Priest had also booked a trip to Istanbul, where she hoped to meet with Khashoggi's fiancée and facilitate the forensics on her phone. Szabolcs Panyi was at home in Budapest investigating the state of relations (warming) between Hungarian president Viktor Orbán and Israeli prime minister Benjamin Netanyahu right around the time NSO licensed Pegasus to Hungarian authorities.

The *Guardian*'s Stephanie Kirchgaessner posted notes from her long off-the-record interview with a source who had deep knowledge of NSO. Stephanie's *Guardian* colleague Michael Safi was investigating India's possible targeting of people within the Dalai Lama's inner circle. "First Macron, now the Dalai Lama," one of Sandrine's friends would joke with her. "Who's next? Jesus?"

Kristof Clerix of *Knack* had joined *Süddeutsche Zeitung* in its reporting on targets selected by Rwanda. Among the people he wanted to see was Carine Kanimba, who had been denouncing the Rwandan government in the lead-up to her father's upcoming trial on charges of terrorism, kidnapping, and murder. Carine's father, Paul Rusesabagina, was the Hotel Rwanda hero who saved more than 1,200 Hutus and Tutsis from murder during the genocide of 1994. His critical stance against the Rwandan ruling party in the intervening years had landed him in 2020 in a Kigali jail, where he had allegedly been tortured and now faced a certain conviction. The Rwandan president was loudly and publicly exclaiming Rusesabagina's guilt in the run-up to the trial.

Miranda Patrucic of OCCRP had already verified a slew of the phone numbers in the data selected by Pegasus system operators in Azerbaijan, including fifteen journalists, twenty-eight civil rights activists and attorneys, and fifty leaders from the Azeri opposition party. Even the deputy minister of defense. The best news from OCCRP was that Khadija Ismayilova might be released from house arrest in Baku later that week. Miranda and a few of Khadija's other colleagues from OCCRP planned to meet Khadija in person in Ankara, Turkey, where it would finally be safe to inform her of the Pegasus infection on her cell phone.

CLAUDIO'S CONFIDENCE IN the Security Lab's forensic findings kept growing, as did his desire to get this investigation over as soon as possible. Claudio and Donncha were literally closing in on NSO. The earliest Pegasus Project forensics had been on phones infected back in 2018 and 2019, in the early days of zero-click exploits. But at least one mobile phone they analyzed in May had been infected within the previous four weeks.

Recently infected iPhones offered new and slightly puzzling findings. It took some deciphering, comparing old backups to newer backups in the same iPhones, but Claudio and Donncha became convinced that NSO was employing a new evasive maneuver. The company's coders and engineers, having realized their zero-click exploits were exposed to cyber-researchers because the infections left discoverable traces of Pegasus in backup files, had added an extra layer of protection. Beginning in 2020, Pegasus exploits appeared to be much more assiduous in cleaning all evidence of attack and infection from a targeted phone and left behind fewer traces.

What was more mysterious, though, and only becoming clear to Claudio and Donncha in the last few weeks of May, was that NSO's Pegasus spyware was now trying to rewrite history. When a device was infected with the most recent version of Pegasus, the spyware was not only scrubbing forensic evidence of the new attack, but also attempting to erase the traces of Pegasus left behind by earlier attacks. This was a win-lose discovery for Claudio and Donncha. On the upside, the Security Lab tool was still able to find old traces because the NSO cleaning agents were not all that meticulous. They scrubbed malicious process names from almost all of the columns in the data-usage logs in the backup files. But not all of them. NSO operatives had been careless, Donncha believed, because they had been arrogant. They seemed to think that they were too good to be caught.

The downside to this discovery, though, was an unsettling confirmation of Claudio's and Donncha's latest fear that NSO might be onto them. "I mean, I don't know exactly what kind of visibility NSO might have [into our forensics]," Claudio told Sandrine and me, "but it would be foolish of them not to have some kind of visibility over a phone they already 'owned.' They could probably see if somebody is doing something."

PALOMA UNDERSTOOD THAT speed mattered more than ever when she headed back to Mexico near the end of May. We had been working the story of Pegasus in Mexico longer than any other, going back to the Cartel Project at the end of 2020. Paloma and the rest of the team had developed a profusion of leads, which had so far turned out to be somewhere between tantalizing and maddeningly difficult to tie down. We were counting on Paloma and our increasingly close partnership with Carmen Aristegui, one of the most admired and popular journalists in Mexico.

Carmen had contacted us with congratulations after the Cartel Project, and we took the opportunity to ask her if she would be willing to join our investigation into NSO. She seemed interested. Carmen had a long and tortured history with the company, its resellers in Mexico, and the government watchdogs who were supposed to protect privacy rights and freedom of the press. The media company she had founded, *Aristegui Noticias*, had been the first to reveal the spread of cybersurveillance in Mexico, back in the summer of 2012, when she and her team published the operational and financial details of contracts between the Mexican army and NSO's reseller in the country at the time, Susumo Azano. Five separate contracts, worth between $350 and $400 million, *Aristegui Noticias* reported, "were processed without bidding and approved by direct assignment to the company Security Tracking Devices, SA de CV." The story had little impact in the moment. The Mexican army ran a pair of cursory audits into the secret contracts and closed the case within months with no explanation beyond "lack of elements."

Carmen's initial report on cybersurveillance, along with her critical reporting on President Enrique Peña Nieto's questionable real estate deals, had drawn heightened scrutiny from Mexican authorities. Carmen herself was one of the first known victims of Pegasus, along with her sixteen-year-old son. Their targeting was confirmed by Citizen Lab in 2017. The criminal complaint she had filed against the Mexican government, however, was still being slow-walked by prosecutors. Carmen had been reporting on the subject of cybersurveillance in Mexico longer than any journalist in the world and knew more about it than almost anyone. But she was intrigued by what little we could tell her over an unsecure phone line, and clearly wanted to hear more. Paloma flew down to Mexico City at the end of March 2021 to explain to Carmen what we had.

We couldn't show Carmen or tell her about all the data we had access to back in March, but we decided the best thing to do was to run the match-a-name game from her contacts file to our leaked list of the fifteen thousand possible targets selected by NSO's Mexican clients. About ten minutes into the exercise, Carmen was astounded. There turned out to be more than sixty matches among her contacts. Scores of journalists, parents of the students detained by local police and killed by the drug lords in Ayotzinapa, the government official who was supposed to be overseeing the dormant investigation into the deaths, more than a dozen powerful political figures, even a Catholic priest who had won human rights prizes for his work with immigrants. "Politicians and journalists and a priest," Carmen joked. "Who can be *our* salvation?"

At certain points in the discussion, Carmen would look at a name and exclaim, "Oh geez," "Oh, no," "Not her," and "Brutal." One surprise was the nefarious and very energetic game of political espionage someone in the Peña Nieto administration seemed to have been playing. The most intimate friends and advisers to opposition candidate Andrés Manuel López Obrador (known as AMLO), who had won the presidency in 2018, were in the data. "He is one of the most trusted men of the current president," Carmen told Paloma, pointing at one match from our data.

"We already have his driver, his cardiologist, the director of his baseball club," Paloma replied.

"Let's see," Carmen said, looking at her own list of matches, "there's his driver and his cardiologist. Then his wife, his three kids. His kids? How many children [on your list]?"

"He has four children," Paloma answered, "and there are three who are on the list."

"Not the little one? Only the older three?"

"Yes."

Some of the matches ended up being inside Carmen's own circle of intimates, most of the people selected at the very time she was first targeted: her personal assistant, one of her longtime producers, even her sister. When Carmen checked in with her sister the next day, Teresa Aristegui pointed to an SMS message she received at the time, which looked to be from a friend. "My father has passed away. We are dismayed. I'm sending you the address to accompany us." Teresa Aristegui was supposed to click on a link. These tracked with the type of SMS messages and links Carmen was also getting back in 2016: "It's been five days since my daughter shows up. I will be grateful if you share this photo. We are desperate." And "Dear Carmen, my brother died in an accident. I'm devastated. I'm sending info for the wake. I hope you will attend."

And worse, one her sixteen-year-old son had received: "Beheaded journalist found in Veracruz after threatening narcos. Details in photos."

"This technology was in the hands of a bunch of operators who were behaving like thugs, and who couldn't resist taunts even as they were trying to infect people," one horrified cyber-researcher had noted.

At one point in the name-matching session with Paloma, it was clear Carmen wanted in on this investigation. She mentioned something very enticing: a cache of more than twenty thousand documents she had received from a source who worked for NSO's suspected sales agent in Mexico, Uri Ansbacher. But Carmen wanted to think about how to use this treasure; she was not yet ready to share all of it with the group.

The biggest moment in the entire session turned out to be pretty early—match number twelve. "This phone belongs to Xavier Olea," Carmen pointed out, obviously intrigued. "He is a criminal lawyer who was the state attorney of Guerrero. . . . He is also the prosecutor who was in charge of the investigation into the death of Cecilio Pineda." Cecilio was a journalist Paloma knew all about. His unexplained murder in one of the most dangerous areas of Mexico—a spot near enough to the mountains to provide good cover for drug manufacturing and near enough to the Pacific Ocean to make for easy export to the hungry US market—was a story Forbidden Stories had been tracking from its first days in operation. Prosecutor Olea, who insisted on around-the-clock protection for his wife and children and traveled in an armored car, would later tell us that he was informed of threats against Cecilio, and that it was pretty obvious he had been killed because of his reporting on the drug cartels, especially on their practice of kidnapping locals and ransoming them for cash. Olea called Cecilio "bold," but the way he said it, it didn't sound like a compliment.

"You know that Cecilio Pineda is also in the data," Paloma told Carmen.

"He might have been spied on?" Carmen asked. "Well, it makes sense. This will be a very important line of research: Cecilio Pineda."

PALOMA DIDN'T NEED to be told this. She had been trying to verify Cecilio's number from day one of the Pegasus Project. She had succeeded only about ten days before her meeting with Carmen at the end of March 2021 and then managed to get a secret phone call with Cecilio's nervous widow, Marisol. "I don't want problems," were the first words out of her mouth. Marisol said she had told her husband to stop his investigations of the drug cartels, but he was stubborn. So was Marisol. "I don't want to know who killed him," she had told Paloma in that first call. "He's dead and won't come back."

Marisol did provide a second source to verify that the mobile phone number we had for Cecilio was accurate, which proved he had been selected for targeting just a month before his murder in March 2017. But forensics weren't yet possible because Marisol didn't have the phone. The police had returned the clothes and shoes Cecilio had been wearing the day of his murder. Nothing else. She told Paloma to check with Cecilio's friend Israel Flores, a fellow journalist who had rushed to the scene of the shooting.

Paloma had reached Israel Flores in early May, and their conversation only deepened the mystery of the phone. Israel said he had seen the device lying on the ground next to his wounded friend when he arrived at the crime scene, but he hadn't thought to pick it up. He left the scene to go with Cecilio to the hospital and was with him when he died in the ambulance. The federal police called Israel in soon after to interview him about Cecilio's death. Israel told Paloma that they had one chief interest; they really wanted to know about that phone. The questions were all about who was nearest to the phone, Israel told Paloma. Where were the EMTs? Who had the phone?

Paloma's final trip to Mexico, near the end of May 2021, was sort of a roller coaster. Further efforts with Marisol, Israel, and the criminal investigators had been to no avail. The phone was still missing. But Paloma had backup from the *Guardian*'s Nina Lakhani, who was back in Mexico after working on the Cartel Project there the previous year. *Proceso* and *Aristegui Noticias* had each put one of their best informed and most capable investigative reporters on the project.

Best of all, Carmen had decided to share her twenty thousand leaked documents with all the reporters on the Pegasus Project. This document dump was set to happen at the very same time we reeled in the final, crucial partner in our investigation, the Israel-based newspaper *Haaretz*.

Amitai Ziv, a telecom and tech reporter from *Haaretz's* financial supplement, had been a very capable contributor to the Cartel Project. Pegasus had been a tiny part of the Cartel Project, and only because of our last-minute confirmation of the targeting of Jorge Carrasco's mobile phone. Amitai had helped the investigation with key contacts at NSO and competitor companies, and around the Israeli tech industry in general. We knew Amitai could provide all those things and more on the Pegasus project. But Sandrine and I had been shy to invite him into the Pegasus Project. Israel's national security policies are a big obstacle for journalists in the country. Military censors had wide latitude to kill off news items, and there was a legal requirement that they be permitted to read anything that touched on national security before publication.

Claudio, meanwhile, had been even more adamant about keeping *Haaretz* at arm's length. He kept warning us that the risk of interception was just too great because Israel was just too small. Cybersurveillance, he explained, is much easier when a target is right around the corner. At the same time, almost all the partners recognized the need for reporters on the ground in Israel. Coming out of our second meeting in Paris, Sandrine and I were hearing that request more and more often. We pressed Claudio again, and he relented.

We contacted Amitai about a week after the second meeting, and he flew to Paris a week later. Amitai appeared quite surprised by the scale of the data leak, the results of the forensics, and the reporting the partners had already done. But when we asked him about the impact the Pegasus Project would have on NSO and the Israeli government, he looked at us with a bit of a side-eye. "Well, nothing," he said, matter-of-factly. "NSO has stories coming at them all the time. It doesn't make a difference." He did offer a more optimistic outlook on another front. Our worries about the military censors were overblown, he insisted, because NSO was a private company. He wouldn't have to share much with the MOD.

Timing matters, and it really mattered in this case. Amitai and *Haaretz* officially came aboard the Pegasus Project on May 26, 2021, which was also the day Carmen delivered a tranche of twenty thousand documents that connected multiple Mexican government agencies, NSO, and NSO's go-to reseller in Mexico, the elusive Uri Ansbacher.

The original leak, Carmen explained, came in the form of two encrypted USB sticks delivered by a whistleblower inside Ansbacher's complicated web of companies. The Israeli businessman worked hard to keep his finances and his business activity veiled from public view. The leaker, who signed all his emails to Carmen "Hunter of Hunters," ripped off that veil. The twenty thousand digital copies of documents he had handed over to Carmen in 2019 included contracts, pages of bank statements, and proof of payments, including enormous payments to "Shalev Holy." The whistleblower had also told Carmen that one of Ansbacher's lieutenants, who received training on Pegasus at NSO offices in Israel, had operated the system on select targets at the request of the sitting government. "They knew absolutely everything about AMLO's life," the source explained. Carmen had seen this lieutenant's mobile phone number in the data back in March. (Pegasus operators often ended up in the data because they used their own phones to provide demonstrations for potential customers.)

Carmen had not been ready to share much of this leaked data with us back in March, before she was officially part of the Pegasus Project, or even in the first weeks after joining. But now, at the end of May, she was all in. Carmen understood that Mexico was part of a much bigger global story, but she also understood that her home country was Exhibit A of what happens when spyware like Pegasus flies wild, for years, without necessary safeguards in place. Her whistleblower was crucial to showing that. We might just be able to prove that a *private* company in Mexico was using Pegasus to perform unwarranted surveillance on people who were neither criminal nor criminal suspects.

Here is where I felt the project getting a new kind of traction. I already knew, from our previous work together, that Amitai could add real texture to Carmen's extraordinary paper trail.

At the end of May 2021, our new partner in Israel told us he was confident he could get an interview with Uri Ansbacher.

CHAPTER SEVENTEEN

"IT'S NOT JUST ME"

The last twenty minutes in the airport were the hardest for Paul Radu. "She's going to be surprised when she sees you," his colleague Miranda Patrucic suggested. "After so long."

"So long," Paul said, almost wistfully, "so long. Yes. . . . She must be so relieved that she's here now. I can't even imagine what the feeling is, to travel after so much time and to be out."

Paul and Miranda were still pacing the polished concourse floor twenty minutes later, not entirely certain their friend had made the flight from Baku to Ankara. The Azerbaijani security services could have detained her at the airport terminal in Baku or even pulled her off the plane at the last minute. But the two were hopeful. "Do you think she will recognize us with these masks?" Miranda asked.

"I was asking myself the same thing," Paul said as he started to nudge forward toward the gates. "People are coming. People are coming. Any moment now. Any moment now."

"It's like a delivery room," Miranda said, watching other travelers from Flight 2162 file out of the gates with their luggage in hand.

Paul cast his mind back to when he last saw Khadija Ismayilova, who had not been permitted to leave her hometown of Baku since 2014. She had spent those years in pretrial detention, then in prison, then living under a government-imposed travel ban. The authorities in Azerbaijan had shown little leniency in that time. When Khadija's mother traveled from Baku to Ankara for cancer treatments, Khadija's request to accompany her was denied. Neither was she allowed to leave the country to be at her mother's deathbed in Ankara some months later.

"Do you know how much time it's been?" Paul said, watching as travelers continued to file out of the arrival gates and into the main concourse. "Almost eight years."

Paul and Miranda finally caught a glimpse of Khadija, in a colorful pink shirt, through the glass doors leading from the gates. She was one of the last passengers to make it into the main terminal, but she was out. Finally. Paul and Miranda ran to their surprised friend and wrapped her in hugs. The three were laughing and crying all at once. Khadija Ismayilova was, temporarily and uncharacteristically, unable to speak.

"Wow, hey," was all Paul could say. "Wow. Wow."

"Finally," Khadija was able to say. "It's been so many years."

"We were counting seven-plus years," Paul answered.

"No, no, it's been less than seven," answered Khadija, who had suddenly regained her composure. She was a journalist first and foremost, by training and by instinct. Above all else, even at the most emotional of times, accuracy mattered to Khadija. "It will be seven in October."

KHADIJA THOUGHT OF Ankara as a temporary way station—her plan was to get back to her work in Azerbaijan as soon as possible—so she arrived as any guest would, as her mother had taught her, with food in hand. She had spent the day before preparing grape leaves stuffed with beef, and her dolma was among salads and baked fish and wine at the table that night, when Paul and Miranda and Khadija and fellow journalist Drew Sullivan and Khadija's sister and a few other friends had a celebratory dinner that lasted into the small hours of the night. It was like old times, Khadija pouring wine and dishing food and describing the method of cooking a proper pilaf. "The walls of the pan should be as hot as the bottom," she would say. If she was in the mood (and it didn't take much wine), Khadija would turn her beautiful singing voice to the "March of Azerbaijan," the national anthem restored in 1992 after the seventy-year enforced hiatus during Soviet dominance in her home country.

Paul had been anticipating the celebration for days, remembering various happy nights with Khadija when he had still been allowed to visit Baku. A founder of the Organized Crime and Corruption Reporting Project, Paul had been working with Khadija for fifteen years, first as a mentor, then as a colleague. "We would go to this bar that was a bit outside," Paul told Miranda as they were driving back from the airport in Ankara. "We partied there, and then we would go to her home to party some more. There would be this huge table, with everything on it, all sorts of foods. And it kept on coming—drinks, food, everything. We had some good parties."

"That's the part, which, for me, is so great about Khadija," Miranda agreed. Miranda had been at OCCRP since 2006 and led its coverage of the Caucasus. She was one of the journalists who picked up Khadija's reporting and made sure her stories kept getting told even when Khadija was blocked by the Azeri government. "She's always partying. I mean, this is kind of in her blood. She has a very strong spirit of friendship."

"She's working hard, but she's also partying, partying, partying," Paul remembered. "And to be honest, I never saw her angry, Khadija. I saw her a little bit upset, you know, discussing something serious, but never angry."

EVERYBODY AGREED THE next day, when the visit turned to business, that the grand arrival dinner had been a rousing success. Khadija, however, started the meeting by apologizing: "My sister told me last night that I didn't let anyone eat. I was speaking nonstop. And people were so polite."

"We ate," Paul insisted. "And it was a lot of really good stories."

"Well, someone should stop me when I talk so much."

The small group did not spend much time joking around because at long last, with Khadija safely out of Azerbaijan, Paul and Miranda and their fellow editor at OCCRP, Drew Sullivan, were able to fill in their longtime colleague about the Pegasus Project. "So I can tell you and solve the mystery," Miranda said to Khadija. "You know NSO? The Israeli company that is selling surveillance software."

"Okay," Khadija answered, a bit puzzled.

Miranda explained the leak and the list, and that more than a thousand of the selections were inside Azerbaijan. Khadija was among the selections, Miranda told her, and there was a good chance her phone had been compromised by Pegasus spyware. Her attorney was also in the data. "It all happens in the background, and you have no idea that you are infected," Miranda told her. "And when you're infected, it's transmitting your messages, your images, everything that's happened on your phone. So it's very, very dangerous because you don't know, and it allows the government or whoever is the client to basically get everything from the person's phone."

"And it's legal to sell it?" Khadija asked.

"Yes."

Khadija agreed right away to let Miranda do the backup of her two iPhones and upload them for Claudio and Donncha to analyze for evidence of infection. She was pleased to hear that they would have results the next day. Khadija professed shock at the number of Azeris who had been selected for possible Pegasus infection ("a waste of public money," she said), but her own presence on the list was no great surprise. She would have been more surprised if she were not on that list.

The fundamental difficulty in Khadija Ismayilova's life, and what landed her on that list, is that she and Azeri president Ilham Aliyev agree on very little, and least of all do they agree on the matter of Khadija Ismayilova. In President Aliyev's view, Khadija has been, as he told the US State Department as early as 2009, "an enemy of the government" and a threat to stability in Azerbaijan. Khadija sees things differently.

KHADIJA ISMAYILOVA CAN tell you exactly when it first began to dawn on her that the official government view did not necessarily accord with the truth, and thus with her own view. She was ten years old, at home in Baku, then the capital city of a Soviet Socialist Republic, observing her parents in a moment of heated passion. They were watching a live televised soccer match between the Soviet Union and Turkey. Khadija's parents were educated and successful professionals, both engineers. Her mother had left her job to stay home with the children, while her father had risen to a high-level post at the Ministry of Energy in Baku.

If her father was taking a cut of the spoils available to any opportunistic official in the most vital and lucrative Soviet ministry in Azerbaijan, it was hard to see. The family did have a comfortable beach cottage, so she and her siblings spent the summers swimming in the Caspian Sea. But like almost every Azeri family in the mid-1980s, the Ismayilovs depended on small government stipends to guarantee the household's supply of butter, meat, milk, sugar, and other staples. Khadija, along with the available contingent of brothers and sisters, was often forcibly marched by her mother to assist with the grocery shopping. Her mom probably wanted the company because she might be facing a four-hour wait in line. Khadija figures she spent about half her waking childhood in line at a market.

Up to the age of ten, Khadija viewed such difficult outings as acts of thoroughgoing patriotism. This was sacrifice for a greater cause, the kind of sacrifice Westerners were too weak to make. The kind of sacrifice that would ensure the eventual Soviet triumph in the Cold War. Khadija enjoyed writing poems about the glory of her empire, the Soviet Union. She was a very dedicated young patriot.

Then, there she was watching this soccer match with her parents in the privacy of their own home, the USSR versus Turkey, and her mother and father were both cheering . . . *for Turkey*. Young Khadija was taken aback. Azerbaijanis were supposed to be proud members of the Union of Soviet Socialist Republics. Why were her parents pulling for Turkey? She asked her mom, who stopped cheering long enough to explain. Turkey was actually their brother country, she said, and the Ismayilovs, like most Azeri families, were of Turkish stock. But wait a minute, Khadija wondered, isn't Russia our brother country? That's what they taught her in school. Khadija's mom kept talking. The Russians had first occupied Azerbaijan, she said, and now we are kind of occupied by the Soviet Union. Khadija's father jumped in with a note of caution, which turned out to be equally jolting. "Don't tell her those things," he warned. "She will go and say something in school, and then we will be harassed. That's going to be a problem."

Khadija had very suddenly and very unexpectedly got hold of some serious unofficial truths. She still laughs whenever she describes the moment the scales fell from her ten-year-old eyes. "I've learned that the Soviet empire was actually a Russian empire and that we were occupied," she would say. "I've learned about our Turkic origin. I've learned about censorship and oppression in our country. All in ten minutes. Before that time, I was writing poems about the Cold War and Lenin. Before that time, I've been very active in school events. Very active in speaking about the Soviet Union and what a good country we have. So that was the day when I stopped writing poems. I stopped going to Communist events at school. I think that was the day I turned into a rebel."

Khadija was a happy warrior in the Azeri national liberation movement in her teens, and by the time the country voted for independence from the Russians and their collapsing empire, she already knew all the words to the "March of Azerbaijan." She started her career in journalism the year after Azeri independence and enjoyed the freedom to write just about anything she wanted—at least as long as she stuck to soft topics like pop culture and human-interest stories. And steered clear of topics like politics and governance.

The Republic of Azerbaijan had lurched pretty quickly from a hopeful democracy to a petrostate controlled by a handful of old Soviet apparatchiks, led by the former head of the KGB in Azerbaijan, Heydar Aliyev. Before he died in 2003, President Heydar Aliyev ensured transfer of power to his forty-one-year-old son, Ilham, who had been educated at university in Moscow and served as vice president of the state-owned oil entity, making deals with the major Western oil companies until his political coronation.

The second-generation Aliyev regime quickly scared off any serious political opposition, bought up most of the media in the country, and sidelined pretty much any journalist who did things a journalist was supposed to do—like figure out how public funds were being spent. The only reporter still trying to do that sort of investigation in 2005, Elmar Huseynov, was assassinated that year, shot six times at point-blank range in the stairwell of his apartment building. The lesson Team Aliyev appeared to be offering anybody working in the field of journalism was quite clear. But then, it had been a long time since Khadija accepted official lessons at face value. This turned out to be the second crucial pivot point in her life. Huseynov "was the only one speaking out about the First Family corruption," Khadija remembers. "He was the only one uncovering the First Family's corrupt businesses. And he paid the ultimate price. He lost his life.

"The night we heard about the assassination, the first thing that came into my mind was, we [other Azeri journalists] are also guilty for that. We are part of the problem because he was the only one, and they thought it's easy to achieve silence by killing one. If there were more of us, they wouldn't count on complete silence by killing one journalist. So we were responsible for his death as well."

Khadija determined to pick up where Elmar Huseynov had left off, though she didn't know the first thing about investigating fraud and corruption in government, or how to follow the money flowing through the state-owned oil company, or how to locate the offshore shell companies used to obscure that money trail. She turned for training and advice to the OCCRP, which was co-founded the same year by Paul Radu and Drew Sullivan. Paul put her onto an early data leak of financial documents out of Panama identifying the owners of shell companies operating in known tax havens around the world. Some of the documents pointed to Aliyev and his family, and Khadija meticulously connected the dots and then bravely published her findings in Azerbaijan. "This was a huge breakthrough," says Paul Radu. "Up to this point, the Aliyev family was operating in the dark. Khadija was the one who pulled the curtain. She pulled it wide so the world could see the corruption of the regime."

Khadija's reports on the apparently precocious and prodigious offspring of Ilham Aliyev were particularly revealing. Working as bureau chief of Radio Free Europe/Radio Liberty (RFE/RL), she unearthed a trail of documents that showed a remarkable portfolio of assets for the children of a man who earned a $230,000-a-year government salary. Aliyev's two daughters managed to accrue between them, and before they hit age twenty-five, major stakes in airlines, banks, a mobile phone company, and a gold and silver mining operation. They also owned another $30 million in real estate around the world. Their younger brother, at the age of eleven, had acquired property in Dubai worth $44 million.

President Aliyev's in-laws, meanwhile, controlled major operations in banking, insurance, travel, cosmetics, car dealerships, and construction, all under the umbrella of Pasha Holdings. The First Lady's family, the Pashayevs, had built a shopping center, a residential tower, the Four Seasons Hotel, the JW Marriott Hotel, and the Amburan Marriott Beach Resort with speed and efficiency that defied long-standing local timelines. Smaller builders were always slowed by tax authorities, fire marshals, and building inspectors who expected to be paid off. "Not surprisingly," noted one foreign diplomat in Baku, "projects by Pasha Construction face few, if any, of these setbacks and are generally among the fastest to be built in Azerbaijan."

Khadija's initial reporting marked her as a figure who required close scrutiny by the people who protect presidential prerogatives in Azerbaijan. The Aliyevs "want to be considered as if they are a respectable member of the family of European democracies," says Gerald Knaus, the founding director of the European Stability Initiative. "So they care much more about their image than European dictatorships used to."

Foreign officials in Azerbaijan and investigative reporters from outside the country began to follow Khadija and do their own digging into Aliyev family finances and its penchant for obscuring and offshoring their wealth. One US State Department official filed a report comparing the Aliyevs to the fictional Corleone crime family from *The Godfather*. (The president seemed to vacillate between the cool and rational Michael and the hotheaded and not particularly bright Sonny, according to the report.) Aliyev's wife came in for some particularly catty and undiplomatic chatter about her personal vanity: "First Lady Mehriban Aliyeva appears to have had substantial cosmetic surgery, presumably overseas, and wears dresses that would be considered provocative even in the Western world," read one 2010 cable from a US diplomat in Azerbaijan. "On television, in photos, and in person, she appears unable to show a range of facial expressions."

Khadija didn't much concern herself with how the Aliyevs spent their fortune but in how they amassed it. Her work for RFE/RL focused on the intersection in Azerbaijan where politics, governance, and corruption converge. She wanted to know how President Aliyev rigged his reelection in 2008. How he convinced the Azeri parliament to do away with term limits—he could be president for life. And how he pushed through new laws to keep information about national finances from public view.

Khadija managed to break the story that the $38.5 million construction contract to build National Flag Square, with the highest flagpole in the world, at a towering 162 meters (six feet taller than North Korea's), had been awarded to a company owned by the president's daughters. The flagpole thing didn't work out so well. Tajikistan built its own new flagpole, which ran to 165 meters high, just two months later. The RFE/RL report that Azerbaijan had lost its world record in such a short time was regarded inside the Azeri government as an attempt to humiliate the nation, and thus its president.

A confidential informant who advised both Ilham and Ilham's father, Heydar, noted the younger man's "exceedingly thin skin" and his rising ire at independent journalists in the country in the wake of the flagpole revelations. "Heydar would never have allowed himself to be goaded into the ridiculous reactions, [the informant] said," according to one diplomatic cable. "Ilham is not inclined to subtlety or deliberation in his response to these kinds of issues. 'I don't feel I have to wipe everybody out,' [Ilham had said.] 'Just my enemies.'"

Aliyev's "obsession with honor means those who criticize and expose corruption will be seen as enemies of the state," Knaus says. "The rulers know that in the end their rule is more fragile than it might appear. If you are insecure, you cannot tolerate any dissent. You crush everything."

The crackdown was swift and energetic. Critics of the Azeri government were harassed, arrested, and imprisoned. A blogger who impersonated Ilham Aliyev in a donkey costume on YouTube ended up in prison for two-and-a-half years. The sentence might appear harsh, Aliyev explained to one EU president, but it was needed "to protect our statehood."

The first big blow aimed at Khadija came in early 2012, while she was investigating the Aliyev family's most recent and towering bit of corruption: siphoning money from the $134 million contract to construct a new 23,000-seat arena for that year's Eurovision Song Contest.

Khadija still remembers the date the unmarked package arrived at her house—March 7, 2012. Inside the envelope were grainy screenshots taken from a videotape. They showed Khadija and her boyfriend engaged in sex. "Whore," read the accompanying note. "Behave. Or you will be defamed."

Khadija's friends warned her to tread carefully, but she didn't listen. She went on her radio show and explained that she was being blackmailed but that her tormentors were not going to intimidate her. She was going to keep reporting. A week later, when the entire video surfaced on an Azeri Facebook page, Khadija was not so sure. She and her boyfriend noted the various angles in the videotape and used them to seek out all the hidden cameras in the apartment. The cameras had been removed, but the cables were still in the walls and led to the bedroom, the living room, and the toilet.

"Then you try to remember what you have been doing [in front of the hidden cameras], and it paralyzes your life," Khadija told us. "I mean, your body stops functioning. I went through this for eight or nine days. I couldn't use a toilet. I mean, not even in public places. [My body] was swelling.

"[The surveillance] had a real impact on my health for almost a year. I couldn't restart any relationship with anyone because I was afraid. I still don't know whether my boyfriend was involved in the scheme or not. You don't trust anyone."

But Khadija decided she would not stand down. She published her investigation into corruption in the Crystal Hall arena less than two months after the sex video was posted on Facebook. "The first family is personally profiting from the massive construction project through its hidden ownership in the Azenco construction company," Khadija reported. Along with the fact that Azenco had been awarded contracts worth $79 million in a single year. "The 2012 Eurovision event will have one other tie to the first family besides the new showcase auditorium:

The president's son-in-law, singer Emin Agalarov, was chosen to enter-
tain the crowds between acts." (Emin did a pretty good job after that of
keeping his name out of other political stories until he made the mistake
of calling Donald Trump Jr. in 2016 to offer him dirt on the Hillary Clinton campaign, courtesy of the Kremlin.)

The entire blackmail episode appeared to have backfired on the
Aliyev family when Khadija was invited to New York to receive the
International Women's Media Foundation's 2012 Courage in Journalism
Award. She took the opportunity to call out the Aliyev government and
others. "Silence is what these regimes need," Khadija said. "Silence helps
them continue to deprive their people of opportunities. With the con-
solidation of power and money, crime and government, accompanied
with disabled justice systems, independent journalists become the main
targets, as they become the only means for resistance for society against
corruption and organized crime."

That appeared to be the final straw for those protecting the stability
of Azerbaijan. Khadija was arrested in Baku a few months later and then
suffered through a series of other arrests, convictions on bogus charges,
nearly two years in prison, and a long travel ban. The trip to Ankara to
meet with Paul and Miranda about the Pegasus Project in the final days
of May 2021 was the first time she had left the Azerbaijan since 2014.

CLAUDIO WAS NOT really looking forward to his call to Ankara to report
his initial findings to Khadija. Sometimes, he would say, he felt like a
medieval doctor: powerless to save anyone, just there to make an accurate body count. Claudio had been delivering so much bad news to so
many victims lately that it was starting to weigh on him. The worst part,
for Claudio, is that he really couldn't offer the instant protection these
traumatized people so clearly craved. He could give them advice but not
a fail-safe to dodge the spyware. "I'm the one that has to tell them, 'You
know, there's nothing I can do for you,'" he admitted to us long after
the Pegasus Project was completed. "'I can't meaningfully provide you
anything to prevent you from being in the same position and getting
infected again in a month or even tomorrow.'"

But Claudio picked up the phone and made the call to Ankara as scheduled, on May 31, 2021, and Khadija didn't waste any time. "So now tell me how bad it is," she told him.

Claudio ran through the basics, while Khadija processed the information. The phone showed evidence of multiple cases of attempted or actual infection starting back in 2018. The attacks continued well beyond the time frame where our leaked data ended, the most recent just a few weeks earlier. Paul, Miranda, and Khadija all had questions about the mechanics of the infections, and Claudio patiently answered them all. Then Drew jumped in with what felt like an attempt to soften the blow. At least Khadija's messages on highly encrypted apps like Signal were still private, Drew suggested, right?

Sorry, Claudio said. Nothing on that phone was beyond the reach of Pegasus. "When you have this sort of spyware running on the device," he explained, "there's not really a whole lot [of encryption] that holds up."

Claudio had promised to spend as much time as they needed on the phone, and he stayed on the line until everybody in Ankara ran out of questions. When he hung up, Khadija stood and walked away from the group.

"Well, that's not great news," Drew said to the rest of the group.

Even back in Berlin, off the line, Claudio knew exactly what Khadija was experiencing. He had seen it so many times already. "First, they are kind of in denial, and then they start to understand, and it becomes a miserable experience because you see them going through a massive sense of guilt. You can see them start thinking not about themselves but what I've cost others. Who else did they compromise? Who else might have been put at risk because of them? They always take it very personally. Like, 'I did something wrong.'"

Claudio was correct, of course. Also in the data, Khadija now knew, were her niece, her sister, even her favorite taxi driver. The thing Khadija could not shake was her communications regarding one particular friend, who had been fighting breast cancer. Khadija had been taking care of her after her surgery. Among the tasks was taking pictures of the surgical wound when she changed her dressings every day and then sending the photographs to her doctor. Some government thug, Khadija feared, may have used Pegasus to intercept those very private photographs. She had been tossing and turning in bed all night thinking about that, even before Claudio had confirmed the presence of spyware on her iPhone for the past three years. "I feel guilty," she confessed to her friends from OCCRP in the hours after the call with Claudio. "I feel guilty for the messages I've sent. I feel guilty for the sources who send me messages thinking that some encrypted messaging ways are secure, and they didn't know that my phone is infected.

"My family members are also victimized. My sources are victimized. People I've been working with, people who told me their private secrets, are victimized. I put so many people in danger, and I'm angry with the government. I'm angry with the companies who produce all of these tools and sell it to the bad guys like the Aliyev regime. It's despicable. It's heinous.

"It's not just me. Like, when the video was exposed, it was just me. Now I don't know who else has been exposed because of me and who else is in danger because of me."

CHAPTER EIGHTEEN

A CHOICE BETWEEN INTERESTS AND VALUES

Laurent

The attacks on Khadija's phone had been relentless, according to further forensic examination by the Security Lab. The first Pegasus infection on her mobile phone appeared to have been on March 28, 2019. The spyware operators were back in the phone just five days later and again in May, June, July, and August. They attacked Khadija's iPhone on four separate occasions in the first few weeks of September alone.

On September 10, 2019, three days after an attack on Khadija's iPhone, NSO Group trumpeted its new corporate governance regime. This updated policy was designed to bring the company into "alignment with the UN Guiding Principles of Human Rights," read the press release, "cementing the company's existing industry-leading ethical business practices." NSO announced the formation of a "Governance, Risk and Compliance Committee," as well as a separate set of outside experts who could offer the company guidance on human rights issues: one former secretary and one former assistant secretary of the US Department of Homeland Security, as well as a French diplomat who had been first secretary at the embassy in Tel Aviv and an ambassador to the US. NSO also announced the hiring of a new general counsel, Shmuel Sunray.

Sunray went in with eyes wide open, he would tell reporters. "We understand the power of the tool, and we understand the impact of

misuse of the tool," he said not long after he started at NSO. "We're trying to do the right thing . . . to find the right balance."

The newly announced policy and personnel were merely a codifica-
tion of protocols already in place, according to NSO. There would still
be a rigid vetting of all potential end users of NSO's weapons-grade
cybersurveillance system. Key to the process was a case-by-case risk
analysis to determine the likelihood of misuse by any country seeking a
license to deploy Pegasus. NSO's attorneys and its compliance committee always took into account the country's record on human rights, rule
of law, freedom of the press and expression, and corruption. (NSO said
it was aware of the "very strong relations between issues of corruption
and the issues of human rights.") The compliance team had a very good
place to start their vetting procedure, which was the annual rankings
assigned by at least seven different international indexes, including the
World Bank's Control of Corruption report and Freedom House's Freedom in the World report.

Azerbaijan was an interesting case in point, index-wise. The Aliyev
government scored somewhere around the bottom 15 percent of countries in the World Bank's Control of Corruption rankings in 2019, when
Pegasus had first been loosed on Khadija—and that was its highest
grade on that comprehensive report card. The country had slid precip-
itously in the Freedom in the World rankings by then and consistently
hovered at the edge of the ten "Worst of the Worst" countries. Azerbaijan scored a bit better than North Korea, Syria, South Sudan, Eritrea,
and Equatorial Guinea; it was on par with Libya, Somalia, China, and
Saudi Arabia. Of the 179 countries in the Reporters Without Borders
annual index, only a dozen scored below Azerbaijan in protecting freedom of the press.

Those were just numbers. The evidence supporting these rankings
was far more compelling, and damning, and relentless. The lede of the
Human Rights Watch annual reports on Azerbaijan had been pretty consistent for nearly a decade: "The government's unrelenting crackdown
decimated independent nongovernmental organizations and media. . . .
Courts sentenced at least 25 journalists and political and youth activists
to long prison terms in politically motivated, unfair trials . . . appalling

human rights record did not improve in 2018 . . . authorities continued to maintain rigid control, severely curtailing freedoms of association, expression, and assembly . . . continues to wage a vicious crackdown on critics and dissenting voices. The space for independent activism, critical journalism, and opposition political activity has been virtually extinguished."

Human Rights Watch also reported specifics of their findings about Azerbaijan. Ilham Aliyev's strongest political opponents tended to get about 3 percent of the vote in both presidential and parliamentary elections so that even the European monitors bribed by the Aliyev government couldn't bring themselves to call the voting free and fair. "The election process itself was organized at a high level" was the best one German observer could offer. Yet somehow, that 3 percent still rankled, so Aliyev's security services remained vigilant in their effort to drive political opposition to the vanishing point.

"These people are in a bad psychological state, and have been for many years," the Azeri president said of his critics. "People who have such a negative attitude of their own nation, their own people and state, can only be called traitors to the nation and anti-national forces."

Opposition figures kept ending up in psychiatric hospitals, often for treatment of their "paranoia." Other alleged traitors to the nation (or more specifically to President Aliyev and his family) were arrested and beaten. One said he had been whacked for an hour with a truncheon "so bad I could no longer feel pain." An attorney who called attention to this extralegal torture had his law license revoked.

Invented charges of "hooliganism" or drug possession landed many of Aliyev's political opponents in prison for extended stays. A conviction of "insulting the honor and dignity of the president" was good for up to five years, thanks to tough new laws enacted by the Aliyev-controlled parliament. Two men who refused to admit to defacing a statue of the president's father were beaten by police, threatened with rape, and sentenced to a decade in prison.

The 2020 Azeri military offensive in a long-running conflict with Armenia, according to reports from international observers, teemed with war crimes—on both sides. The Azeris attacked residential areas with cluster munitions, which had been "banned because of their wide-spread indiscriminate effect and long-lasting danger to civilians." Armenian POWs were deprived of food, water, sleep, and medical care. The prisoners reported being burned with cigarette lighters, subjected to electric shocks, and punctured with metal rods.

Journalists didn't fare much better than POWs. The public reporting suggested a love-hate relationship between President Aliyev and the press in Azerbaijan. The president loved the Azeri media he controlled, which was almost all of it by 2019. He had once gifted 255 apartments to reporters and then showed up to accept his third "friend of journalists" award from Baku's local Press Council. He hated the writers and editors who were critical of him and his family and their unexplained wealth. Those journalists did not get free apartments. They got harassed, threatened, and intimidated, even after fleeing the country.

A female reporter living in the United States got the Khadija blackmail treatment in 2019. Someone from Azerbaijan sent her intimate photographs of her and her boyfriend and told her to cease her broadcasts about the president's finances. "You have seven days to show you have quit," read the message to her, "or we will expose you."

Afgan Mukhtarli, the husband of Leyla Mustafayeva, Khadija's friend who had helped me get my tapes out of Azerbaijan back in 2014, was kidnapped in the country of Georgia in May 2017 (their investigations into the Aliyev family corruption made it too dangerous to stay in Baku). The kidnappers blindfolded Afgan, broke his nose and his ribs, put €10,000 in his pockets, then handed him off to Azeri law enforcement, who threw him into a jail in Baku. He was convicted of "smuggling contraband" (the €10,000) and served almost three years in prison.

President Ilham Aliyev's extremely thin-skinned, dictatorial comportment and his well-deserved low ratings on the scale of human rights, rule of law, freedom of the press and expression, and corruption was an awfully large and ungainly lump for NSO Group and others to sweep under the international carpets, and had been for years. President Aliyev, one US diplomat admitted, "complicates our approach to Baku and has the unfortunate effect of framing what should be a strategically valuable relationship as a choice between US interests and US values."

■■■■■■■

By 2019, ILHAM Aliyev had a pretty good idea of where the democracies of the world would land on this difficult and tortuous choice between their interest and their (professed) values. He'd been given plenty of glimpses behind the curtain over the previous twenty-plus years, starting when he was invited to headline a Strengthening Democratic Institutions Project seminar at the Kennedy School of Government at Harvard University in 1997. Turned out the notions of democracy and human rights and freedom of expression didn't really come up much. Rule of law got some play, at least where financial instruments and business contracts were concerned.

Ilham Aliyev was wearing two hats at that seminar: he was the only son of the sitting Azeri president, and he was first vice president of the State Oil Company of the Azerbaijan Republic (SOCAR). Both the emcee of the event and the first speaker after Ilham were current Kennedy School professors and past and future officials in the US Department of Defense. The other speakers were executives at six oil companies already doing business in newly independent Azerbaijan. The recent US assistant secretary of defense Ash Carter made a brief talk about the West's desire for strong military partnership with Aliyev's father and the geopolitical necessity of security and stability in Azerbaijan. "I want you all to do a thought experiment and imagine there were no oil in Azerbaijan," Carter said. "If there were not oil in Azerbaijan, it would still be an important place; it would be a geopolitically important place to the United States. We would still have an interest there, and we should still have a security strategy there."

The next six speakers at the Kennedy School event put the lie to that proposition. Oil and natural gas were the entire point of the seminar because oil and gas were the crucial point of engagement between Azerbaijan and the West. Europe and the US were a bit skittish about the shrinking supply of the commodities so crucial to their citizens' creature comforts and their countries' industrial output. Expectations at the time were that oil production in Europe was going to shrink by almost 2 million barrels per day over the next decade, while demand there

would be increasing by that amount. The US was also girding for a drop
in its domestic oil production and a rise of prices at the pump. Meanwhile, three countries sitting on about 250 billion barrels of proven oil
reserves—Iran, Iraq, and Libya—had proven unreliable trading partners. Azerbaijan was among the key untapped sources of oil and gas in
the old Soviet republics. So major oil companies from Europe and the
US stood ready to do their part in the tapping and to reap the profits.

SOCAR VP Ilham Aliyev had already overseen production-sharing
agreements between his company and many of the biggest oil-producing
companies in the world. The "contract of the century" had flooded Azerbaijan with the cash and know-how needed to get that black gold out of
the Caspian seabed and off to needy European markets and beyond. The
plan was to build three separate pipelines to move Azerbaijan's valuable
export.

The first crude oil produced by the partnership had been sucked out
of the Caspian and into a newly constructed shore terminal just nine
days before the Harvard seminar, and this promised to be but a drop
in the new and growing bucket. The most optimistic estimates of the
oil reserves under the Caspian Sea ran to more than 200 billion barrels,
enough to fuel all of Europe for almost forty years. Saudi Arabia–type
numbers, a development executive from Pennzoil noted. Even if most
of those reserves properly belonged to Iran, Kazakhstan, Turkmeni-
stan, and Russia, Azerbaijan's proven 7 billion was a still very alluring little honeypot all on its own. "For Exxon and for the rest of the
industry, we have two jobs to do in Azerbaijan," one of the seminar
speakers explained. "First is to find and size the resource, the remaining reserves, and then hopefully develop multiple routes to multiple
marketplaces. A slogan that has become popular with the industry,
and with SOCAR now, is 'Happiness is multiple pipelines.' We support
that concept."

The six oil company executives at Harvard heaped copious praise
on the progress Azerbaijan had made in just six years of independence
from the Soviet Union. The Western oilmen in Baku could find restaurants serving excellent Chinese food and Mexican and Cajun. They
could buy Italian suits, French wine, and other luxury goods. The Azeris

were working hard to learn the language of international commerce—English. The speakers at the Kennedy School forum, to a man, also heaped praise on Ilham's father for farsighted policies that not only attracted foreign investment but placed it under legal and judicial protection: "Azerbaijan's prosperous secular government serves as a model for other governments in the new independent republics. . . . Azerbaijan is a very reliable partner for industrial development, not only in our business but, I think, in all business. . . . The progress is unprecedented, certainly in my business experience and probably in the history of our industry."

Just over twenty years later, and sixteen years into Ilham Aliyev's own oil-industry-friendly presidency, the lessons he had first learned still applied. His very low rankings in human rights, rule of law, press freedom and expression and his very high rankings in personal corruption were generally beside the point. As long as Azerbaijan helped feed the gaping maw of the European oil and gas market and spread the profits among a handful of powerful European and American corporations, nobody was going to deny him much of what he wanted. Or call him out too loudly on his most heinous behavior.

I had witnessed this firsthand back in early 2014, on my reporting trip to Baku with President Hollande and French energy company executives who arrived with their hands out. That politicians, human rights activists, and journalists in Azerbaijan were being surveilled, blackmailed, tortured, and imprisoned was not a subject of discussion on that trip. When I sought out the victims of Aliyev's vicious campaign against his detractors, I became a target for harassment and theft (the Azeri security services confiscated our computer drives) and was later dragged into a French court and unsuccessfully sued for libel. President Aliyev objected to us calling Azerbaijan a "dictatorship."

I tried to raise the question of human rights in Azerbaijan at a joint appearance of President Hollande and President Aliyev at the Élysée Palace later that same year. This was a breach of protocol at the palace, where reporters are not supposed to shout questions during photo ops, but sometimes protocol be damned. There were more than ninety Azeri citizens being held in prison for criticizing or challenging Aliyev. Leyla

Yunus, one of the most outspoken human rights activists, whom Hollande and I had both met in Baku, had been jailed six months earlier on questionable fraud and tax evasion charges. She was also being denied much-needed medical care. "Mr. Hollande," I yelled, from behind a cordon about thirty feet away, as the two men walked toward Aliyev's waiting limousine. "Have you considered asking your counterpart to release political prisoners in his country?"

"We have discussed it," Hollande answered.

"And what was his response?" President Aliyev barely even glanced at me. He kept his eyes on Hollande.

"That he was going to look into the matter in detail," Hollande answered.

"About the case of Leyla Yunus, who you met in Baku?" I asked, which did draw Aliyev's attention for just a flash. He didn't speak much French, but he clearly recognized the name.

"That's been done," Hollande insisted, meaning, I guess, he had raised the issue. The two leaders smiled at one another, shook hands, and parted, Hollande back inside his residence and Aliyev across the graveled driveway toward the open door of his waiting limo.

I kept trying, now with Aliyev, in English. "Are you planning to release political prisoners in your country?" He just kept walking toward the car, as if I wasn't even speaking. "What are you planning to do about Leyla Yunus?"

Ilham Aliyev clearly felt no need to answer such a question, and certainly no obligation. He drove off without acknowledging my presence. Hollande refused my later request for a formal interview to discuss human rights violations in Azerbaijan.

The status quo held.

Ethics officials in the US waved off the fact that SOCAR had spent $750,000 to wine and dine American congressmen at the recent "US-Azerbaijan: Vision for the Future" conference. Members of the congressional delegation had been gifted silk scarves, crystal tea sets, rugs, and free travel. Lobbyists in the US and Europe happily accepted millions of dollars to quash a damning report on political prisoners in Azerbaijan. Aliyev's operatives reportedly spent €30 million to persuade members of the Council of Europe, whose sole mission was to bolster democracy on the continent, to ignore the long and continuing Azeri record of human rights violations.

In October 2017, the European Bank for Reconstruction and Development approved a €450 million loan to help fund SOCAR's (and partners') gas pipeline from Azerbaijan to western Europe. The following March, the European Investment Bank signed off on a €930 million loan for the pipeline. "The EIB did not condition the loan on the improvement of human rights," wrote Human Rights Watch, "even though its obligations under the EU Charter of Fundamental Rights mean it should not finance projects that would encourage or support human rights violations."

Exactly a year later, and not long after the new pipeline went into operation, the long-suffering Khadija Ismayilova was subjected to an entirely new and systematic invasion of privacy, courtesy of Pegasus. And now, at the end of May 2021, more than a year and a half after NSO announced its industry-leading Human Rights Policy, its all-star Governance, Risk and Compliance Committee, and its robust vetting program—and as the company was preparing its first ever *Transparency and Responsibility Report*—Khadija Ismayilova remained under constant cybersurveillance by the Azeri security services. When Claudio and Donncha executed a jailbreak on Khadija's phones in the first week of June, they found evidence of more than a hundred separate attacks over eighteen months.

All this thanks to the growing excellence of the relationship between President Ilham Aliyev and the leaders of the country that proudly declares itself the one and only bastion of democracy in the Middle East.

THE WEEK BEFORE Khadija left Baku for her reunion with her OCCRP colleagues, President Ilham Aliyev appeared at a web conference sponsored by a foreign policy NGO in the Azeri capital. Aliyev was in fine fettle that day, still in the glow of the success of his military's lightning forty-four-day offensive against Armenia. He had already inaugurated a museum commemorating this victory, leading a state-run camera crew through the rows of captured Armenian military equipment and through an arch lined with helmets worn by killed and captured Armenian soldiers. Aliyev was happy to credit the key allies who helped the Azeri army retake land lost to Armenians twenty-five years earlier, in the earliest days of his father's presidency. He made a point to recognize the Israeli contribution during the Q&A portion of the web conference in Baku in late May 2021. Israel had provided billions of dollars of sophisticated military equipment over the previous five years, including the drones that had proved pivotal in Aliyev's recent triumph.

"Our relations are very diverse," Aliyev said of his country's relationship with Israel. "We are active trading partners, and the volume of our trade is increasing. Azerbaijan has full access to Israeli defense industry products. It is not a secret. And now we are in the phase of new development in that area."

Prime Minister Benjamin Netanyahu had been nurturing this relationship with the Republic of Azerbaijan for years. He had made pilgrimage to Baku in 2016 to exercise his preferred brand of foreign relations. Commerce, in Netanyahu's view, was the necessary precursor to any international alliance. Israel was already a leading importer of Azeri goods by 2016, trailing only Italy and Turkey in raw volume. Israel was buying Azeri gold, tomatoes, and, of course, oil and gas, while promoting Caspian Sea vacation packages for tourists from Jerusalem, Tel Aviv, and Haifa. Azerbaijan was importing Israeli agricultural technology and military hardware by the billions of dollars. Five years later, wrote one Middle East expert and diplomat who worked at the European Parliament, this advanced weaponry proved "instrumental" to Azerbaijan's victory over Armenia.

Israel's energetic efforts at trade and diplomacy in Azerbaijan were no different from its efforts all across the Middle East. At the end of May 2021, judging by the evidence the Security Lab and the reporters in our consortium had turned up from the leaked data, military-grade spyware was nested in the package of goodies Israel had to offer its prospective allies. Azerbaijan, Morocco, the United Arab Emirates, and Saudi Arabia had all been operating NSO's Pegasus systems under licenses approved by the Israeli government. The former defense and intelligence officials we were talking to at the time were happy to explain the calculus; it all boiled down to the promotion of one thing, and that was Israeli security, which also boiled down to one thing: neutralizing the country that had been promising for generations to wipe Israel from the earth: Iran.

All the trade with Azerbaijan, which included the licensing of Pegasus, was a security swap. Aliyev gets the tools he needs to maintain control of his near total domestic power and fence off his neighbors. And Israel, according to that Middle East expert from the European Parliament, "gains a foothold on Iran's northern borders for intelligence gathering or even a launching pad for a potential military attack on Iran."

The same calculus applied to Israel's attempts at improving relations with Morocco, Saudi Arabia, and the United Arab Emirates. Netanyahu was working to create a united front against Iran in the Middle East, according to former Israeli government officials, and access to cutting-edge Israeli arms, including cyberweapons like Pegasus, was among the incentives the prime minister could offer. "Of course, it helps," says Israeli national security expert Yoel Guzansky.

Netanyahu's government lacked easy and open channels to spread those kinds of incentives in the capital cities of Rabat, Riyadh, and Abu Dhabi. No embassies, no consulates, no foreign service officers on the ground. Israel's chief point contact with these wary allies was its international intelligence service, the Mossad. "Mossad is in charge of building diplomatic connections with the regimes where we don't have a diplomatic relationship," one former Israeli intelligence commander explained to us. When their intelligence counterparts in these countries started asking for Unit 8200–level spyware technology to fight ISIS or homegrown terrorists, the Mossad had to demur. The Israeli military did not share its technology with anyone, not even close allies like the US and the UK. But Mossad could offer the next best thing, which was Pegasus. NSO's technology was top-shelf, and NSO could be trusted to keep their collective mouths shut about who was buying and operating its spyware system.

So tight-lipped were the officials at the top of NSO, in fact, that they even kept the identity of potential clients from the members of the company's new outside human rights advisers who were supposed to provide guidance in vetting potential clients and in investigating claims of misuse. The updated compliance regime, which seemed more like an updated set of talking points, had been pushed hard by the new majority owner of NSO Group, the recently hatched London-based hedge fund Novalpina.

More established firms had taken a hard look at buying NSO and bailed. The partners at Novalpina thought of themselves as buccaneers; willing to take chances on high-risk businesses others were afraid to touch. "They told me it was a new fund that was supposed to be special-izing in problem companies because usually they are underlisted and they make big money," says one potential investor.

The three principals in the fund were thrilled to be able to help Shalev Hulio and Omri Lavie buy out Francisco Partners in early 2019, and then they embarked on a campaign to refurbish the company image, which was in pretty poor shape after the revelations in Mexico and the allegations surrounding the Khashoggi case.

For membership on the new compliance committee, the Novalpina moneymen wooed a number of respected European and American diplomats and intelligence specialists, promising them that they would have real impact on company policy. One of the potential human rights consultants, former French diplomat Gérard Araud, was given a one-day tour of the NSO offices just before he signed on in September 2019. "A modern tower in the northern suburbs of Tel Aviv, the chic district where they have a lot of embassies," Araud remembers. "They have the top three floors of a hypermodern building. Everyone is in T-shirts and shorts. People are all between twenty-eight and thirty-five years old. They arrive on scooters."

The visit came with a brief rundown of Pegasus but no demo of the system itself. "I got some not very precise slides," he says. "The presenta-tion they gave me was for children, really."

Araud says he and his fellow human rights consultants had no real input into company business. A group of investors had once let slip to him that more than forty client countries had licensed Pegasus, but nobody at NSO ever divulged to him the names of these countries. Or even the names of prospective licensees.

The NSO vetting process was an in-house operation, handled by the Governance, Compliance and Risk Committee and run with the exigencies of the Israeli Ministry of Defense in mind. "The [government] mostly looks at it in the spectrum of what's good for Israel," says one cybersecurity expert we talked to in Israel. "It's not about the ethics of the sales. They just want to make sure it won't be used against Israel."

There was an acute sensitivity among Israeli authorities to the moods and responses of the governments of the United States and Russia. No US phone number could be attacked by Pegasus, the Ministry of Defense and NSO claimed, nor could any phone be attacked by Pegasus while it was on US territory. Somebody at the Ministry of Defense or at Prime Minister Netanyahu's office scotched Pegasus licensing deals to Ukraine and Estonia, according to reporting in March 2022 by Ronen Bergman and Mark Mazzetti of the *New York Times*, for fear of Vladimir Putin's reaction if it were found to have been used against officials in his Kremlin.

North Korea, China, and Iran were deemed beyond the pale but not many others. Not even Saudi Arabia. Not even in the aftermath of the Khashoggi killing. The Saudi rulers might be anti-democratic and serial violators of human rights, and even outright murderers, but they were becoming more aggressive in their efforts to help with what Israel most desired—checking Iranian power. You can't always choose your allies, was Netanyahu's take. Interests trump friendship in the existential matter of national security.

HOLGER STARK, FROM our partner *Die Zeit*, arrived in Tel Aviv on the same day Khadija Ismayilova touched down in Ankara, May 29, 2021. Three days later, and the day after Claudio confirmed that Khadija's iPhone had been targeted by Pegasus, Holger was busy confirming basic facts: NSO had clients in more than forty countries. The company had about 860 employees and 550 of those, give or take, worked in research and development. More than half of NSO customers were government agencies in European countries. NSO officials estimated its value at about $1.5 billion, a bit less than what was being reported in the financial press.

Novalpina now owned 70 percent of NSO; Shalev and Omri maintained personal interest in the company worth about $10 million each. The Pegasus system represented about 65 percent of NSO's business, but the company hoped it would soon be less than half. Drone technology was the next big thing.

Holger did find himself, suddenly, in the same room as Shalev Hulio at one point in the trip. He used it as an opportunity to press the NSO CEO. "Okay, to make sure," Holger asked, "Pegasus was not used either before or after the Khashoggi murder to target the people around him?"

Shalev answered: "No, not his wife, not family . . . never, ever, ever, ever and never and again. I am willing to do a polygraph on that. None of our technology actually had been used in that case."

CHAPTER NINETEEN

"THIS IS GOING TO BE BIG"

Sandrine

Donncha Ó Cearbhaill was back home in Ireland, back inside the Ring, in the middle of June 2021. He was there to visit his family and friends, but the trip could hardly be counted as vacation. Donncha spent much of his time in Birr at his parents' kitchen table, his laptops and notebooks splayed out in front of him, bent to his work. The scene in their kitchen may have given Donncha's parents reason for pause, given his complicated history in the cyberworld. Donncha could not confide in his parents exactly what kind of work he was doing, but they did know this much: when their son spent this much time on his computer, wrapped up in secret projects, it had not always resulted in happy outcomes. "Is this all legit?" his father asked him at one point in the visit.

Donncha had little choice but to stick to his private business, whatever his parents' concern. The Pegasus Project was gaining momentum every day, as if the entire eighty-person team was just starting to accelerate toward a long final kick to the finish line. I felt it in Paris, and no doubt Donncha felt it, too. He represented an entire half of the project's crucial forensics team, and the journalists working on Pegasus were piling more on his shoulders every day.

One of the imperatives we had set for ourselves involved a numbers game. We had already verified the identities of close to 1,000 of the 50,000 selections in the data. The verifications included about 150 journalists, and our goal was to get that number up to 200 before publication. The deadline we had set for that task was July 6, just three weeks away. We were also working hard to confirm as many people as possible who had been victimized by Pegasus attacks or actual Pegasus infections, which meant a steady flow of backup files from mobile phones (or the physical phones themselves) was washing into the Security Lab.

The daughter of the hero of Hotel Rwanda, Carine Kanimba, had provided backup files from her two iPhones a week earlier, for instance. (Hannes Munzinger, from *Süddeutsche Zeitung*, had approached Carine after the German newspaper had found the mobile phone number of her father's attorney in the data. Because Carine was a vocal spokesperson defending her father, and a vocal critic of the Rwandan regime, Hannes believed she might also be a Pegasus target.) There was no clear evidence of Pegasus infection on either iPhone but enough suspicious activity that we asked her if she would send the phones to Berlin for a jailbreak analysis.

Stephanie Kirchgaessner, from the *Guardian*, had persuaded a second exiled human rights defender from Rwanda to allow Claudio and Donncha to run forensics on his cell phone logs. Pegasus Project reporters were approaching people in the data from all over the world. Siddharth and his team from the *Wire* had found four possible victims in India willing to submit their phones to forensics—a human rights lawyer, a human rights defender, a labor union official, and a journalist. Phineas found two more journalists from India who agreed to the forensics and to go public if the Pegasus targeting was confirmed. A third said no, thank you, telling Phineas that he was in the middle of very sensitive reporting and wasn't willing to risk compromising it.

The wife of a Moroccan political dissident who was serving a thirty-year prison sentence said yes to the forensics. Frederik Obermaier, Bastian Obermayer, and Szabolcs Panyi all had new candidates for analysis in Hungary. A reporter from *Süddeutsche Zeitung* thought she had a chance to get the iPhone of a young Azeri dissident who had drowned in Istanbul just a month earlier; his number was selected back in 2019, not long after Khadija Ismayilova was first targeted.

The most urgent forensics at that moment in mid-June revolved around the Jamal Khashoggi case. Traces of evidence in the Android phone belonging to Khashoggi's wife, Hanan, suggested she had been targeted by Pegasus spyware before his murder but did not prove a successful infection. So Dana Priest of the *Washington Post* was flying to Istanbul with Arthur Bouvart from Forbidden Stories on June 15 to meet with Khashoggi's closest contacts in Turkey, including his fiancée, Hatice Cengiz, who had been waiting outside the consulate in Istanbul at the time of his murder. Hatice was also in our data. If things went as planned, Claudio and Donncha would be analyzing her mobile phone any day.

On top of the ongoing requests for forensic analyses, the two cybersecurity researchers were just beginning to pull together a report detailing their findings to present to NSO before publication. We had an obligation as journalists to give the company a chance to comment on, dispute, or correct any of the facts we deemed solid enough to publish. Amnesty International and the Security Lab felt ethically bound to give NSO the opportunity to respond to specifics in the forensic findings as well.

Claudio and Donncha were also preparing the materials they would be releasing to the public at large when the Pegasus Project went live on July 18. The pair had decided to do something fairly unprecedented in the short annals of cybersurveillance research. They were going to be completely transparent. They weren't going to merely show their findings; they meant to show their work, in detail, to the world. There would be a comprehensive report on Security Lab methodology, including the design, development, and implementation of their forensic tool. Claudio and Donncha were also preparing to report in detail the evidence they had found for each and every confirmed attack or infection, and to expose all the zero-click and zero-day exploits they had identified, as well as all the Pegasus-generated process names and fake accounts that NSO made available to its clients for delivery of the malicious spyware payload.

The reports were still evolving because Claudio and Donncha were gathering new evidence almost every day. On June 14, while Donncha was in Ireland and Dana Priest and Arthur Bouvart were heading out for their trip to Istanbul, Claudio was in his office in Berlin jailbreaking one of Khadija Ismayilova's cell phones. Miranda Patrucic had carried the phones to Germany for further analysis after her reunion with Khadija in Ankara. Claudio had one of Khadija's iPhones wired into his laptop that sunny late-spring morning, while Miranda peered over his shoulder, trying to make sense of the impenetrable lines of code filling the screen, highlighted in different colors. "This is what it looks like really," Claudio explained. "I mean, this is just the output of our tool. So essentially, we see processes that we know are connected to Pegasus. We'll see some iMessage accounts that are connected to the attacks . . ."

"Is it new ones or the ones you've seen before in her backup files?" Miranda wanted to know.

"I believe these are the ones we've seen before, but I'm going to have to basically later sit down and go through the ones I may not have seen," Claudio explained, pointing out different lines on the screen. It was all pretty standard fare, lines of code he and Donncha had observed dozens of times by now. "This might indicate what the entry point is," he said, and then suddenly, "What the fuck? . . . That's weird. . . . There are some new traces that we have not seen before. . . . They might be indicative of some other exploits that we've not seen before."

He told Miranda he needed a little extra time "to do some more digging."

Donncha had a look as well, and the two partners agreed. This *was* something new, an exploit neither had ever seen before. NSO researchers had apparently found a vulnerability related to Apple Music sometime before the summer of 2020 because the Pegasus system used it as the entry point for delivery of malicious spyware payload to Khadija's iPhone as early as July 10 of that year. The evidence in Khadija's phone didn't allow Claudio and Donncha to determine exactly where in the exploit chain Apple Music fit—whether it was the vehicle for the final delivery of the payload or just an early stage in prying open a back door—but it pointed to an NSO-created domain Claudio and Donncha had identified back in 2019. And the URL pattern used to download the payload showed another key link between the attacks

on Maati Monjib's phone in 2019, Khadija's in 2020, and the Pegasus zero-click exploit chain being used in 2021. This late discovery meant a whole new section that Claudio and Donncha would have to write into their *Forensic Methodology Report*: "Apple Music Leveraged to Deliver Pegasus in 2020."

DANA PRIEST AND Arthur Bouvart arrived in Istanbul the next day, June 15, 2021, and shuttled back and forth to Ankara over the next few days so they could meet with both Khashoggi's fiancée, Hatice Cengiz, and his good friend Yasin Aktay, a Turkish government official. Aktay was not only Khashoggi's emergency contact in Turkey; he was also a key aide and confidant to Turkish president Recep Tayyip Erdoğan. When Dana explained to Aktay that he was in our data, he expressed no surprise. In the aftermath of Khashoggi's murder, he said, he had been told by agents from the Turkish Interior Ministry that his phone had been hacked. He didn't ask who had compromised his phone at the time, and he waved off Dana's request that he make that ask now. Aktay agreed to sit for an interview, but he refused to let us run forensics on his phone. His life and his professional dealings were an open book, he said, and he'd long ago changed to a new phone.

Aktay did not appear to be a wary man by nature, but he was wary of the ruling families in the Kingdom of Saudi Arabia and the United Arab Emirates, for whom he had little good to say. Nobody had ever tried to assassinate him, he told Dana, but he wasn't taking any chances. He had a personal bodyguard and a big Mercedes with darkly tinted windows, maybe bulletproof. When he took Dana to the airport, Aktay's driver pushed the limo up to 120 miles per hour. "It is very hard to have an assassination plan when you go fast," he said.

Hatice Cengiz had been forced into her own tight security bubble after Jamal Khashoggi's killing. She was protected at all times by a security detail provided by the Turkish Interior Ministry but rarely went out in public even with her armed guards. Hatice did consent to meet with Dana and Arthur, and she did agree, after a lot of gentle cajoling by the two reporters, to let the Security Lab run the forensics on her iPhone.

She seemed skeptical that the forensics would turn up anything because she had been told that the iPhone was a very secure device.

Donncha was sitting at the kitchen table at his boyhood home in Birr—right down the hall from the room where he learned his cyber-skills, where he had pranked Rupert Murdoch ten years earlier, and where the local police had first burst in to question him about his alleged "cybercrimes"—when the upload of Hatice's iPhone backup commenced in that third week of June. Claudio was outside on his balcony in Berlin, on the line with Dana, talking her through the process, and also on a separate line with Donncha. When the files uploaded, the Security Lab forensic tool dug out the goods in no time.

Claudio and Donncha, separated by 2,000 kilometers, could both see it all, at the same time. They knew exactly what they had found. There was the CrashReporter file, and the bh process, and a data extraction, and another Pegasus-generated process name. Hatice's phone had no doubt been attacked and successfully compromised by Pegasus spyware. There was evidence of attack and/or infection on three separate days over a six-day span in early October 2018. The first attack was four days after MBS's Saudi thugs murdered Jamal Khashoggi.

"This was like a turning point," Claudio remembered of that moment. "We had already found a lot of cases by then, but for me, it just clicked. 'Fuck. This is going to be big.' It's not just a bunch of journalists in some country nobody ever heard of or nobody cares about. This will have impact. Because of the gravity of the story in which [Hatice] was involved and because of the fact it had been repeated [by NSO and Shalev] ad nauseam that it was all bullshit."

Donncha had the same reaction. "This is not overhyped, the Khashoggi thing," he remembers thinking. "It is actually really real. This disproves all the lies NSO has been saying for years that they didn't have anything to do with the murder. I remember standing up from my table and almost being like, 'Oh wow. We found the evidence.'"

THINGS WERE HAPPENING so fast now that it was real work to keep track. There were around eighty journalists on the project, and we had

separate investigations going in Europe, Asia, Africa, the Americas, and the Middle East. Nina Lakhani of the *Guardian* was just back from Mexico; she hadn't had any more luck than Paloma locating Cecilio Pineda's phone, but Nina had filled out the story about Cecilio's final bits of work and the threats against him in the weeks before his still-unsolved murder. Siddharth had met with a political opponent of Indian prime minister Narendra Modi, Rahul Gandhi, who confirmed the reports that someone (and Gandhi made it sound like it might have been someone inside NSO) had warned him that he had been targeted.

Kristof Clerix of *Knack* in Belgium was going back to talk to Carine Kanimba to get her phones for another round of forensics. I spent hours at my flat with a reporter from Radio France, who was headed to Rwanda, trying to game out how she might approach known Pegasus targets there. This was no easy task. Rwanda was a dangerous place for a foreign journalist to work. She knew she would likely be watched and followed by government security services. Even after decades developing sources in the region, she had no one there she could absolutely trust to maintain the necessary secrecy.

The *Washington Post*'s Craig Timberg was getting good background material from cybersecurity specialists who at least had some limited vision into the vulnerabilities in Apple's iMessage app. "Send unlimited texts, photos, videos, documents and more," was how Apple marketed the app. This one-service-does-all program was a remarkable convenience for the user, but that convenience came with a cost few users understood. When iMessage was just an Apple version of SMS, it was pretty locked down, according to one cyberexpert, but once the app allowed iPhones to download video and GIFs and games, it became significantly less secure. As Apple added more and more facets to iMessage, it created a larger "attack surface."

Martin Untersinger from *Le Monde* was able to add to Craig's reporting with a source who had spent some time on Apple's security team. "In the beginning the iOS had few vulnerabilities, but the past few years have gotten worse," Martin offered the team as general background. The iPhone was likely the most secure mobile phone on the market, and Apple still had a "colossal" team playing defense, he explained, but that team had a lot coming at them, both in terms of outside researchers hunting flaws and coders accidentally creating them. "Developers introduce bugs when they code badly, when they start off with a complicated codebase, or because they're pressed to work fast. Apple releases have accelerated in the last few years."

Holger Stark was just back from Tel Aviv with sackfuls of very useful reporting, including confirmations of some key facts about NSO and its relations with the Israeli government and its intelligence services. National security reporter Shane Harris and another of his colleagues from the *Washington Post* had scheduled their own trip to Israel for early July. Amitai Ziv, meanwhile, was on his way to interview Uri Ansbacher about his questionable dealings in Mexico, which he knew a lot more about now, with access to the leaked documents Carmen Aristegui had shared with the group. Amitai had just gotten a call from Shalev Hulio's founding partner in NSO, Omri Lavie, who wanted to sit down for a coffee the last week of June. Amitai had just published a story in *Haaretz* on NSO's recent financial woes, so it was likely Omri was trying to do damage control on that front. But the invite still made me wonder for a second whether or not NSO was onto us.

My nerves were already a little twitchy when Laurent came in on June 17 and showed me a disquieting message from Fabrice Arfi, our friend and colleague from *Mediapart* who had helped convince Edwy Plenel to let us do the forensics on his phone back in April. Fabrice had sent Laurent a text saying that he had heard some loose talk around Paris about Edwy's Pegasus infection. Neither Fabrice nor Edwy were happy about it. *Mediapart* was doing its own reporting on cybersurveillance separate from our consortium, but they had made the collegial offer to hold their stories until after we published. Fabrice was worried that a story about Pegasus infections inside *Mediapart* would leak, and it would embarrass the respected site. Edwy was nervous. Fabrice was nervous. I was a bit concerned myself. We were still a month away from publication, and it was my job to make sure this investigation remained a close-held secret until we were ready to hit the go button.

∎∎∎∎∎∎∎

KRISTOF CLERIX WAS determined to nail down the Carine Kanimba story for *Knack* when he went to see her in Belgium on June 24, 2021. Kristof had been an enthusiastic partner on the Pegasus Project, and he knew Carine was living in Belgium at the time. Her father, Paul Rusesabagina, had been kidnapped by Rwandan authorities a year earlier, was currently being tried on very questionable charges, and it looked like he was going to be railroaded into a sentence that ensured he would die in prison.

Carine had left Rwanda as a young girl, shortly after surviving the genocide there; she had gone to college in the United States and worked in New York for part of her career. But she had been living in Belgium since her father's kidnapping. Carine carried two phones, one with a Belgian number and one with a US number. Neither phone proved particularly cooperative.

Kristof had already gone to see Carine three times in Belgium in the previous three weeks to facilitate the forensics on her two phones, but the analysis was still not completed to anyone's satisfaction. On the first visit, when Kristof tried to make a backup of one phone, the file was just too big; on the second visit, a key file went missing in the upload to the Security Lab. The plan for Kristof's fourth visit was to get a more complete backup of the Belgian phone for Claudio to analyze. Further complications arose that day. When Kristof tried to collect the diagnostic logs from Carine's phone, the process froze, something Claudio had never seen before. "I was like, well, that's strange," Claudio remembers. He suggested that Carine shut down the phone and restart it, which she did, and this time the log extraction worked without a hitch. It occurred to Claudio that day that maybe the phone was compromised with Pegasus at the very moment he had tried to extract the data, and the malware was blocking him. When he checked the diagnostic logs in the timeline he found the Pegasus process executions he had seen over and over the previous few months: otpgrefd, launchafd, vrn_stats. "There were records right up until the minute that I told her to shut the phone down. She was getting infected every few days, and we happened to be there."

"We thought we were on their tail when we had started finding cases a month old," Donncha says. "Then we started finding cases a week old.

Then [with Carine], we found somebody whose phone was hacked at the very moment we were analyzing the phone. Okay, now we're really going head-to-head. They're targeting, and we're actively finding infections that are happening right now. We're really, really on their tail."

By now, after almost four months of forensics, the increasing proximity to the attacks had paid off. As Claudio and Donncha moved from looking at historical cases to active targeting and live infections—crimes in progress, you could call it—they had developed enough evidence, on enough different mobile phones, to be able to piece together the zero-day, zero-click iMessage exploit chain that Pegasus had been employing throughout 2021. Claudio and Donncha called this sophisticated new attack Megalodon, a name in their Pegasus evidence file. (Megalodon was also the name of the largest species of shark that ever lived, which was probably not lost on NSO exploit developers.) The Security Lab forensic tool had first turned up evidence of Megalodon on the mobile phone of a French human rights lawyer back in March, and Claudio and Donncha had seen it on other phones in April, May, and now at the end of June, in Carine's iPhone.

The problem, of course, was that if the Security Lab could see the best new version of Pegasus operating live inside the phone, it increased the odds that Pegasus could see the Security Lab operating live inside the phone as well. Claudio and Donncha had been anxious to wrap up this investigation as quickly as possible for weeks. Now they were really anxious to get it done.

I had a great and growing appreciation for those concerns, especially after Amitai Ziv contacted me a few days later to say one of his sources in Israel, connected to the cyber industry there, asked him if we had "a list." There were apparently rumors floating around Israel about a list connected to NSO.

I asked Amitai to set up a call for me with his source. I suggested Amitai tell him we wanted his technical insights into the cyberexploit industry as it was practiced in Israel.

The guy seemed to be a bit of a gadfly around the cyber circuit in Israel when I did a little research on him—a self-described security expert who was always in attendance at the big cyber conferences where Prime Minister Netanyahu did his cheerleading for the industry. But he talked as if he was interested in policing cybersurveillance tools like Pegasus, so who knew. Maybe I was being paranoid. Maybe he would have something worthwhile to add.

When I got him on the line, he said he wanted to be helpful to us, but the conversation very quickly got weird. The first strange thing he did was offer up a ludicrous math formula suggesting that the total number of people targeted by NSO clients added up to maybe 1.8 million over ten years. A classic red herring.

Then he started fishing for information. He never actually asked me about a list, but he did push for specifics about our investigation. "Sandrine, you haven't told me what this story is about," he said.

"It's about cyberthreats against journalists," I said, explaining as much as I could to somebody outside the consortium of reporters and editors. "Like our Mexican story and our Moroccan story, basically. We're following what we started and really trying to find out what are the kinds of cyberthreats that are possible against journalists and who can be targeted. And basically, technically, how this works."

This wasn't good enough for him, he said. He wanted something more "concrete," like maybe new "signs" he could check for us against his own database. I told him I'd send him a list of questions, which he could answer by email. Then I got off the line.

He was persistent and not very subtle. "If you do have the database that was leaked, which is probably just a rumor," he wrote after we ended the call, "can you please look for my name there?" Now I found myself wondering if he was acting on behalf of NSO.

A few days later, we heard from Shane Harris, one of a dozen or so reporters the *Washington Post* now had on the project. Shane had decided to scrub his planned trip to Israel. A new government had just taken charge a few weeks earlier. Netanyahu was out as prime minister, and Naftali Bennett was in. But it seemed very unlikely that the new administration would be any less protective of NSO Group. The *Post* thought that Israeli authorities knew something was heating up around the company and its technology, and Bennett's administration was worried about a "big mess." The *Post* was starting to hear talk inside Israel of a Pegasus-related "victim list."

We were still three weeks away from publication, which seemed like a very long time to keep this investigation secret, and I wasn't entirely sure we would all get to safe harbor.

CHAPTER TWENTY

"WE'RE ROLLING"

Sandrine

Anxiety about keeping the Pegasus Project under wraps for a few more weeks and keeping our source out of harm's way before, during, and after publication was causing me some restless nights. The chief worry among the other partners in the last days of June was the question of the forensics. Claudio and Donncha had been calm and steady hands throughout the investigation, and anybody in the consortium who had watched them work up close, or sat in on their presentations, walked away confident in their technical expertise. But every one of these journalists had editors back home to answer to, and each of their publications had attorneys who were paid to be skeptical, and to demand as much proof as could be obtained, and to keep their clients out of court. The editors and the lawyers all wanted some serious reinforcement of the Security Lab's findings, and we had all agreed at our conference back in May that the best possible reinforcement was a peer review of the forensics.

There was a single best possible option for the technical review. The gold standard of independent cybersecurity research facilities was Citizen Lab. The institution and its personnel were known in the field and respected around the world. So everybody on the project was pleased when Citizen Lab and its lead computer scientist, Bill Marczak, signed on to conduct the peer review. The head of Amnesty Tech, Danna Ingleton, set up the mechanics with Ron Deibert, the director of Citizen Lab in Toronto. The first stage of the two-part review was forensic analyses on a few of the iPhones in which Claudio and Donncha had found evidence of compromise by Pegasus. The review would be done blind, using Citizen Lab's own forensic tools, without any knowledge of the methodology the Security Lab had used in its analysis. The hope was that Citizen Lab would replicate the Security Lab's findings. The second part of the peer review would be a more general audit of the methodology Claudio and Donncha had employed. Kind of like an outside coach watching game film after the fact and grading the plays.

I didn't foresee any problems, but that didn't mean I was free of worry. Any unexpected issues in the peer review could be devastating to the investigation. If Citizen Lab was unable to replicate our findings, or found serious problems in our methodology, salvaging the Pegasus Project would be an uphill battle. We sent off three separate iPhone backup files to Toronto on June 24, with the permission of the owners—Khadija Ismayilova, Szabolcs Panyi, and Edwy Plenel—and asked for a quick turnaround. The first results came back four days later, which felt like a very long four days.

Bill Marczak and his colleague John Scott-Railton called to let us know what they'd found and then sent us their written report. When I opened the file, I skimmed through the short section containing the Pegasus-generated process names that Citizen Lab had recognized in each of the three new analyses and went straight to the money paragraph: "We conclude with high confidence," it read, that all three iPhones "were successfully infected with NSO Group's Pegasus spyware during the dates mentioned. Our high confidence conclusion stems from the fact that we have never seen the above process names used in a benign context, and we have only ever seen the above process names used in high-confidence cases of infection with NSO Group's Pegasus spyware."

I posted my synopsis of the first stage of the peer review on the secure site that each of the partners could access, along with a pdf of the report Citizen Lab had forwarded, and I anticipated the collective sigh of relief from Pegasus Project collaborators all over the world. Craig Timberg posted a comment almost immediately. "This is tremendous news!" he wrote. "Well done!" Miranda Patrucic from OCCRP seconded him: "This is excellent."

Neither Claudio nor Donncha was going to crow about this validation of their work, in part because neither of them was angling for the spotlight. The two had remained low-key, nose-to-the-grindstone craftsmen throughout our partnership. That wasn't going to change. But when Claudio got on a secure call two days later to be interviewed by a small subgroup of the partners who wanted quotes from him for their opening-day stories, now just eighteen days away, he seemed almost buoyant. He may have even smiled a few times. Claudio was on the line for an hour and a half, patiently taking questions, prepared to explain anything from the first draft of the eighty-page report he and Donncha were planning to release on our publication date. Claudio had provided the draft to all the partners earlier that day.

He was hearing the same questions he had fielded from some of these same reporters already, sometimes over and over—*How do you know it is Pegasus and not some other spyware?*—but he seemed happy to answer. "These process names are very unique. Very peculiar. There are only a few dozen of these, and they are not legitimate iOS process names. And I can say it for a fact because I also did the exercise of downloading every single version of iOS which was released since 2016, and I checked every single file that was released with it. And none of these actually appear on it. So we know that these processes that appear are not legitimate processes. They're malicious processes. We know that they are Pegasus processes because they are connected to the network infrastructure we've seen."

He went back over the intrusive capabilities of NSO's spyware: "When an iPhone is compromised, it's done in such a way that allows attackers to obtain so-called root privileges or administration privileges on the device that virtually allows anything to be done on the phone." That meant *anything*, adding a new thought to the discussion. If somebody wanted to know how fast you were moving while driving your car, Claudio explained, all the NSO engineers had to do was write the code and slip it into the infected phone.

Claudio answered questions about the dynamics of the battle between

NSO and mobile phone manufacturers like Apple, which was probably still the best at playing defense. "Credit where credit is due," he said of Apple, "but someone that is very talented out there, motivated by the very high remuneration they get from finding these issues, is working in all possible ways to bypass and find workarounds." He reminded the reporters about the goody bag of workaround exploits NSO could offer their Pegasus licensees. "I imagine there's a good chunk they discover and develop themselves," he explained, "and there's probably a good chunk to be acquired from external researchers and brokers."

By the end of the interview, I couldn't help reflecting on the value of this collaboration between journalists and technical experts. Whatever wariness Claudio, Donncha, Laurent, and I had had about one another in that first meeting in Berlin back in 2020 had evaporated. We had each made the others better at our jobs, and that was no small thing. Claudio and Donncha's technical expertise not only provided the reporters on the project a much more nuanced understanding of the Pegasus system and NSO and the entire cybersurveillance industry; it had also opened an avenue to help them find the most emblematic and powerful personal stories. And by getting out in the field and scaring up more than sixty different phones for forensic analysis, the reporters on the Pegasus Project had managed to deliver to the resident empiricists at the Security Lab the means to new discovery. "The more attack records you see, the more you compare traces, the more clear the picture becomes," Claudio told the group that day. "You start putting together all the pieces of the puzzle, and it starts becoming more obvious. So it all kind of adds up."

THINGS STARTED GETTING really real for me after that, in the first week of July, because it was my job to coordinate the massive five-day, worldwide, multiplatform publication—involving seventeen independent newsrooms, each with its own prerogatives and its own editors and its own attorneys. We were still wrangling details of the order of the rollout of the stories ten days before our publication date. For maximum impact, and minimum blowback, the rollout had to be synchronized, and the content needed to be as uniform as possible. The general outlines of the schedule I mapped were acceptable to all. On Day One, the consortium would lay out the scope and scale of the use of NSO's Pegasus spyware system, but the focus would be on journalists and human rights defenders who had been victimized. Almost all the partners planned to make the targeting of Jamal Khashoggi's family members (wife, fiancée, and one son), friends, and colleagues the lead story that first day. But not all. *Direkt36* preferred to lead with the story of its own reporters being spied on with Pegasus, courtesy of the Orbán government; the *Wire* would headline stories about journalists being cybersurveilled in India, including those compromised in their own newsroom. OCCRP planned to highlight the Khadija Ismayilova story.

The partners all agreed to hold the names of world leaders and government officials selected for targeting by NSO until Day Three, to make sure the more serious issues about cybersurveillance of private citizens weren't overwhelmed by dog-bites-man headlines about geopolitical spy games. The odds of that happening had increased immensely just a few days earlier, when the team from *Le Monde* had finally been able to confirm that a mobile phone number in the data was, in fact, that of sitting French president Emmanuel Macron. *Le Monde* had confirmed the selection of more than a dozen other key members of the Macron administration. There were a handful of other presidents and prime ministers in the data that we had been able to confirm with multiple sources and could now identify in print.

The final request for a change in schedule came from the *Wire*, in India. The original plan was to save the story of Pegasus being used to spy on Rahul Gandhi, the most serious political rival of Prime Minister Narendra Modi, until Day Five. Exposing the Modi government for what looked like the criminal act of surveilling a political opponent was a potentially explosive revelation in the world's largest democracy. We all wanted to give the story its own space, where it didn't have to compete for attention. But the editor at the *Wire*, Siddharth Varadarajan, didn't think his website could hold the story for four days. He was afraid Gandhi would talk to other news outlets in India as soon as the Pegasus Project went live, and the *Wire* would lose the biggest scoop in its home territory. I sent a query to the partners about moving up the Gandhi report. "We know it's an important story for the *Wire*," I explained, "and that they have done important work investigating it." Everybody agreed to move Gandhi to Day Two, making the headline story of Day Five the potential targeting of people close to the Dalai Lama.

The other tricky bit of coordination was making sure the partners stuck to the same language in paragraphs describing the nature of the leak and the central conclusions of the investigation. In the first case, we needed to make sure we continued to protect the personal safety of our source. In the second, we needed to make sure none of the partners overstepped the boundary lines of what our forensic evidence and our reporting revealed about NSO and its clients. The editors and lawyers of each partner could determine for themselves just how far they wanted to go, but we needed them all to know there were lines that could not be crossed—both to ensure accuracy and to meet the professional standards we all shared. A person on the list we had confirmed, for instance, we could say was "selected" for possible Pegasus attack by a client of NSO. "You should NEVER imply that someone was successfully targeted UNLESS we can prove so through forensic analysis of the phone," I wrote in a fact sheet distributed to all the partners.

We did, by then, feel confident in reporting the extraordinary fact that the data we had been given access to contained about fifty thousand unique phone numbers. Our confidence came from the forensic work Claudio and Donncha had done, in spite of limitations. It was impossible, for instance—given time constraints, the danger of exposing our investigation, or the very real possibility of putting the source in harm's way—to approach everybody we could confirm in the data and ask them to let us do the forensics on their mobile phone. But we had been able to safely run technical analyses on more than sixty phones belonging to journalists, lawyers, and human rights activists—none of whom were criminals, terrorists, or pedophiles. According to the forensic analysis by Claudio and Donncha, 85 percent of the iPhones in our data being used at the time of selection showed evidence of infection. Nearly nine out of ten.

"We know that we see records of phone numbers selected by NSO clients before Pegasus infections," I explained in our fact sheet. "We know infection always occurs AFTER a selection . . . in quite a few cases there is approximately 30 seconds between selection and iMessage look-ups on the device. The time varies between seeing the iMessage lookups and Pegasus process on the device, but it's in the range of five minutes to one hour. . . . Conclusion we can make is phone numbers we see were entered in a system used by NSO clients before a Pegasus attack."

LAURENT AND THE lead editor of the Pegasus Project at the *Guardian*, Paul Lewis, got Edward Snowden on the phone the first week in July. Paul had worked on the Snowden story back in 2013, when the former US government contractor revealed that the NSA was monitoring com-munication traffic, if not actual conversations, en masse, and had the capability of building a "pattern of life" profile on anybody who used a cell phone or the internet. Those revelations had real consequences, both intended and unintended. Tech companies like Apple began to put a pre-mium on encryption of communication to ensure privacy, and marketed their ability to provide a new layer of personal security. Law enforce-ment agencies around the world then made pleas for a "back door" into encrypted devices like laptops and cell phones so they wouldn't "go dark" and lose their ability to track terrorists and other criminals. The tech companies rightly refused, pointing out that if they created and distrib-uted back doors to self-proclaimed white hats like the FBI, the black hats were sure to get them, too, and could then do damage to innocent people. NSO and other private companies stepped into that breach, learning how to exploit software vulnerabilities in mobile phones and selling to law enforcement and intelligence agencies the tools to catch the bad guys.

"The centerpiece of this is a leak of data from NSO Group," Paul told Snowden in their Zoom call on July 5, 2021. "We have fifty thousand phone numbers."

Edward Snowden is not easily shocked by stories about the spread of cybersurveillance, but he seemed taken aback. He was silent for a couple of seconds, while the number sank it. "*Fifty* thousand," he said. "Wow."

"Yeah, more than fifty thousand," Paul explained.

"It's a completely different scale," Snowden mused. "You know the general argument that the NSA and also these commercial companies that are trying to do the same thing, is that it's targeted, you know, it's only used against criminals, it's only used against bad people. To have fifty thousand phone numbers that have been targeted just puts the lie to that kind of argument."

"NSO has always maintained the line: our clients are contractually bound to only use this technology against terrorists and criminals," Paul said. "What we found is that on a pretty sort of widespread basis across the world, these governments have been using a technology to spy on or target journalists, activists, lawyers, human rights defenders, academics, businesspeople, senior religious figures, politicians up to and including some heads of state. Sort of everyone, really."

Not a major surprise, Snowden responded, but then, "*Fifty* thousand people. It's, uh, I just kind of keep repeating that number to myself. A company like [NSO] really shouldn't exist. . . . These are devices that exist in every context, on every desk, every home, all over the world, and we are dependent. We cannot work, we cannot communicate, we cannot trade, we cannot go about our lives in a normal expected way today without using these. . . . The only thing that the NSO group does, their only product is trying to discover weaknesses in these devices that we all rely on and then sell them commercially. . . . There's no limitation. There's only Israel pinky promising that they're going to have their Ministry of Defense or whatever review the export license."

Just ten minutes into the call, Snowden was on a roll. The fix, as he saw it, was some kind of global regulation to bring the cybersurveillance industry to heel. Maybe the EU would be moved, finally, to act. NSO is "not trying to save the world," he continued. "They're not trying to do anybody any good. They're trying to make money despite their public claims to the contrary. When you create the means of infection, and you start passing them off to the highest bidder, as the NSO Group has done and is doing and will do tomorrow—if nothing changes, you're creating, you are *guaranteeing* that the world will be less safe tomorrow than it is today."

Before he signed off, Snowden told Paul he would be happy to assist the Pegasus Project any way he could. "If you guys want me to help, like, just announce it," Snowden said, "because this is a story."

PAUL LEWIS UNDERSTOOD as well as any of our partners the potential impact of this story, as well as the potential for damage. Given the libel laws in the United Kingdom, the *Guardian* was likely to be among the most exposed of our media partners. Paul was mindful of one of the final key pieces of business for the Pegasus Project: composing a letter to NSO asking for response and comment on what we intended to report. The letter was a must, legally and ethically; it offered NSO the opportunity to speak to all the key facts that the consortium would be reporting. The most difficult balancing act in this effort was a matter of timing. A few of the partners had wanted to send our request for response to NSO weeks in advance. But there were partners still reporting, and we didn't want to give NSO or its clients the chance to scuttle that work before we were ready.

Laurent and I were aiming to send the letter to NSO on July 10, which would give them four days to respond to specifics in our upcoming publication, and still leave another four days for further discussion with NSO and for any necessary refinements or emendations of our stories before the project went live. The partners were also working on separate drafts of requests for response to be sent to all the governments that had, by pretty clear evidence, licensed and used Pegasus.

The team at the *Guardian* took the lead in writing the first draft of the request for response; the joke around the office in London was that they had the perfect man for the job. David Pegg's first big job at the *Guardian* was on an investigation in 2015 into allegations that the Swiss bank HSBC helped its wealthy banking customers conceal assets and dodge taxes. As the junior member of the team, David was assigned the thankless task of composing request-for-response letters for more than 150 people implicated in the SwissLeaks scandal. David signed the letter himself, and what followed was an avalanche of threats from rich and powerful folks sent to the *Guardian's* editors and lawyers. *Do you have any idea what this fellow David Pegg is doing?* David laughs about how he had been very truly and rightly intimidated at first, but pretty quickly became desensitized to it. "I still think of it as a happy memory, strangely," David told us at one point. "My friends all think I'm weird."

Anyway, David took on the job of drafting the request-for-response to NSO with Paul's help. The two organized the letter in four separate categories: individuals targeted by Pegasus; NSO's dealings with the clients who appear to have misused its spyware; conclusions that could rationally be drawn from the reporting we had done; and a catchall of other salient facts we had turned up about NSO's business deals and its relationship with the Israeli government. Claudio and Donncha, meanwhile, were finishing up a twenty-three-page report laying out their findings for NSO to see. Titled *Technical Analysis of Forensic Traces and Network Measurements,* the report included the NSO-generated domain names, process names, iCloud accounts, and specific exploits that the Security Lab had discovered and tied to the Pegasus system. This would also give NSO the opportunity to refute any of the specifics of the Security Lab's forensic analyses.

Nobody on the Pegasus Project believed that NSO would respond in any meaningful or professional way. Amnesty International, the Security Lab, and Citizen Lab had sent similar prepublication letters to NSO for various investigations going back to 2016 and received little by way of serious answers to serious questions. "We on our side publish very detailed, peer-reviewed, evidence-based reports," Ron Deibert, the founder of Citizen Lab, told us. "Their responses have been mostly ad hominem attacks, slagging us for some imagined bias that we have that's never clearly articulated." Claudio had had similar experiences with NSO and other private cybersurveillance companies, so expected more of the same but didn't sound intimidated. "We are right [on the forensics]," Claudio said. "If they start challenging us, they are challenging us with empty words. They can't deny evidence."

Paul Lewis didn't think NSO would answer any of the specifics we had turned up in the forensics or in the reporting, but he was convinced the letter would change the dynamics of the investigation. The minute the letter landed in Herzliya, NSO would see the Pegasus Project as an existential threat to the company. There was no upside for NSO to engage in a rational conversation about our questions, our findings, or our conclusions, journalistic or forensic. Paul expected them to attack.

THE LETTER TO NSO was to go out under the signatures of Laurent and me, as agents of Forbidden Stories, but we invited back-and-forth discussions with the partners about the tone and the specific language in the letter. Paul thought it best to be aggressive, to make sure we didn't pull any punches, so nobody at NSO could say we misled them or softpedaled what we intended to publish. "Our research suggests NSO's technology has been used by multiple governments to systematically abuse the human rights of individuals whom those governments have no justifiable basis to place under surveillance," was some of the language we agreed on. "Our reporting suggests this abuse is systematic, widespread, and ongoing. We strongly believe it is in the public interest to reveal this information, which has serious implications for privacy rights of all people around the world, and the ability of people to communicate freely with one another without fear of surveillance or repression, particularly in societies where human rights abuses are likely."

The letter named the specific countries our reporting had identified as licensed users (and proven abusers) of NSO's military-grade spyware, including Azerbaijan, Bahrain, Hungary, India, Kazakhstan, Mexico, Morocco, Rwanda, Saudi Arabia, Togo, and the United Arab Emirates. We also named individuals whose phones showed clear evidence of compromise by Pegasus.

We ended up delayed by a day, but Laurent and I were ready to hit the Send button on the letter to NSO when the sun came up in Paris on Sunday morning, July 11, 2021.

AMNESTY INTERNATIONAL HAD decided to take some extra precautions in Berlin just before we sent the letter and alerted NSO of the investigation and the imminent publication date. The bosses at Amnesty were a little concerned about Claudio and Donncha. The two cyber-researchers, soon to be spotlighted as the team that caught NSO and its client states red-handed, were ambivalent about the stepped-up security regimen. Claudio, for one, didn't think there was much danger that they would be hacked by NSO spyware. He was careful to keep his work separate from his private life, didn't have a personal cell phone number, and rarely used social media other than Twitter, and then only under his nom de plume. "I don't have a very digitally rich life," he joked. On top of that, he told Laurent and me later, "I would hope it would be a dissuading factor for some, knowing that, you know, we are the ones equipped to catch them in the first place."

Donncha was no more worried than Claudio about being hacked, but he did have his own safety concerns, which seemed understandable for a man who had memories of being rousted from bed in the middle of the night by an angry posse of Irish lawmen. He wasn't as worried about the technical capabilities of NSO as he was about the nasty proclivities of some of NSO's clients, who were to be informed any day of the Pegasus Project and of the Security Lab's role in it. These were some brutal regimes, who had proven willing to commit ugly acts of intimidation and violence without fear of consequence, on their own soil and off of it. The Kingdom of Morocco had been holding Omar Radi in prison, often in solitary confinement, for more than a year, and he was only now getting his day in court. The crown prince of Saudi Arabia had ordered the killing of Jamal Khashoggi, a man who had done nothing more than criticize him.

Donncha had also been reading news reports about the case of Mahammad Mirzali, a twenty-seven-year-old Azeri blogger who had fled Baku and settled in Nantes, France, 5,000 kilometers away. Mahammad thought he would be safe enough in France to continue to post messages critical of President Aliyev's financial corruption and the bloody war in Armenia on his YouTube channel, *Made in Azerbaijan*. But the distance had not put Mahammad or his family beyond the reach of Azerbaijan. His parents also fled to France after his father and brother-in-law were threatened and encouraged to stifle Mahammad. His sister had suffered the indignation of having an illegal recording of one of her intimate moments circulated online, a shrill echo of the blackmail attempt on Khadija Ismayilova. Mahammad himself was shot at while sitting in a parked car in October 2020, and in March 2021, he was attacked in Nantes and stabbed ten to fourteen times—the medical reports released to the public were uncertain. (Aliyev has publicly stated that there is not enough evidence for him to deign to respond to what he called "groundless and biased accusations" that his government was responsible for the attacks on Mahammad. Three of the four men charged with the crime a year later, however, were Azeri nationals.) Mahammad Mirzali survived, after a six-hour surgery, only to receive a text a week later. "This is the last warning," it read. "We can kill you without any problem. You've seen that we're not afraid of anyone. . . . We'll have you killed with a bullet to the head fired by a sniper." The threats had continued into June, according to the latest reporting, and Donncha suspected they were probably ongoing.

So when Amnesty International offered to relocate Claudio and Donncha from their homes to undisclosed safe houses for the week leading up to publication, both of them accepted. The attacks on the Azeri dissident were in Donncha's head. "He's writing satire about the [Aliyev] government, and the government is going to try to kill him, twice, *in France*," Donncha says. "If the Azerbaijanis know that [the Pegasus Project] is going to come out, are they going to do anything to try to stop us? And it's not just Azerbaijan."

LAURENT AND I hit the Send button on the letter to NSO a little after eight o'clock on Sunday morning, July 11, 2021. "As fair and responsible journalists we would like to invite you to comment on the above information, and let us know if you dispute any of it," read the conclusion of the ten-page letter (which was accompanied by twenty-three pages of technical notes authored by Claudio and Donncha). "Please respond no later than Wednesday, July 14, 2021, at 6 p.m. French time. Any substantive comment will be fairly reflected in any coverage. Please note that we do not accept generalised assertions of 'inaccuracy' as substantive."

The moment was actually a bit disorienting. "It feels a bit like being at the top of a hill in a car and removing the hand brake," Paul Lewis texted us that morning. "We're rolling."

CLAUDIO AND DONNCHA were in their office that Sunday night, after dark, when a Security Lab server suddenly went offline. The server had been running every day for two years, twenty-four hours a day, and it had never crashed. And now, the day the letter goes out to NSO, boom, an unexplained hardware failure. Claudio flashed back to some slides he had seen years earlier from a report the US intelligence services had published; they described an attack on servers that could cause immediate failure on the network card. This felt like that kind of attack. Donncha was thinking the same thing. *Oh, shit! Maybe somebody got into the offices and cut a cable; maybe somebody actually stole the server.* Donncha raced over to see if the server was still there.

That was a very tense evening at the Security Lab in Berlin, trying to figure out what the hell was going on. Neither Claudio nor Donncha believed NSO or anybody else could breach their system or steal the Pegasus-related data they had accumulated, but it sure felt like someone was trying to sabotage the project. Donncha found himself thinking a very unexpected thought while he checked the server and then the logs: *Something happens to me, okay. But I want to make sure the Pegasus Project succeeds.*

CHAPTER TWENTY-ONE

"THIS IS REALLY HAPPENING"

Laurent

"Are you all stressed out? Or excited?" Sandrine asked our small team at the Forbidden Stories office on the Monday morning after we had sent the letter to NSO. This was the group of young reporters who had been on the project with us from the beginning, sworn to absolute secrecy, working long hours on difficult tasks for seven months without cease. "I mean, how are you doing?"

"In between," Audrey Travère answered. "There will be my name on the article on NSO. I really want it to come out, and I really want everyone to discover this story and all these outrageous abuses. But at the same time, there is fear."

"There are three of us who are going to have our own names on articles dealing with NSO," Phineas added. "Is there something we can do in preparation?"

"For your safety?" I asked.

"Yes," Phineas said. "In terms of security. And also legally."

"Argentina!" I offered. "Tomorrow night. Terminal F in Roissy. We've got your plane tickets. We have collected your passports. We're all going to Argentina. It's just six months of our lives. Right? We're going to leave for six months."

The laughter was loud, almost fierce, which I was happy to hear.

Because I knew it was going to take plenty of good cheer and camaraderie to get through the next few weeks. The publication date was less than a week away, and I could sense ill winds gaining force around us.

Sandrine and I spent some of this short meeting at Forbidden Stories reiterating the same admonitions we had been making since the first hours of the investigation. Talk to no one outside the project, do not say anything even to one of our reporting partners that might suggest a path to the source of the leaked data, and make sure if your mobile phone is compromised that there is nothing on the device pointing to the Pegasus Project. (Sandrine and I had started having Claudio and Donncha do regular checks on our phones for signs of Pegasus infection, including three in the final week alone.) The anxiety in our office was real, and it was not an entirely bad thing because we all needed to be on our toes—no matter how tired we got.

Some of the most admired newsrooms in the world had been impressed with their work, and there would be time, Sandrine promised the crew that morning, "to savor this moment. There aren't so many in a journalist's life, so take advantage of it." But not yet, I added: "This is really the moment when we can expect a hard bit of, not of fight, but of intense confrontation."

Sandrine and I didn't expect to have an answer to our letter to NSO for another couple of days, but we had a pretty good idea of what was heading our way. The night before we emailed our request for response to Herzliya, we had received a very odd call from an acquaintance who was in touch with Shalev Hulio. The caller thought we should know that Shalev had said he was onto "True Stories," as he kept calling us, and knew all about the "list." Shalev wanted to warn us that the list had nothing to do with Pegasus, and if we published, we would do great damage to our professional reputation.

"Shalev Hulio is mad at what he calls the 'True Stories,' which he believes is preparing an imminent attack on NSO," I explained to the Forbidden Stories team at our Monday-morning meeting. "In the words of Shalev, according to [the caller], 'They are totally wrong, True Stories. In fact, what they have is not what they think they have.' He told us to be very careful because there is a real gap between what you think you have and what you really have. Be very careful."

There wasn't anything to do, however, until we got a real and official response from NSO. What we could do while we waited was go about our business.

SOME OF THE partners were beginning to upload early, unedited drafts of their stories into the Pegasus Project central database shared by all, which gave each of the partners the option of publishing stories authored by other reporters in the consortium. A few of the early drafts had unanticipated surprises. We knew Szabolcs Panyi had done really good reporting in Hungary for *Direkt36*, but his main story for the Pegasus Project was much more than we expected, in part because of his own personal experience of having been a victim of cybersurveillance. He described being outraged, ashamed, and somewhat proud. "While the Orbán government simply ignores my official media requests most of the time, it turns out they do appreciate my reporting after all, although their way of showing interest is maybe a little bit creepy. . . . "

He also touched on his feelings about being the victim of spyware created by an Israeli company and licensed with the approval of the Israeli Ministry of Defense. "Like many Hungarians of Jewish origin, I never attached much meaning to the state of Israel," he wrote. "It's just another foreign country I've never seen. My only real tie to Israel is a brother of my grandmother, who went there after surviving Auschwitz and became a soldier. I know it is silly and makes no difference at all, but I would probably feel slightly different if my surveillance had been assisted by any other state, like Russia or China."

Direkt36's reporting out of Hungary was enormously bolstered by Bastian Obermayer and Frederik Obermaier, as well as other journalists from Germany, the UK, and France, all of whom had done serious work in and around Budapest. A reporter from *Le Monde* had elicited an interesting response just a few days earlier from the Hungarian minister of justice, when he asked her about the apparent authorization of surveillance on journalists or politicians critical of Orbán. "What a question," she shot back, in spirited non-denial. "That in itself is a provocation!"

Statistics on the number of people in our data who had been selected for targeting, attacked with Pegasus, or actually infected were still being updated in the final days. Of the 50,000 phone numbers in the data, we had been able to verify, with multiple sources for each, the identities of more than 1,000 people from fifty countries. The count included more than 600 politicians and government officials, including 3 presidents, 10 prime ministers, and 1 king. There were 65 businessmen, 85 human rights activists or attorneys, and 2 Emirati princesses. Craig Timberg's last-minute addition of an American reporter working in Saudi Arabia pushed our count of journalists to 192.

As of Monday, July 12, Claudio and Donncha had done forensics on sixty-five mobile phones that appeared in the leaked list. Thirty-five showed evidence that they were attacked and/or infected by Pegasus. Almost all the others were either Android phones or new iPhones that were not being used at the time of targeting, so could not offer conclusive findings. The forensic success rate with iPhones being used at the time of selection was still above 80 percent.

At that point, in the last week of the investigation, we had evidence of successful Pegasus infections on the phones of journalists, human rights activists, and human rights lawyers. We did not have evidence that proved an attack or infection on any politicians in the data because we had deemed it too risky to alert these people early in the project by reaching out to request their phones for analysis. But we had not given up hope on that front, and we had a small window of time to make it happen.

The team at Le Monde was trying to confirm traces of Pegasus on the mobile phone of the French politician François de Rugy. Siddharth Varadarajan, the editor of the Wire, was on a mission to add an Indian politician to the list of confirmed targets. Siddharth had tried with the chief political foe of Prime Minister Narendra Modi, Rahul Gandhi, but Gandhi no longer had the iPhone he was using near the time of his selection. Siddharth made one last try on July 12, this time with Prashant Kishor, who happened to be in Delhi that day to meet with

Rahul Gandhi. This meeting between Kishor and Gandhi could not have been happy news to Kishor's former client, Narendra Modi. Kishor was among the most ambitious and media-savvy political operatives in India, and he first made a name for himself boosting Modi's rise to power. For the last seven years, though, Kishor had used his considerable talents to put the brakes on Modi and his increasingly authoritarian brand of governance. Word in political circles in India was that Kishor would be working hard to unseat Modi and his adherents in the next big election cycle. Modi's team was paying attention.

Siddharth had no trouble convincing Kishor to submit his phone to forensic analysis, which promised a poetic closing of a circle for our investigation. Sandrine and Sandhya Ravishankar had talked Siddharth into allowing the Security Lab to do the forensics on his own phone four months earlier, and his device had delivered to the project the first solid forensic evidence of Pegasus infection in the data; now here was Siddharth talking Prashant Kishor into one last chance for our consortium to get crucial forensic evidence before publication.

It worked. On July 14, the day after Donncha confirmed traces of Pegasus on Rugy's phone, he found evidence of Pegasus infection on Kishor's phone. So now we had two politicians confirmed, both from democracies. One from the world's largest democracy.

THE SECURITY LAB was still capable of conducting business at their office in Berlin, even after the terrifying server crash. Turns out, after some intense worry and some deep diagnostics, the problem was simply a strangely timed hardware failure: the equivalent of your carburetor needing replacing, as opposed to somebody pouring sugar into your gas tank. Our two technical experts were working down to the wire just like the rest of us, still with big things to finish. They were, for one, preparing to release a version of the forensic tool they had used in the Pegasus Project. This felt to me like harnessing the power of Luke Skywalker's *Star Wars* lightsaber and gifting it to the masses—a most democratic weapon to do battle with a most undemocratic foe. The Mobile Verification Toolkit (MVT) would allow anybody, anywhere, to do a quick diagnostic check on their mobile phone and identify traces of a Pegasus infection. The MVT was not foolproof, and it would have a limited shelf life, Claudio admitted, but it was the best thing available and downloadable, for free. Claudio and Donncha hoped it would level the playing field just a bit and maybe afford a little peace of mind to a whole lot of people.

The Security Lab crew was also making the final editorial changes to their *Forensic Methodology Report*, which had a lot of moving parts. The list of countries hosting the most servers where Pegasus attack vectors originated had to be updated with raw numbers. The UK, Switzerland, France, and the US were high on that list, but Germany stood atop it. "Some of the biggest hosting companies are in Germany, as well as some of the cheaper ones," Claudio says. "Pretty common destination when you want to set up infrastructure on a large scale." Claudio and Donncha were also able to report that NSO had recently—and ill-advisedly—started using Amazon Web Services as a host for at least seventy-three of their servers.

A forensic find on Prashant Kishor's cell phone, just four days before publication, provided Claudio and Donncha new and disturbing detail. Pegasus had exfiltrated nearly 100 megabytes of data from the iPhone in the previous week alone—right around the time Kishor was meeting with the Indian prime minister's chief political opponent. There was evidence of an infection on that very day, July 14, 2021. Which meant NSO's software could still sneak past Apple's current system of safeguards on an iPhone with the most up-to-date protections. "Most recently," Claudio and Donncha added to the introduction of their report, "a successful 'zero-click' attack has been observed exploiting multiple zero-days to attack a fully patched iPhone 12 running iOS 14.6 in July 2021."

I CHECKED MY email inbox again and again as the appointed hour neared. The results were always the same. Nothing there, or at least nothing I was looking for. Sandrine and I had asked NSO to respond to our letter by 6 p.m. French time, on Wednesday, July 14. At five minutes past 6, I checked my inbox again, and still no response. So I picked up the phone and called the company's press liaison.

"How are you?" I said when she picked up her phone.

"Very good," she responded, sounding surprisingly nonchalant.

"Thank you for taking the time to take the call," I said. "I was just wondering if you are planning to answer."

"Yes," she answered, still curt. "You can see it in your email now."

I checked my inbox again. Still nothing new. "You just sent it?" I asked, continuing to refresh my email. "I don't see anything. Can you just check? . . . You sent it like a few minutes ago?" And then, suddenly, there it was. "Okay! I see it."

"Thank you, bye," was all she said, and she was off the phone.

I read the response aloud to Sandrine, trying to make sense of it as I went. "NSO Group firmly denies false claims made in your report which many of them are uncorroborated theories that raise serious doubts about the reliability of your sources, as well as the basis of your story. Your sources have supplied you with information that has no factual basis, as evidenced by the lack of supporting documentation for many of the claims."

The entire missive was barely more than a page, a typical NSO rejoinder—a standard answer to a very nonstandard letter. Except, not even really up to standard. There were a handful of typos and grammatical errors, as if Shalev had tossed it off in about twenty minutes while dealing with other business. The company had not denied, refuted, added context, or attempted to explain a single of the dozens of specifics in the letter. "When making such incendiary claims, readers would naturally expect you to provide some modicum of proof," I continued reading to Sandrine. "Instead, it appears you are simply furthering the salacious narrative about NSO Group that has been strategically concocted by several closely aligned special interest groups."

The unsigned email from NSO.com simply repeated the Khashoggi denial, the assertions that Pegasus was only sold to "vetted foreign government[s]," that "no customer has ever been granted technology that would enable them to access phones with US numbers," that NSO can and does terminate the system if the company discovers misuse. "Simply put," the letter concluded, "the NSO Group is on a life-saving mission, and the company will faithfully execute this mission undeterred, despite any and all continued attempts to discredit it on false grounds."

Sandrine was as nonplussed as I was. They seemed to let stand almost every fact in our letter.

"That's great for us," she said.

"It's really good," I agreed, as Sandrine walked me through how to forward it to our partners.

The long wait was over.

"That's it?" Sandrine mused.

"They have no answers," I said. "In fact, they're just trying to catch points that are fragile, but they're not addressing the strengths, or the gist, of our questions. It's incredible."

"It's crazy."

We went out for a drink to celebrate, and I wasn't sure how to feel, except oddly weightless. I found myself thinking about the movies I wanted to see, the books I wanted to catch up on, the chance to get back to normal life and see my family. To actually talk to my family and let them in on the big secret I'd been keeping from them. I took the train home that night, forty minutes removed from the tumult of the office, and got the first good night's sleep I'd had in a very long time.

THERE WAS A slew of new messages on my phone when I woke up Thursday morning. The first email I opened was from Drew Sullivan, at OCCRP, who had attached a letter he wanted me to see. Our partners had gotten a very different message from NSO, or rather from the company's hired lawyer in Washington, DC. "Our firm is defamation counsel to NSO Group," was the opener. "It is evident that Forbidden Stories has already formulated (and intends to publish on its own platform) a false, preconceived, and highly damaging narrative regarding NSO Group—and that it intends to do so regardless of the actual facts. . . . We are putting OCCRP on formal notice that Forbidden Stories will publish defamatory falsehoods about NSO Group in its series of articles and that, should OCCRP elect to publish or republish any portion of those articles, OCCRP runs a substantial risk of publishing defamatory falsehoods."

The NSO's hired attorney offered a brief primer on journalistic ethics and pointed out seven questions from our letter he deemed "false and defamatory accusations." But he did not explain exactly how they were inaccurate, let alone defamatory. The new letter did speak to a few specifics: the defamation counsel asserted that the numbers in our data were not "a list of numbers targeted by governments using Pegasus, but instead, may be part of a larger list of numbers that might have been used by NSO Group customers for other purposes." (He did not explain what these other purposes might have been.) He denied Saudi Arabia had targeted the lawyer of Jamal Khashoggi's fiancée. He denied that NSO had "lost control" of Pegasus in Mexico, or that any nongovernmental users had the opportunity to abuse the spyware in that country, or that NSO Group is "a tool of Israeli diplomacy" or a back door for Israeli intelligence.

His letter was a little hard to decipher—the denials appeared to be dancing around or fuzzing the actual facts presented in our questions to NSO—but his strategy was clear. Divide and conquer. Each of our Pegasus Project partners had received its own version of the threatening letter.

I took the first train back to Paris that morning, carrying enough clothes to stay in the office for several nights on end. The next four days were going to be a big fight with NSO and a series of smaller skirmishes with the lawyers working for our various partners. In among the idle threats from NSO were some useful hints about where we might have a weakness in our understanding of the Pegasus system, and where we might refine and sharpen our language.

Crisis points reveal good journalism, I've discovered over and over in my twenty-five-year career, and they make it better. There are no mistakes until a story goes live; until then, a writer or an editor always has the chance to improve the story. The best journalists are willing to admit where they've gone wrong and to fix it before publication. There is no honor in covering up mistakes.

So we had four days to make sure we got everything right, to the satisfaction of the entire consortium. We each had to make sure that nothing we published overstepped the boundaries of the evidence we had gathered and that the language in every Pegasus Project story was clear and precise.

The *Guardian*'s Paul Lewis was one of the first calls we had that Thursday morning. "So obviously we've all read the letter," he said when we got on the phone. For Paul, as for the rest of us, the letter didn't answer many of our questions, but it did raise some. He wanted to know more about the mechanics of NSO's bar on infecting mobile phones with US phone numbers, and he wanted more precise information about Khashoggi's fiancée's attorney. He really wanted to hear more from NSO about the other purposes a client might have for entering a phone number into the Pegasus system.

More than anything, though, Paul wanted to move quickly to compose a new letter to send to NSO asking for clarifications. The deadline was approaching, and he wanted the clearest answers he could get. "I think it needs to get there in their morning and give them a deadline of 6 p.m. that night," he told us.

DONNCHA ENDED UP being the forensics point person in the final days and hours before publication, trying to reassure editors and lawyers at media companies across four continents and many more time zones. He was living in the alien hotel room where Amnesty International had stashed him for safekeeping, going on his second week in a room that made him feel like he was living in 1985. It sported a plush carpet and pieces of furniture that seemed unrelated to their surroundings and to one another. Donncha had to put each of his three phones on silent mode so he could get a little sleep every night. He'd conk out long after midnight, after a sixteen-hour workday, and wake up the next morning, somewhere around eight o'clock, with fifty messages on each of his cell phones to answer.

The stress was intense, Donncha remembers, but he tried to talk to every reporter, every editor, and every media lawyer to reassure them of the strength of the forensics and how he and Claudio had connected the evidence in the mobile phones to NSO and Pegasus. For security reasons, Donncha felt it best to do all these calls in the bathroom. "Whenever the light was on in the bathroom there was a loud fan buzzing," he says. "So I had a choice of yelling over the noise or taking the calls in the dark." He "endured" those final days, Donncha told us long after the project was over. "[Claudio and I] had put so much hard work in this for so many years," he said. "I can't let this blow up. We can't let NSO win by pushing back with [the threat of] lawsuits."

FRIDAY, JULY 16, just two days to get to the finish line, and there were newsrooms all over the world pushing toward the publication of the Pegasus Project. The rollout of stories would stretch across five days, but the real grind was now. Editors and reporters were buttoning up all the stories for the week, and lawyers were over their shoulders, doing the vetting. "It's a bit tense here, if I'm honest," an editor in one of those far-flung newsrooms admitted. The editor was already suffering from overwork and missing his family, but he did not have time to stop worrying over headlines, graphics, front-page layouts, video packages, digital promos, and the explainer capsules describing the project, the technology, the victims, and NSO and its clients. ("We have to run [the explainer capsules] in every day's paper," he told a graphics editor.)

In the middle of it all, the editor summoned as many of his reporters as he could for an important call, to give them a heads-up on the schedule. "All going well, um—and if we're proceeding with this project," he explained, "[then] on Sunday you've got to be around for checks and tweaks and the like, and we'll have the final sign-off decision. But I think the crunch point really is going to be in the next twelve hours."

There was one phrase that clearly caught the attention of everybody on the line. "If we're proceeding?" somebody asked.

"Yeah."

"Is that in doubt?"

"Well, it's never confirmed," the editor said, "until it's confirmed."

NSO's LAWYERS AND spokespeople played a good cop–bad cop game right up to the hour of publication, the net result being a corporate filibuster. They refused to address all but a few specific questions we had put to them in our letters asking for comment and clarification, and they steered very wide of any discussion of the forensic evidence that the Security Lab had presented to them. They could not reveal the identities of their clients, they reminded the consortium; they reiterated their great umbrage at any misuse of Pegasus and insisted on their ability and their efforts to root out any such abuse if they received credible reports. Of the twenty-eight specific victims we identified to them, they refuted only a few—"a technological impossibility," they said of one. As for the rest, they claimed we had not given them sufficient time to check. They tried to throw a lot of sand in our eyes about the data we had access to, but they had a hard time keeping their explanations consistent.

The partners, meanwhile, bent to the work of including NSO's responses in the bodies of their stories, as well as providing links where readers could see the NSO letters in full.

There were more than eighty journalists on call to answer editors' questions or tweak language right up to the last minute before publication. But only a few trail bosses were actually herding their stories through the editorial chutes, each with dozens of features and sidebars and graphics packages to finalize, and most of them were flagging. "Ah, my brain's going slightly dead," one editor admitted.

Another had to stop for a moment to answer a text from his parents, who seemed to have lost patience at having been put off for so long. "Problem?" his colleague asked.

"I'm just saying I'm not going to be able to call her tonight because I'm at work and I'm very busy," he said. "I haven't told her everything because I was afraid she would worry."

"Are you talking about your mom?"

"My mom. The last time I went to see my parents, I said, 'I'm working on a big thing right now. A cybersurveillance story.' She said to me, 'But why do you always get into complicated things?'"

The work went on in that newsroom, as the reporters and editors worked together to finalize language and make sure the relevant NSO responses made it into the first-day package. Then a phone call. "Oh, hell, it's my mom. . . . 'Hello? Hi! Not now. Not unless it's extraordinarily urgent, and someone's dead. . . . Okay, can I call you back? Thanks a lot. Kisses.'"

"I took my afternoon off [yesterday] because, by the way, it was my wedding anniversary," one of the colleagues said, commiserating. "So I was at a restaurant. And as a result, I missed the call from the Moroccan embassy."

Our own reporters at Forbidden Stories were still reaching out for last-minute comment. We wanted to include the voices of as many people selected in the data as possible in our first-day stories. Audrey Travère managed to get one journalist on the phone on the last day of reporting and explained to her that her number had been in our data, making her a possible target of Pegasus spyware. She stayed on the line for forty minutes with Audrey, describing herself as a "paralyzed journalist" unable to do her job because she no longer felt safe in her home country. She believed her work had even put her family in danger.

Audrey gently explained to the woman that we had no evidence that the cybersurveillance was ongoing, and also offered to help with forensics on the journalist's mobile phone to be sure she was now in the clear. In the end, however, the journalist told Audrey she was too frightened to be identified by name in our report. "Of course, we will not name you," Audrey told her. "I, of course, respect your decision, and it is totally understandable, and I'm just so saddened that you cannot pursue your passion of being a journalist."

"Audrey, trust me, one day I will talk," she said. "I will talk." Then she started to cry. "But right now, I cannot. I have a lot inside my heart . . . but I don't know you, and I don't trust anyone. . . . They silenced us."

AT A FEW minutes before 6 p.m. French time on Sunday night, Paul Lewis was still working on last-minute changes. He had been at this for days, and he was now standing over the shoulder of the *Guardian*'s chief lawyer, who was doing a final check. "So what's next?" she asked.

"Okay," he said, pointing to a small box that held a key explainer capsule. "Here's a simple one. Like three hundred words. Totally fine, I'm sure."

The investigation was into more than NSO, Paul's colleague pointed out, while reading the lede of the explainer.

"Could we say 'NSO Group and its clients'?" Paul suggested.

"Yes," she agreed. "'And its clients.' Stick in 'and its clients.'"

Three minutes later, the *Guardian*'s series into NSO, its clients, and a whole lot more, went live. "Oh f-ing hell," Paul announced. "That was ridiculous."

DONNCHA WAS IN his rented time-warp hotel room in Berlin that Sunday evening, July 18, 2021, which, he noted to himself, happened to be the ten-year anniversary of his prank on Rupert Murdoch. He was still fielding messages from journalists in the consortium that evening because there were still four more days of stories to come. "I was answering all the questions on my two laptops," Donncha told us later, and also constantly refreshing various web pages. *Le Monde.* The *Guardian.* The *Wire.* The *Washington Post. Die Zeit. Süddeutsche Zeitung. Knack. Daraj. Direkt36. Aristegui Noticias. Proceso.* And the rest. Seventeen media outlets in ten different countries, all right on schedule. The Pegasus Project was bannered across the front pages of them all. Donncha experienced a brief moment of realization, almost five years in the making: "This is really happening."

And then: "Okay. All right. Back to work."

DAMIEN LELOUP AND Martin Untersinger at *Le Monde* had been through the same fresh hell as Donncha and everybody else. They had the added difficulty of needing a reaction from the Élysée Palace to the revelations that President Macron and most of his cabinet had been selected for possible targeting by a foreign government that was supposed to be an ally. The two *Le Monde* reporters had been key members of the first circle that Sandrine and I roped into the Pegasus Project, which meant they had been working on this story nearly as long as we had.

A few minutes after the first stories went live at *Le Monde*, they had a Twitter alert.

"Snowden?"

"Snowden," Damien said, reading the tweet from Edward Snowden.

"'Stop what you're doing and read this. This leak is just going to be the story of the year.'"

"Nice!"

THE TEAM AT the *Guardian* was already refreshing the websites of the partners at a few minutes after 6 p.m. French time, and Paul Lewis picked up the phone to call Craig Timberg at the *Washington Post*. These two contemporaries worked for a couple of the most respected English-language journalistic organizations in the world, and they were normally fierce competitors for stories on both sides of the Atlantic. Today was different. "Hi, Craig," Paul said, and rolled into some friendly ribbing. "You guys haven't published yet? . . . Ah, you have now, okay. We just wondered. We thought you might have got cold feet."

Craig suggested to Paul he should check out the *Post*'s Pegasus Project video feed.

"Oh, I'm going to have to subscribe," Paul answered, pulling up the feed. "No, I do subscribe. Oh, nice graphics. Very nice graphics."

Craig seemed not to be sure if Paul was still joking.

"No, I really like it," Paul insisted. "You've got the scrollies. We ran out of time for the scrollies. My scrolly people are going to be furious when they see this.

"Oh well, look. Congratulations for getting it over the line."

I WAS ABLE, in an instant, to access scores of stories spooling out across the globe, and there was a particular name I found myself looking for; it belonged to the person who had been an inspiration and a spur for the Pegasus Project. The first name I had identified in the data, back in that rented flat in Berlin at the very first meeting Sandrine and I had with Claudio and Donncha: Khadija Ismayilova.

There was something very gratifying to know her story was spreading across continents, suddenly accessible to hundreds of millions of people. Khadija, meanwhile, was back in Baku that day. She might not be able to free herself from government surveillance (or the attendant harassment and intimidation), but I hoped Khadija was at least a little better protected because of the consortium's reporting. She was, of course, already at work on her next investigation into the Aliyev government, waging her lonely battle for democracy in the home she refused to abandon.

There was a quote from Khadija in one of the Pegasus Project's first-day stories that caught my eye: "It is important that people see examples of journalists who do not stop because they were threatened. It's like a war. You leave your trench, then the attacker comes in. . . . You have to keep your position, otherwise it will be taken and then you will have less space, less space, the space will be shrinking, and then you will find it hard to breathe."

EPILOGUE

Laurent

We woke to a lot of news on the second day of publication, much of it generated by the Pegasus Project rollout, some of it not. Not all of the news was good, especially a story out of Casablanca that morning: Omar Radi had been convicted of "undermining the internal security of the state" and of rape and sentenced to six years in prison. Omar continued to declare his innocence. His family and supporters decried the Moroccan court's obstruction of any credible defense and the prosecution's flimsy evidence. After more than a year in jail while the legal proceedings ground their way to their inevitable conclusion, Omar was already in declining health and often despondent. It was hard to imagine him emerging unbroken after another six years in prison. And this was clearly what King Mohammed VI and his coterie were counting on. Omar was not merely being silenced; he was being held up as an example of what could happen to anybody who might attempt the practice of independent journalism in Morocco—anyone "lacking due respect to the king."

Omar was being supported by journalism foundations and civil society NGOs whose members were at a safe remove from the Kingdom of Morocco, but there was no serious protest made by any government, anywhere. The US secretary of state had reportedly raised general concerns with Moroccan government officials about the kingdom's poor performance on human rights and press freedom several weeks earlier, but nobody was divulging what was said behind closed doors. It reminded me of what Khadija Ismayilova had said after one of her arrests in Baku. Either stand up and defend freedom of the press and the right of privacy aloud, in public. Or don't bother. "I don't want any private diplomacy for my case," she had said back in 2015. "People of my country need to know that human rights are supported."

Backlash against the Pegasus Project itself came from the expected parties that week, with Shalev in the lead. He was conciliatory at times. "The company cares about journalists and activists and civil society in general," he said in interviews. "If somebody says, I found a better way to get criminals, get terrorists, get information from a pedophile, I will shut down Pegasus completely." He hammered on his talking points: NSO is a software company and doesn't operate Pegasus; the company sells to government entities only; it has no real-time visibility into its clients' targets; the Israeli government regulates all licenses of the Pegasus system. But as media outlets all over the world ran with and followed up on the stories our consortium published over the next four days, and it was clear the investigation was going to have real impact, the response from NSO grew angrier, and more conspiratorial. Shalev said the list of numbers had no relation to NSO, and the number of selections on the list was "insane." He said our forensics were all wrong but did not point to a single actual error in the detailed reports that the Security Lab had provided the company. Three days into publication, NSO threw up its hands and emailed a statement to media organizations across the world: "Enough is enough. In light of the recent planned and well-orchestrated media campaign led by Forbidden Stories and pushed by special interest groups, and due to the complete disregard of the facts, NSO is announcing it will no longer be responding to media inquiries on this matter."

NSO and its defenders had by then opened its playbook to a dog-eared, oft-used page. Forbidden Stories and Amnesty International were either leaders of, or tools of, an anti-Israel, anti-Semitic conspiracy, they suggested. One Israeli Army reservist and cyberspecialist told reporters that the Pegasus Project was "an orchestrated effort to harm Israel by smearing one of its cybercompanies." The "deliberate hand," as Shalev called it, might be the pro-Palestinian BDS movement (Boycott, Divestment, Sanctions) or Qatar. "Al Jazeera, I noticed, gave much attention to [the Pegasus Project reports]," said one Israeli professor. "I'm sure the [Ministry of Defense] knows exactly who's behind it."

SANDRINE WAS AT the office early on the morning after NSO's "Enough is enough" diatribe and received a courier delivering an official document from the Moroccan ambassador in Paris. The deliveryman was an amiable and easygoing sort. The document he was carrying was not. The Kingdom of Morocco was suing me for defamation. I had been sued for defamation by a foreign government before and knew that the Kingdom of Morocco, like the Republic of Azerbaijan, had no real case. But the lawsuit was not the point. The point was the free publicity generated by the news that the case had been filed and was headed to trial. This was just part of a public relations campaign Morocco was mounting in the face of the embarrassing revelations about its use of spyware. The kingdom had already denied its use of Pegasus against anyone, and now it was unleashing its paid agents to destroy the messengers. Morocco's lawyer in France filed defamation suits against *Le Monde*, *Mediapart*, Radio France, and later *L'Humanité*; the kingdom also filed an injunction against *Süddeutsche Zeitung* in Germany.

The kingdom's subsidized media mouthpieces went after Sandrine and me personally, without ever addressing the specifics of Morocco's cybersurveillance program that we had helped to reveal. I was, in this telling, a money-hungry mountebank, obsessed with Morocco, financed by George Soros's Open Society (which is true, in part, and I am proud of it), whose aim is to finance projects to "destabilize Arab countries" (which is a lie). The kingdom's lawyer in Paris granted interviews to a slew of media organizations and attacked me, Forbidden Stories, the consortium, and our reporting because, as he said, the Moroccan state "wants all possible light cast on these false allegations."

The kingdom did have good reason to kick up some dust. The morning I was served with legal papers, President Emmanuel Macron, who had just been alerted that he and many of his ministers were among the people on our list, called an urgent national security meeting. Prosecutors in Paris were already investigating possible criminal activity in France by Moroccan authorities.

OUR PHONES DIDN'T stop ringing that first week, and many of the callers had the same frantic request. Please check for me. Was my phone number on the list? The French government and the French prosecutors were determined to get a look at the list itself, and the police sent a single officer over to make the case to me in person. I agreed to meet him outside a café near the Gare de Lyon, and he pulled up on a motorbike, full of bonhomie. He made some small talk about biking in Paris. He told me he had read the Pegasus Project in full and found it enlightening. He said we were on the same team. Then he made his pitch for why I should hand over our list to the French government. He said we were both looking out for victims and potential victims. "All these people," he said. "Don't you want to protect them?"

The talk remained friendly, even when I explained that we were journalists and not government agents. We had done our part by alerting the world to the dangers of Pegasus. But this was not our list to hand over, and we had made a pledge not to reveal our source, who was still in danger. The police officer said he understood the ethics of journalism, of course, and he was sympathetic to our professional obligation to protect our source. But he warned me that if I didn't cooperate, French law enforcement would probably get a subpoena commanding me to hand over the list, or a search warrant to seize it.

I kind of felt bad for him, since they sent him alone, and he had to play both good cop and bad cop. He wanted me to understand all the pressure he was under from the prosecutor. There were a lot of important people on that list. Couldn't we help out? Wasn't it our patriotic duty? He pushed for a while, but when it became clear I wasn't going to budge, he reverted back to good cop. He said he understood our position, and he agreed it was proper. If the prosecutor really did try to get a subpoena or a search warrant, he told me, he would stand up for us. Before he departed, he asked the question I knew was coming. Could you check a few numbers for me? See if they are on the list?

I received the subpoena the next day, and later a message from the cop, who told me he was really upset that we didn't want to protect the victims. If I didn't comply with the subpoena and hand over the list, things would escalate.

"We're not far from getting a search warrant," he said.

"I thought you said you would defend us," I answered.

In the end we were not compelled by law enforcement to hand over the list, and prosecutors didn't even try to get a search warrant. But I was able to do a favor for one very high-up French government official who was closely following the case. He wanted me to check a small set of numbers against our list. The numbers he gave me had only six digits, not the usual ten, which meant they would be unidentifiable to me. I agreed to check for him but only because I was hoping he would do the honorable thing and reveal the names to Forbidden Stories for eventual publication. It seemed pretty obvious that these were numbers of French officials whose phones had showed evidence of spyware infection after the government did its own forensic analysis. Some were on the list, I was able to tell him later, and some were not.

"It's worse than I thought," he said when I gave him the news.

"Do you have positive results for ministers that we did not mention?" I asked.

He said yes. "I've started to ask myself," he said cryptically, "if there are any who have escaped."

OFFICIAL CONFIRMATIONS OF Pegasus attacks that we had reported, or brand-new confirmations of previously unknown attacks, started coming out in the first weeks after our publication and continue to come out to this day. Reporting threads we had started were being picked up by other media organizations around the world. We felt like this story was not going to fade away anytime soon. Forensics by the National

Cybersecurity Agency of France (ANSSI) supported Claudio and Donn-cha's findings on Edwy Plenel and Lénaïg Bredoux, and added a journalist from France24 Television to the list of Pegasus victims. *Mediapart* later broke the story that ANSSI also confirmed the "presence of suspicious markers" in the phones of five French government ministers. ANSSI would eventually confirm almost all the French citizens we identified as victims and more we had not. The Security Lab turned up evidence that a British lawyer defending an Emirati princess had suffered a Peg-asus attack. Court papers released in London in early October revealed that the emir of Dubai had likely used Pegasus to spy on his estranged wife, her famous divorce attorney (a member of parliament), and a few others in the royal wife's entourage. A Dublin-based NGO caught Israel using Pegasus to spy on six Palestinian human rights activists. (Citizen Lab and the Security Lab both confirmed those findings separately.) The Israeli government had conveniently designated the workplaces of three of the victims as "terrorist organizations" a few weeks before the report but long after they had conducted their warrantless surveillance.

Thanks to Carmen Aristegui and her informant, Mexico arrested a former employee of Uri Ansbacher in early November 2021 and charged him with using Pegasus to spy on at least one journalist, Carmen herself. This was the first known instance of a private company using Pegasus to spy on a private citizen. Which is apparently what can happen when nobody in a country controls the use and spread of this military-grade cyberweaponry. But the Mexican government was promising trans-parency now and had already begun releasing startling details to the public. "Last week, the government's top anti-money laundering inves-tigator said officials from the previous [Mexican] administrations had spent about $300 million in government money to purchase spyware," the Associated Press reported. "The head of Mexico's Financial Intelli-gence Unit said the bills for programs like Pegasus spyware appear to have included excess payments that may have been channeled back to government officials as kickbacks."

The Polish government was found to have used Pegasus to spy on its political opponents, and so, too, the Spanish government, which put these two in league with Mexico, Hungary, and India, to name a few.

Apple started playing a little offense. The company patched the Megalodon exploit chain that Claudio and Donncha had discovered and that Citizen Lab had actually then captured. Apple then went to work engineering a Lockdown Mode to safeguard its new iPhones, iPads, and computers from surreptitious spyware attacks. The company also filed a lawsuit against NSO at the end of November 2021, calling the company "amoral 21st century mercenaries. . . . NSO's malicious activities have exploited Apple's products, injured Apple's users, and damaged Apple's business and goodwill. NSO's malicious products and services have also required Apple to devote thousands of hours to investigate the attacks, identify the harm, diagnose the extent of the impact and exploitation, and develop and deploy the necessary repairs and patches to ensure that Apple servers, products, platforms, applications, and experiences remain safe and secure for more than a billion individuals and entities."

Apple also announced a new policy of proactively alerting its iPhone users when they had been attacked by cybersurveillance weapons, then immediately revealed that eleven employees at the United States embassy in Uganda had been hacked by Pegasus. (The names of active iMessage exploit accounts the Security Lab had shared with Apple, the company techs told Donncha, had been "foundational" in its ability to track NSO spyware and send out accurate notifications.) The United States government may have already known of the hack in Uganda because it had by then "blacklisted" NSO, which made it nearly impossible for the company to buy crucial technology from Dell, Intel, Cisco, and Microsoft. This was an unprecedented step. The US had, without warning, cut off from all trade a private company in an allied country.

"The United States," said Commerce Secretary Gina M. Raimondo, "is committed to aggressively using export controls to hold companies accountable that develop, traffic, or use technologies to conduct malicious activities that threaten the cybersecurity of members of civil society, dissidents, government officials, and organizations here and abroad."

NOVEMBER 2021, FOUR months after our publication, was when NSO began taking on serious water, and without properly functioning bilge pumps. The man who agreed to come in and right the NSO ship fled a week after news of the blacklisting, before his official start date. "In light of special circumstances that have arisen," Isaac Benbenisti wrote to the NSO board, he "would not be able to assume the position of CEO with the company." Novalpina, the private equity company that had become majority owners in 2019, had collapsed in on itself, and a new set of consultants were now looking after the interests of shareholders invested in NSO. The employee pension fund of the state of Oregon, for instance, was understandably shaky about continuing its large equity position in what the US government called a tool of "transnational repression."

NSO employees soldiered on and kept up a good show. *We save lives!* They could point to their invitation to the company-wide Hanukkah retreat Shalev was throwing at a Red Sea beach resort as a sure sign that NSO would endure. But software coders and engineers in Tel Aviv were swapping stories of NSO employees going sheepishly silent when asked to recount their workweek at Shabbat family dinners on Friday night.

Sales of Pegasus slowed to a trickle, and Moody's pronounced the company in danger of defaulting on its debt. There was some doubt that NSO could make its November 2021 payroll. Thanks to some excellent reporting by the *Financial Times*, we know what was happening inside NSO at that dire moment. Shalev boldly announced a new plan to boost revenue—start selling to those "elevated-risk" customers again. NSO's new financial minders at the Berkeley Research Group were understandably alarmed. BRG hadn't even received necessary security clearances from the Israel government, so it had no real vision into the arms export sales that NSO specialized in. "You are demanding that [BRG] blindly sanctions the sale of . . . Pegasus . . . to elevated risk customers without a thorough governance review," read a letter the *Financial Times* reporters saw. "Please note that in no circumstances is [BRG] prepared to do so."

Shalev was in a full snit. When BRG insisted that "the plan was fraught with risk," according to the *Financial Times*, "[Shalev] quipped back that it was risky to miss a debt payment too."

The best Shalev could get out of BRG was a $10 million loan that helped to cover the payroll for a time. He has since concocted something NSO insiders call the "phoenix plan." NSO could split off all the ugly liabilities inside the company's Pegasus system and sell them on the open market, maybe even to a US defense contractor. By the middle of 2022, it was pretty clear that NSO was not going to rise from the ashes. The company had ridden its signature product, Pegasus, to the top of the mountain, but the wings on the stalking horse appeared to be irreparably broken.

"Hulio keeps telling everybody that the company is on the verge of a turnaround," the *Financial Times* quoted one Israeli official. "It is not."

THE DEMISE OF NSO is a cautionary tale for the current traffickers of these military-grade cyberweapons and the wannabe traffickers. But it is also a cautionary tale for all the spyware critics and the human rights defenders who hope to forestall the Orwellian future where cybersurveillance is a baked-in fact of our civic life. NSO might be crippled, but the technology it engineered is not. The issues of protecting privacy and freedom of expression and freedom of the press might have been raised, but the solutions are not even in the works.

A dozen or so governments around the world held hearings and commenced investigations and convened courts of law to get to the bottom of the problem of unwarranted cybersurveillance and make recommendations for solving it. There has been a surfeit of official lip-flapping in the eighteen months since the publication of the Pegasus Project and very little actual regulation. The truth is, in terms of legal restrictions, the cybersurveillance industry still operates without any real guardrails.

Oh, and NSO might not live to fight another day, but there are plenty more private spyware companies out there. The UAE has created its own in-house spyware monster, DarkMatter, thanks to help from coders and engineers they hired away from NSO and from some mercenary former agents from the world's premier signals intelligence organization, the United States' National Security Agency.

Finally, it is worth recognizing that while the for-profit "Intrusion as a Service" industry might see the need to be more careful after all the unsightly press of the past few years, the clients of that industry do not share that need for caution. Why would they? I have not seen a single instance of a democratic government crying shame on the regimes who used Pegasus, for years, as a tool of vicious repression against their own citizens. The worst of them—Azerbaijan, the UAE, Morocco, Rwanda, Saudi Arabia—have suffered little to no consequences.

Consider this story of the CEO of a private company specializing in cybersecurity. His company does not traffic in spyware, but they have the coding and engineering talent to do it, and everybody in the market knows that. He has been courted for years by Middle Eastern potentates who fly him on private jets to their capital cities and offer him tens of millions of dollars to provide them with cybersurveillance tools on par with Pegasus. He has always said no. But he told us things have changed in the wake of our investigation, when NSO could no longer license its wares in Bahrain, the UAE, Saudi Arabia. The effect he described was not what I expected. "If you want to understand what happens because of the Pegasus Project," he told us last year, "like four months ago, Saudi Arabia came to us and offered us two hundred million dollars." He turned them down again and says he will continue to do so, but . . . "One deal, for two years, I get two hundred million dollars," he says, "so now you understand the economics of this industry."

ACKNOWLEDGMENTS

This book is the child of the Pegasus Project, and we would like to thank all the people who made that project possible. They each and all contributed to this book as well.

Thank you to the source of the leaked list, whose courage led to the revelation of a major scandal, and to the many victims of Pegasus we met along the way during our investigation. We think in particular of Khadija Ismayilova and Omar Radi, who shared their personal stories.

A tremendous thank you to Claudio Guarnieri, Donncha Ó Cearbhaill, and Danna Ingleton from Amnesty International's Security Lab, without whom the Pegasus Project would never have existed. Without their perseverance in tracking down Pegasus, their unique expertise, and their trust, the scope of the abuses in the use of the spyware would never have come to light. For their involvement in the project and their *crucial* work within Amnesty International, we warmly thank Agnès Callamard, Etienne Maynier, Fanny Gallois, Katia Roux, Likhita Banerji, Raed Labassi, and Tom Mackey.

A heartfelt thanks to our young and yet so talented team at Forbidden Stories: Cécile Schilis-Gallego, Phineas Rueckert, Arthur Bouvart, Paloma de Dinechin, Audrey Travère, and Clément Lemerlus, who worked for months at our side to make this list the worldwide scoop that it has become.

How can we not mention the members of the Pegasus Project who worked in the utmost secrecy to reveal the scale of the scandal to the entire world? Alia Ibrahim, Amitai Ziv, Andras Petho, Anuj Srivas, Astrid Geisler, Bartosz Wieliński, Bastian Obermayer, Carmen Aristegui, Craig Timberg, Damien Leloup, Dan Sabbagh, Dana Priest, Drew Harwell, Elodie Guéguen, Frederik Obermaier, Hala Nouhad Nasreddine, Hannes Munzinger, Holger Stark, Jacques Monin, Jean-Baptiste Chastand, Joanna Slater, Joël Matriche, Jorge Carrasco Araizaga, Julien Bouissou, Kabir Agarwal, Kai Biermann, Kristof Klerix, Lilia Saúl Rodriguez, Madjid Zerrouky, Martin Untersinger, Mary Beth Sheridan, Mathieu Tourliere, Michael Safi, Michal Kokot, Miranda Patrucic, Niha Masih, Nina Lakhani, Omer Benjakob, Paul Lewis, Pavla Holcová, Peter Jones, David Pegg, Sam Cutler, Sascha Venohr, Sebastian Barragan, Shane Harris, Shaun Walker, Siddharth Varadarajan, Souad Mekhennet, Stephanie Kirchgaessner, and Szabolcs Panyi.

We are very grateful to the editors and partners who believed in the Pegasus Project from the start: Alexandre Marionneau, Anne Grolleron, Anne Poiret, Cameron Barr, Caroline Monnot, Drew Sullivan, Fabrice Puchaullt, Grégoire Allix, Jeff Leen, Katharine Vinner, Paul Radu, Phil Bennett, Philippa Kowarsky, Raney Aronson-Rath, and Sally Buzbee.

We are thankful to Anne Poiret, who kindly allowed us to use some of the interviews she did for the documentary on the Pegasus Project.

We also owe a debt to the Citizen Lab team for their help. John Scott-Railton, Bill Marczak, and Ron Deibert have been tracking Pegasus around the world for such a long time. Without their relentless efforts and their expertise, NSO customers could have continued to abuse the spyware for years.

We deeply thank Laurie Liss, our literary agent, for her unfailing support, and Deborah Kauffman for her much appreciated advice. Also, from Henry Holt, our editor, Tim Duggan, for his always calm guidance and his expert advice; Tim's sharp-eyed assistant, Anita Sheih; and Hannah Campbell and Carol Rutan for their care with this manuscript. Also, Holt editor-in-chief, Sarah Crichton, who assembled all those resources and more.

This book would not have been possible without the talent and the invaluable contribution of Mark Zwonitzer, whose expert writing and editorial skills were invaluable to us, not to mention his enthusiasm and his support. Our eternal gratitude to you, Mark.

Finally, and most important, this book would not have been possible without the support of our families whose boundless patience allowed us to dedicate ourselves to this challenging and time-consuming investigation:

My wife, Aurélia, and my children, Marius and Swann. My parents, André and Danièle. My brothers, Guilhem and Olivier.

My husband, José, my daughters, Lilie and Apoline. My parents, Christian and Shahira. My sister, Carole.

INDEX

ABOUT THE AUTHORS

LAURENT RICHARD is a Paris-based award-winning documentary filmmaker who was named the 2018 European Journalist of the Year at the Prix Europa in Berlin. He is the founder of Forbidden Stories, a network of investigative journalists devoted to continuing the unfinished work of murdered reporters to ensure the work they died for is not buried with them.

For more than twenty years, Laurent Richard has been conducting major stories for television. He is the author of numerous investigations into the lies of the tobacco industry, the excesses of the financial sector, and the clandestine actions of Mossad and the CIA.

Since its creation, Forbidden Stories has received numerous awards, including a prestigious European Press Prize, two George Polk Awards, and a RSF Impact Award for the Pegasus Project, published in 2021.

SANDRINE RIGAUD is a French investigative journalist. As editor of Forbidden Stories since 2019, she coordinated the award-winning Pegasus Project and the Cartel Project, an international investigation of assassinated Mexican journalists. Before joining Forbidden Stories, she directed feature-length documentaries for French television. She has reported from Tanzania, Uzbekistan, Lebanon, Qatar, and Bangladesh.